ASSORTED BIBLICAL TOPICS

Clarifications, Difficulties, 'Discrepancies', Poison

Wilbur N. Pickering, Th.M., Ph.D.

Copyright, 2017

CONTENTS

Chapter I: Clarifications.

Chapter II: Difficulties?

Chapter III: Discrepancies?

Chapter IV: Poison.

Chapter V: Doctrinal topics.

Chapter I: CLARIFICATIONS

The purpose of this section is to take up passages in the Sacred Text that have not always been adequately interpreted or understood. Generally speaking, the context has not received the careful attention it requires. An occasional practical application is offered.

Two desperate women

A twelve-year hemorrhage

The relevant texts are: Matthew 9:20-22, Mark 5:24-34 and Luke 8:42^b-48.

> Matthew 9:—20 And then, a woman who had been hemorrhaging for twelve years came from behind and touched the hem of His garment. 21 For she kept saying to herself, "If only I may touch His garment I will be healed". 22 But Jesus, turning around and seeing her, said, "Take courage, daughter; your faith has made you well". And the woman was healed from that *very* hour.

> Mark 5:—24 A large crowd was also following Him, and they were pressing around Him. 25 Now a certain woman— who had been bleeding for twelve years, 26 and had suffered many things under many doctors, and had spent all that she had, yet instead of getting better she grew worse—27 when she heard about Jesus, she came from behind in the crowd and touched His garment. 28 (She had kept saying, "If I can just touch His clothes, I will be healed".) 29 Immediately the flow of her blood was dried up, and she knew in her body that she was healed from the affliction. 30 And instantly Jesus perceived within Himself that some power had gone out of Him, and turning around in the crowd He said, "Who touched my clothes?" 31 So His disciples said to Him, "You see the crowd pressing around you, yet you say, 'Who touched me?'?" 32 But He kept

looking around to see who had done it. 33 So the woman, fearing and trembling, knowing what had happened to her, came and fell down before Him and told Him the whole truth. 34 And He said to her: "Daughter, your faith has saved you. Go into peace and be healed from your affliction."

Luke 8:—Now as He was going, the crowds were pressing against Him. 43 And a woman—suffering with a flow of blood for twelve years, who had spent her whole livelihood on physicians, but could not be healed by any—44 approaching from behind touched the border of His garment; and immediately the flow of her blood stopped! 45 So Jesus said, "Who touched me?" When all denied it, Peter and those with him said: "Master, the people are pressing against you and crowding in, and you say, 'Who touched me?'?"[1] 46 But Jesus said, "Someone <u>did</u> touch me, because I noticed power going out from me". 47 Now when the woman saw that she could not hide, she came trembling, and falling down before Him she told Him in the presence of all the people the reason why she had touched Him, and how she was healed immediately. 48 So He said: "Courage, daughter, your faith has healed you. Go into peace."

Here we have a moving account of faith, determination and perseverance; perhaps it will have some practical lessons for us. My discussion will attempt to follow the actual sequence of events. Matthew's account is abbreviated, so I will depend mainly on the other two.

1) The street was presumably not very wide, and both Mark and Luke inform us that it was filled with a crowd that was pressing around and against Jesus. Indeed, Mark 5:31 and Luke 8:45 reinforce the observation. Obviously this represent-

---

[1] Perhaps 1.5% of the Greek manuscripts, of objectively inferior quality, omit "and you say, 'Who touched me?'?" (as in NIV, NASB, LB, TEV, etc.).

ed a problem for the woman; how could she get to Jesus through that crowd, the more especially if it was made up mostly, if not entirely, of men? For any woman to push through a crowd of men would be unacceptable, but she had an added problem.

2) From Matthew 9:1 and the context we may conclude that this episode transpired in Capernaum, which really was not all that big a town. The point is, that woman would be a known person. The available space was packed with people, the crowd was on both sides of Jesus, as well as behind, so she would have to force her way through. However, this represented a difficulty beyond just being rude. According to Leviticus 15:19-27, any discharge of blood made a woman 'unclean', and verse 25 deals with prolonged hemorrhage—anyone who touched her, or even her clothes, became 'unclean' as well. So everyone she touched on her way through the crowd became 'unclean'! Now she and her problem were well known, so the people she touched were NOT happy. She no doubt got plenty of dirty looks, and maybe a few elbows, as well as some choice expressions. It would have been easy to give up, but she kept repeating her expectation to herself (Matthew 9:21) to keep up her courage, and she was desperate.

3) So why was she desperate? She "had been bleeding for twelve years, and had suffered many things under many doctors, and had spent all that she had, yet instead of getting better she grew worse" (Mark 5:25-26). In other words, she was at the end of her financial resources and of any medical hope. Mark almost seems to be accusing the doctors of malpractice. Luke, himself a doctor, is more cautious: "a woman suffering with a flow of blood for twelve years, who had spent her whole livelihood on physicians, but could not be healed by any" (Luke 8:43). No wonder the woman was desperate, but then "she heard about Jesus" (Mark 5:27), and all of a sudden she had hope!

4) Well, she managed it. She wormed through the crowd and "touched the hem of His garment" (Matthew 9:20). "Immediately the flow of her blood was dried up, and she knew in her body that she was healed from the affliction" (Mark 5:29). Note that all she had to do was touch; this sort of thing, people getting healed just by touching His clothes, happened repeatedly during the Lord's earthly ministry. Jesus could have let the incident pass, but He chose not to. He stopped and turned around.

5) "Instantly Jesus perceived within Himself that some power had gone out of Him, and turning around in the crowd He said: Who touched my clothes?" (Mark 5:30). When Luke writes that "all denied it" (8:45), we may understand that it was by their silence; no one spoke up. But Jesus insisted, "He kept looking around to see who had done it" (Mark 5:32). When the disciples protested that He was being 'touched' all the time by the jostling crowd, Jesus said, "Someone <u>did</u> touch me, because I noticed power going out from me" (Luke 8:46). He was referring to a purposeful touch. The woman had evidently withdrawn into the crowd, and may even have been hidden behind others. But Jesus did not let her get away with it.

6) "Now when the woman saw that she could not hide, she came trembling, and falling down before Him she told Him in the presence of all the people the reason why she had touched Him, and how she was healed immediately" (Luke 8:47). That was not easy, in front of the crowd, but Jesus gave her no choice. Was He just being mean? No, He was doing her a big favor. The people knew who she was, and about her physical problem; Jesus was declaring her healing, and therefore her cleansing, to the assembled multitude, and by implication those who had been 'contaminated' by the woman could relax on that score.

7) Then Jesus said to her: "Courage, daughter, your faith has saved you. Go into peace and be healed from your affliction"

(Mark 5:34, Luke 8:48). That is what the Text says, 'into peace' not 'in'. To go 'in peace' is to leave on good terms, no hard feelings. But what might going <u>into</u> peace be? I would say that you take the peace with you; you live within an atmosphere of peace. Now that is a proper 'blessing'! Sovereign Jesus never said 'go in peace'; He always said "go into peace"—He was giving the person a new life. How about a doxology!

A crumb for a 'puppy'

The relevant texts are: Matthew 15:21-28 and Mark 7:24-31[a].

> Matthew 15:—21 Going out from there Jesus withdrew into the region of Tyre and Sidon. 22 And then, a Canaanite woman coming from those parts cried out to Him saying: "Have mercy on me, Lord, Son of David! My daughter is severely demonized." 23 But He answered her not a word. So His disciples came and urged Him saying, "Send her away, because she is crying out after us". 24 But in answer He said, "I was not sent except to the lost sheep of the house of Israel".[1] 25 So she came and worshipped Him saying, "Lord, help me!" 26 But in answer He said, "It is not good to take the children's bread and throw it to the little dogs". 27 So she said, "Yes, Lord, yet even the little dogs eat the crumbs that fall from their masters' table". 28 Then Jesus answered and said to her: "O woman, great is your faith! Let it be to you as you desire." And her daughter was healed from that *very* hour.

> Mark 7:—24 Then He got ready and went from there into the region of Tyre and Sidon. He went into a house and did not want anyone to know it, but He could not escape notice. 25 In fact, as soon as she heard about Him, a woman whose little daughter had an unclean spirit came and fell at His feet. 26 Now the woman was a Greek, a Syro-

---

[1] Although His ultimate mission included the whole world (see the Great Commission in Matthew 28:19-20), His earthly ministry was directed to the "house of Israel".

Phoenecian by birth, and she kept asking Him to cast the demon out of her daughter. 27 But Jesus said to her, "Let the children be filled first; it is not good to take the children's bread and throw it to the little dogs". 28 So she answered and said to Him, "Yes, Lord, yet even the little dogs under the table eat from the children's crumbs". 29 So He said to her, "Because of this saying you may go; the demon has gone out of your daughter".   30 She went away to her house and found that the demon was gone and the daughter had been placed on the bed.   31 Again, departing from the region of Tyre and Sidon, Jesus came to the Sea of Galilee by way of the Decapolis region.

Here we have a moving account of faith, determination and humility; perhaps it will have some practical lessons for us. My discussion will attempt to follow the actual sequence of events.

1) To begin, we observe that Jesus left the Jewish Galilee and went to the Gentile Tyre and Sidon. Now why do you suppose He did that, since He would presently say, "I was not sent except to the lost sheep of the house of Israel" (Matthew 15:24)? In that case, what was He doing in Tyre? Well, maybe He just wanted to get away and rest a bit; upon arriving "He went into a house and did not want anyone to know it, but He could not escape notice" (Mark 7:24). A group of thirteen foreigners would tend to attract some attention, even if they tried to keep a low profile. Still, the Text plainly says that Jesus tried to avoid being noticed. How then did the 'puppy' know that Jesus was coming before He even arrived?!

2) From Mark's account one could assume that the woman appeared after Jesus was in the house, but Matthew's account tells us something else. Notice verse 23: His disciples came and urged Him saying, "Send her away, because she is crying out after us" (Mark does say that she kept asking, verse 26). They were still on the road, and the woman was following them. Further, she addressed Him as the Jewish Messiah: a

Canaanite woman coming from those parts cried out to Him saying, "Have mercy on me, Lord, Son of David! My daughter is severely demonized" (Mathew 15:22). "Son of David"—as a Canaanite she appealed to the Jewish Messiah, upon whom she had no claim. But how did she know that? I suspect there is more to this story than meets the eye. The only explanation that I can see is that the woman received divine orientation; she was told where to go and what to say. In that event, helping that woman may have been the purpose for the trip.

3) The woman began with, "Lord, Son of David", to which Jesus returned no answer, since she had no claim upon Him in those terms. However, since she would not stop, and did not keep her voice down, she was 'blowing their cover'. So the disciples appealed to Jesus for relief, to which He replied, "I was not sent except to the lost sheep of the house of Israel" (Matthew 15:24). The Lord spoke loudly enough for her to hear, since His answer was as much, if not more so, for her as it was for the disciples. So she came and worshipped Him saying, "Lord, help me!" (Matthew 15:25). She got the message, because she now dropped the appeal to the Messiah. Mark 7:25 tells us that she "fell at His feet", so either Jesus had stopped or she had run ahead so she could stop Him.

4) Now we come to an unusual conversation. Our Lord's choice of terms would probably strike most readers as being unexpectedly harsh. "It is not good to take the children's bread and throw it to the little dogs" (Matthew 15:26, Mark 7:27). Dear me, Jesus called her a dog (and a 'little' one at that)! To be sure, at that time Jews commonly referred to Gentiles as 'dogs', but why would Jesus follow suit? I imagine that He was testing her humility, since she had already, as I believe, received a special dispensation of grace. (One is reminded of Cornelius.) And she passed the test! So she said, "Yes, Lord, yet even the little dogs eat the crumbs that fall from their masters' table" (Matthew 15:27). Big dogs would not be in the house, so these would be little house pets, or perhaps puppies. Then Jesus answered and said to her: "O

woman, great is your faith! Let it be to you as you desire. Because of this saying you may go; the demon has gone out of your daughter" (Matthew 15:28, Mark 7:29).

5) "She went away to her house and found that the demon was gone and the daughter had been placed on the bed" (Mark 7:30). The verb 'place' is perfect passive; evidently the child was too small, or too weak, to have gotten there by herself.

6) "Departing from the region of Tyre and Sidon, Jesus came to the Sea of Galilee" (Mark 7:31). We are not told whether Jesus did anything else while in that region. If not, He apparently went there just to help that woman. But why would He do something like that?—it involved time and inconvenience. Well, consider 2 Chronicles 16:9. "For the eyes of the LORD run to and fro throughout the whole earth, to show Himself strong on behalf of those whose heart is loyal to Him" (NKJV). God's 'search' covers the whole earth, so is not limited to nation or place, and not to time either. Cornelius is a biblical example, but there have doubtless been many others down through history (I have seen it myself). So if you are needing some 'strong' help, here is the key—the language of the Text indicates that God is just waiting to give that help. How about another doxology!

This episode always moves me. In effect, Jesus called the woman a 'dog' (that is what Jews called Gentiles), and she accepted the classification. She was determined to get her 'crumb', and she did! And she left us a great example of humility, determination and faith!

Poor Pilate—wrong place, wrong time

According to John 18:12, there was a *chiliarch* among those who went to the Garden of Gethsemane to arrest Jesus. Well now, a *chiliarch* commanded a thousand men (or perhaps a cohort, about 600). There would scarcely be more than one of them stationed in Jerusalem, so he was presumably the top commanding military officer in town. So what was the top military commander doing in Gethsemane at 2:00 a.m.? If he was there, it was because the governor, Pilate, had sent him. And why would Pilate do something like that? He had his reasons.

As governor, Pilate represented the Roman Empire. He was responsible for keeping the peace, according to Caesar's interests. In those days the city of Jerusalem was not very big, and keeping well informed would not have been difficult. Pilate was doubtless well aware of Jesus, and would have followed His career with attention. Someone with a large public following could be a threat. Moreover, since it was the chief priests' man who led the expedition, and they kept the prisoner, it is clear that they had gone to Pilate and convinced him that Jesus represented enough of a threat that something needed to be done about it. (Jesus had used violence in cleansing the temple, as well as totally disregarding their authority. Why would He not do the same against Rome?) Even so, just why Pilate decided to send his *chiliarch* is hard to say; perhaps to be sure that things were done professionally, as well as to form a professional opinion as to the nature of the threat. Certain it is that Pilate and the chief priests had agreed on a plan of action, as John makes clear, a plan that included death by crucifixion.

Both Mark 15:1 and John 18:28 inform us that it was early morning when Jesus was taken to Pilate, but John 19:14 states that it was around 6:00 a.m. when Pilate pronounced sentence. Even allowing that 'around' 6:00 was perhaps five or ten minutes after the hour, it could not have been later than 5:30 when the chief priests pounded on Pilate's door. Now then, we all know that one just does not go pounding on a governor's door at such an hour, especially a conquered people. Not only that, Pilate was dressed and waiting. Actually, he had doubtless been up, waiting for the *chiliarch*'s report. But at that point he changed the game-plan. He went out and asked, "What accusation do you bring against this man?" (John 18:29). Their reply was petulant, "If he were not an evil-doer we would not have handed him over to you." They thought that they had an agreement, but something had made Pilate change his mind.

To understand what happened, we need to go back to Geth-semane, and the *chiliarch*. The traitor had told them that there would be eleven men besides Jesus, and that they had two swords (Luke 22:38). But they were country bumpkins with no fighting ability. Even so, the *chiliarch* probably had over twice as many men, and all were armed—he doubtless expected some attempt at resistance. When they arrived and stated their business, Jesus calmly identified Himself, but at His word they all fell to the ground (John 18:6). Later, after the traitor's kiss, Peter managed to slice off an ear, but not only did Jesus tell him to quit it, He healed the ear (Luke 22:51)! Then the disciples abandoned Jesus, and He allowed Himself to be bound, without resistance. So what sort of report would the *chiliarch* give to Pilate? It was more than obvious that Je-sus was no wild-eyed insurrectionist. He had supernatural power, and yet submitted peacefully. And Jesus was impres-sive! Pilate had to conclude that the picture that the chief priests had painted was wrong, and so the agreement could not stand.

Now a *chiliarch* was a hardened and seasoned warrior, not easily impressed. He probably told Pilate that if it were up to him, he would leave Jesus alone! But Pilate had to deal with the chief priests, and he knew it would not be easy. In Acts 3:13 Peter affirms that Pilate was determined to let Jesus go, but the chief priests got what they wanted in the end. Close attention to the Record makes clear that Peter's affirmation is correct. Pilate wanted no part of killing Jesus! He made re-peated attempts to 'get off the hook'. Consider:

1) Pilate answered their petulant response with, "<u>You</u> take him and judge him according to your law". To this they re-

sponded, "We are not permitted to execute anyone". This exchange indicates that execution had been in the agreement, but Pilate also rubbed salt in their wound, making them recognize that they were a subjugated people. Even so, he told them to do the judging, which would make them responsible.

2) Luke 23:2 probably gives the first concrete accusation: "We found this fellow perverting the nation and forbidding to pay taxes to Caesar, declaring himself to be Christ, a king." The part about taxes was a plain lie, but the part about the Christ was true. In any case, Pilate could not safely ignore such accusations, so he interrogated Jesus.

3) Matthew 27:11, Mark 15:2, Luke 23:3 and John 18:33-38 all refer to this first interrogation. It revolved around the kingship of Jesus, which could be a crime against Caesar. Jesus affirms that He is a king, but His kingdom "is not of this world" (John 18:36). A kingdom that was not of this world would not represent a threat to Rome. So Pilate went out and said to the crowd, "I find no crime in him at all". If there was no crime, there should be no punishment.

4) This led to a barrage of further accusations, to which Jesus did not answer, which surprised Pilate (Matthew 27:12-14, Mark 15:3-5 and Luke 23:5). But among the accusations they mentioned Galilee, which allowed Pilate to learn that Jesus was a Galilean, thereby belonging to Herod's jurisdiction. As 'luck' would have it, Herod was in town and nearby. (He had doubtless been informed about what was afoot, since he also was up and dressed at that early hour.)

5) So Pilate sent Jesus to Herod, probably hoping that Herod would take responsibility. Luke is the only one who records this side-trip (23:7-12). But Jesus refused to speak; and what can you do with someone who won't talk? From the Lord's point of view, Herod was irrelevant; it was Pilate who had the authority to crucify. So, frustrated, Herod sent Him back, only now arrayed in a gorgeous robe. The whole side-trip probably took no more than fifteen minutes.

6) Poor Pilate, what was he to do? Next he tried the 'releasing a prisoner at Passover' gambit, hoping to release Jesus, but the crowd demanded Barabbas. (Both Matthew and Mark record that Pilate knew that the chief priests had acted out of envy.) In the middle of this proceeding, Pilate received a message from his wife, about her dream (Matthew 27:19) [she had probably been told why he didn't go to bed that night]. When Pilate asked what he should do with Jesus, they demanded that he be crucified. When Pilate asked what evil Jesus had done, they just yelled all the louder. Luke gives us a little further information. Pilate affirmed that neither he nor Herod had found guilt in Jesus, but because of their fury he offered to flog Jesus, hoping that would appease them.

7) Matthew, Mark and John give some account of the treatment Jesus received from the soldiers. They made a crown of thorns, probably poisonous, and then drove the thorns into His scalp by beating on the crown with a rod. The poison would cause the scalp to swell, and blood would ooze from the wounds. They covered His face with spittle. Although none of the Evangelists mentions it, Isaiah 50:6 was presumably fulfilled as well—a soldier grabbing a fistful of beard and giving a violent yank would tear away the skin holding the hair, which would leave a painful and ugly wound. The total effect must have been horrible, leaving Jesus unrecognizable—Isaiah 52:14 was literally fulfilled. Then Pilate had Him brought out and said, "Look at the man!" (He had repeated that he found no crime in Him.) Pilate was hoping that when the crowd saw how much Jesus had already suffered, they would be satisfied, but it only made them worse!

8) To their "Crucify! Crucify him!" Pilate answered, "You take and crucify him, because I find no crime in him". The Jews answered him, "We have a law, and according to our law he ought to die, because he made himself 'Son of God'!" That statement made Pilate more afraid than ever (John 19:6-8). So he took Jesus inside for a second interview. Although Pilate represented the greatest temporal power at that time, Jesus calmly affirmed that there was a higher power, and that He, Jesus, represented that higher power. It appears to me that Pilate at least half believed Him, because John 19:12 says, "From that moment Pilate really tried to release Him". But the Jews did an 'end run'.

9) They kept shouting: "If you release this fellow you are no friend of Caesar's! Whoever makes himself a king is opposing Caesar!" Ooops! Pilate owed his position to Caesar's good graces, and simply could not afford to do something that could be construed (even with a little twisting) as treason. He was beaten and knew it. But he still managed to get them to declare that their only king was Caesar.

10) Sitting on the judgment seat, Pilate called for water, washed his hands in front of the crowd, and said: "I am innocent of the blood of this righteous man. It's your problem!" So in answer all the people said, "His blood be upon us and upon our children!" (Matthew 27:24-25). Terrible, terrible, terrible! This may well be the worst curse that any parents ever placed upon their descendants. Since Pilate declared Jesus to be righteous, and since the Jews took full responsibility, I suspect that God will not hold Pilate responsible. After all, he was fulfilling the Plan: Jesus had to die by crucifixion.

Before bringing this article to a close, I would like to call attention to several further items that bear on Pilate's attitude.

1) Pilate had Jesus' 'crime' posted in *three* languages; he evidently wanted as wide an audience as possible. All four Gospels mention this, and from them we may understand that the full Accusation was: This is Jesus the Natsorean, the King of the Jews. That Pilate put "**the** Natsorean" (<u>not</u> Natsarene [Nazarene]) indicates that he had researched Jesus. The reference is to Isaiah 11:1; Jesus was David's Branch, the Messiah. Pilate was making a statement. When the chief priests complained, he answered, "What I have written, I have written!" (John 19:21-22).

2) All four Gospels mention the burial, but only Mark registers that when Joseph of Arimathea asked Pilate for permission to remove Jesus' body, Pilate was surprised that Jesus was already dead. So he summoned the centurion to confirm the fact (15:44-45). As soon as Jesus died, the centurion most probably had left the scene, going back to headquarters, leaving the four soldiers to guard the two malefactors. Of course Pilate had experienced the three hours of darkness, and had felt the earthquake, but he was not on the scene. He knew that a person on a cross dies from asphyxiation. The weight of the body pushes the diaphragm against the lungs and he can't breathe. Nailing the feet was a sadistic procedure that prolonged the agony—rather than die they would push against the nail to get a breath. Finally, when too weak to do that they would die for lack of air. (That is why they broke the legs of the two thieves; they then died within a few minutes.) Jesus had been on the cross for six hours, but victims could last several times that long. Whether just then or later, Pilate doubtless got a full report from the centurion. Jesus had given a great shout and then died. Obviously, if you are dying without air, you can't shout! The centurion knew that the cross had not killed Jesus. But what mere human can just tell his spirit to leave? 2 + 2 = 4. Jesus had to be the Son of God.

3) Only Matthew mentions the sealing and guarding of the tomb (27:62-66). The chief priests went to Pilate requesting that the tomb be made secure until the third day. To this Pilate replied, "You have a guard; go make it as secure as you can!" His turn of phrase is interesting, "make it as secure as you can". In other words, he was hinting that it would not make any difference. I rather suspect that Pilate believed that Jesus would do what He said.

We learn from Tertullian that Pilate wrote a letter to the emperor suggesting that Jesus be added to the roster of Roman deities. Now to make a suggestion like that involved an element of risk. But evidently Pilate was sufficiently convinced that he took the risk. If I someday meet Pilate in Heaven, I will not be surprised. If his experience with Jesus resulted in his salvation, Pilate would likely suggest a different title for this study: Blessed Pilate—right place, right time!

Harmonizing the accounts of the Betrayal and Arrest

1) The crowd arrives—Matthew 26:47, Mark 14:43, Luke 22:47[a], John 18:3. The four accounts state the fact, while Luke emphasizes that Judas was leading them, also implied by John.

2) Jesus knocks them down—John 18:4-9. I take this to be a 'cyst' of supernatural intervention, to make clear that the Father has not lost control of the events. I say 'cyst' because then the crowd carries on as if nothing had happened. A person delivered from demonic control often does not remember what he did while under that control; this may have been similar, only on the other side.

3) The kiss—Matthew 26:48-50[a], Mark 14:44-45, Luke 22:47[b]-48. Only three of the four accounts take up this pitiful episode. I offer the following harmonization:

> Now His betrayer had given them a signal, saying, "Whomever I kiss, he it is; seize him and take him away securely".[1] So upon arriving he went directly to Him. So Jesus said to him, "Friend, what brings you here?"[2] Judas said, "Greetings, Rabbi!" and kissed Him. So Jesus said to him, "Judas, are you betraying the Son of the Man with a <u>kiss</u>?"

---

[1] Why the 'securely'? Judas had seen so many manifestations of Jesus' power that he should have known better, but of course he was under Satan's control at that time. However, it appears that they expected resistance.

[2] Jesus knew perfectly well why Judas was there, so why did He call him "friend"? Perhaps to show that He held no personal animosity against him. The Plan was being fulfilled.

4) They grab Jesus—Matthew 26:50[b], Mark 14:46. Judas served as guide, but I take it that Malchus was actually in charge of the operation. He may have taken the lead in grabbing Jesus, which was why Peter swung at him. This grabbing precipitated the reaction that followed.

5) Peter's sword—Matthew 26:51-54, Mark 14:47, Luke 22:49-51, John 18:10-11. All four of the accounts take up this episode. I offer the following harmonization:

> When those who were around Him saw what was about to happen, they said to Him, "Lord, shall we strike with the sword?" Then Simon Peter, having a sword, drew it, struck the high priest's servant and cut off his right ear. (The servant's name was Malchus.)[1] Then Jesus reacted by saying, "Allow at least this!" and touching the man's ear He healed him.[2] Then Jesus said to Peter: "Put your sword back into its place, for all who take the sword will die by the sword. Do you actually suppose that I cannot call upon my Father right now and He will place beside me more than twelve legions of angels?[3] But how then would the Scriptures be fulfilled that it has to happen this way? The cup that the Father has given me, must I not drink it?"

6) Jesus addresses the crowd—Matthew 26:55-56[a], Mark 14:48-49, Luke 22:52-53. Only three of the four accounts take up this episode. I offer the following harmonization:

> Then Jesus said to the chief priests, officers of the temple, and elders who had come against Him: "Have you come out with swords and clubs as against a bandit, to arrest

---

[1] The Text has 'the servant', so the high priest had probably put him in charge of the operation. John probably knew him personally. Obviously Peter was not used to wielding a sword.

[2] Peter's attack caused them to release Jesus, so His hands were free to do this. If the Lord had not healed that ear, things would probably have been nastier for Peter in the 'courtyard', if not already in the garden.

[3] That would be a minimum of 36,000—probably enough to handle the situation, don't you think?

me? I used to sit daily with you in the temple, teaching, and you did not seize me. But all this has happened so that the Scriptures of the prophets should be fulfilled. This is your hour; even the authority of the darkness!"[1]

7) The disciples run away—Matthew 26:56[b], Mark 14:50. The two accounts state the fact.

8) Jesus is taken away—Matthew 26:57, Mark 14:53[a], Luke 22:54[a], John 18:12-13[a]. The four accounts state the fact. The first three are in essential agreement, but John offers some new information. First, there was a Roman detachment, with its commander, there in the garden. The word here (*chiliarch*) refers to a commander of a thousand men (or of a cohort = about 600); this could only be a Roman officer of high rank, and there would only be one of them in Jerusalem. So how did they get him to come along? Obviously Pilate had been informed and was participating. Second, they took Him to Annas first, because he was the father-in-law of Caiaphas,[2] who was high priest that year. A careful look at the parallel accounts makes clear that all of Peter's denials took place at Caiaphas' palace, as also all the recorded questionings, etc., so after showing Jesus to Annas they took Him on to Caiaphas. That interim was probably also used to gather the Council, who would not want to be dragged out of bed until Jesus was actually in hand—it was probably between 3 and 4 a.m.

Harmonizing the accounts of the burial

The relevant passages are: Matthew 27:57-61, Mark 15:42-47, Luke 23:50-56 and John 19:38-42.

---

[1] This was Satan's hour, being part of the Father's Plan; 'the darkness' refers to Satan's kingdom; 'your hour' means that they were part of that kingdom.

[2] The bigger reason was that Annas was the real high priest, according to the Law (the office of high priest was for life). He was the power behind the throne, so to say. Caiaphas was the political high priest (that year), for purposes of dealing with Rome.

1) Joseph of Arimathea was an important man in town. He was 'rich' (Matthew 27:57) and a prominent member of the Sanhedrin (Mark 15:43). Any self-respecting governor would make it his business to know who were the important people within the area of his jurisdiction, so Pilate doubtless knew who Joseph was, whether or not he had ever met him— evidently Joseph experienced no difficulty in obtaining an audience. Joseph was 'a good and righteous man' (Luke 23:50) 'who himself had become a disciple of Jesus' (Matthew 27:57), but who had not declared himself openly 'for fear of the Jews' (John 19:38).

He had been waiting in the wings. Just as with the owner of the donkey, and the owner of the upper room, who were doubtless advised in advance that their services would be needed, Joseph had been prepared. He did not just 'happen' to have a tomb he didn't know what to do with, complete with a large stone just right for sealing. Since he had the wherewithal, he had purchased the divinely indicated plot and had the tomb carved into, or out of, the sedimentary rock (Matthew 27:59, Mark 15:46, Luke 23:53). According to Isaiah 53:9, Jehovah's Servant was to have a rich man's grave, not whatever the common criminals got (the Father did not allow the Son's body to suffer that humiliation).

2) Nicodemus was a Pharisee and 'a ruler of the Jews' (John 3:1), the one who 'came to Jesus by night' (John 19:39). Since he started his interview by declaring that Jesus was 'a teacher come from God' (John 3:2), he no doubt became a disciple. Since he defended Jesus openly (John 7:50-51), his sympathies were presumably well known. He also had been prepared to assist Joseph with the burial procedure. He had purchased 'a mixture of myrrh and aloes, about a hundred pounds' (John 19:39), which represented a significant investment, and had placed them within the tomb in time to help Joseph with the body. Al- though the Text does not mention it, he was presumably also the one who furnished the linen strips for wrap-

ping the body. Obviously all preparations had to be completed before the time for the burial.

3) At the right moment, Joseph 'went boldly in to Pilate and asked for the body of Jesus' (Mark 15:43). As already mentioned, he was evidently given an audience without difficulty. "Well Pilate was surprised that He was already dead; and summoning the centurion he asked him when He had died" (Mark 15:44). As soon as Jesus died, the centurion most probably had left the scene, going back to headquarters (he had probably received special instruction about Jesus). He probably felt he should inform Pilate about the unusual events, but somehow Joseph got ahead of him (but evidently not by much—had the centurion arrived first, he presumably would have been already reporting to Pilate when Joseph arrived). Well, Joseph was primed for action, watching from a distance, and as soon as Jesus dismissed His spirit Joseph headed for Pilate. "Upon the centurion's confirmation, he granted the body to Joseph" (Mark 15:45).

4) Then Joseph and Nicodemus met at the cross and removed the body. Joseph had purchased a linen sheet for the purpose, and the two used it to transport the body to the tomb (Matthew 27:59-60, Mark 15:46, Luke 23:53, John 19:39). Obviously the tomb had been prepared beforehand, as already stated. Matthew and John say that it was 'new', while Luke and John add that it had yet to be used (Matthew 27:60, Luke 23:53, John 19:41). John adds that it was in a garden near Golgotha.

5) Once within the tomb, they prepared the body for burial. "Then they took Jesus' body and wrapped it in linen strips, with the aromatic spices, according to the burial custom of the Jews" (John 19:40). How many linen strips would it take to wrap up 100 pounds of spices? The result would have looked something like a cocoon, except that it did not include the head, which was covered with a facecloth (John 20:7).

6) When they had finished their task, they 'rolled a large stone against the door of the tomb and left' (Matthew 27:60, Mark

15:46). If they rolled it, it was in the form of a wheel; there would be a track in which it rolled, with a bit of incline, so that Joseph and Nicodemus could roll it down into place, where it would stop; but it would take several men to roll it back up and away, 'because it was very large' (Mark 16:4).

7) Mary Magdalene and Mary the mother of Joses 'followed along', saw where the body was placed, and sat down opposite the tomb (Matthew 27:61, Mark 15:47, Luke 23:55). That is, they saw where the body was taken, but obviously had not looked in the tomb—there were 100 pounds of spices in there, with enough linen strips to tie it all in. This is clear from Luke 23:56, "Then they returned and prepared spices and perfumes; but they rested on the Sabbath according to the commandment." They evidently did not realize that the men had already done what there was to do.

8) Although subsequent to the burial itself, the guarding of the tomb is important; it is recorded in Matthew 27:62-66.

> 62 The next day, which is after the Preparation, the chief priests and the Pharisees went together to Pilate 63 saying: "Sir, we remember that that deceiver, while still alive, said, 'After three days I am going to rise'. 64 Therefore command that the grave be made secure until the third day, lest His disciples come by night and steal Him and say to the people, 'He was raised from the dead', and the last deception will be worse than the first." 65 So Pilate said to them, "You have a guard; go make it as secure as you can!" 66 So they went and secured the grave with the guard, having sealed the stone.

Was Pilate happy? No he was not! And maybe, just maybe, he wasn't as stupid as some might like to think. From Mark 15:44-45 we know that he debriefed the centurion, who had to explain why Jesus died sooner than expected! "Make it as sure as you can." Right. Ironically, those great champions of the Sabbath had to violate the Sabbath to secure the tomb. They thought they were being shrewd, but only played into God's hand. Their effort only made the evidence for the resurrection all the stronger. Well, for starters, who removed the stone? The soldiers would not touch a stone with a Roman seal, and they had no reason for doing it, in any case. The women were physically incapable of doing it. So who removed the stone?

Harmonizing the accounts of the post-Resurrection appearances

I will attempt to discuss the appearances in chronological sequence, although the evidence available does not always permit a clear decision. The first five occurred on Resurrection Day.

1) The first appearance is related in Mark 16:9 and John 20:14-17. Mark simply records the fact, stating clearly that it was to Mary Magdalene. John gives further detail about the encounter.

2) The second appearance is recorded only by Matthew, 28:9-10. This appearance was to Mary the mother of James, Salome, Joanna and 'the others'; the Text does not specify that it was the second, but the only other possible candidate would be Peter (Luke 24:34), and there simply was not enough elapsed time to fit him in here. According to verse 7, the disciples were to go to Galilee to see Jesus, verse 10 giving the same instruction to His 'brothers'. In Matthew 26:32 Jesus Himself had said to them, "After I am raised I will go before you into Galilee".

3) I arbitrarily give the third appearance to Peter, but it could have been to the Emmaus disciples—between them they are the third and fourth. The fact is mentioned in Luke 24:34 and 1 Corinthians 15:5; just the fact and no more.

4) The episode on the road to Emmaus is recorded in Mark 16:12, but related in Luke 24:13-32 (Luke's account is most interesting).

5) The fifth, and last, recorded appearance on Resurrection Day was to the Eleven (although only ten were present), as recorded in Mark 16:14-18, Luke 24:36-49 and John 20:19-23 (1 Corinthians 15:5). I assume that Mark's record refers to that first Sunday, although the 'later' that begins verse 14 could also apply to the second Sunday (the eleven at the table would presumably have to be one of the two Sundays). The content of Mark's record seems to me to fit better with the first Sunday. Luke makes clear (verse 33) that there were others besides the Eleven in that upper room. Verse 36 makes clear that this was the first Sunday. Strictly speaking, verses 44-49 could have been uttered at a later date, but if not, then verse 49 requires special handling. "You must stay in the city of Jerusalem until you are clothed with power from on High." Since Jesus had instructed them to meet Him in Galilee, and did in fact meet with them there, then this amounts to a directive to return to Jerusalem after the meeting(s) in Galilee. John's account clearly refers to the first Sunday, and provides new information, as is his custom (from him we learn that Thomas was absent). The reference to 'the Twelve' in 1 Corinthians 15:5, probably refers to the first Sunday, but could have been the second, or even in Galilee. (I take it that both 'the Twelve' and 'the Eleven' were used as technical terms referring to the apostolic 'college'.)

6) The next recorded meeting is found in John 20:26-29, taking place on the following Sunday, in the same upper room, to the complete 'Eleven'.

7) The breakfast on the beach (John 21:1-23) must be the seventh, because verse 14 states: "This was already a third time that Jesus appeared to His disciples after He was raised from among the dead." This would presumably be the first appearance in Galilee, following the two in the upper room.

8) 1 Corinthians 15:6 states that "He was seen by over five hundred brothers at once", and subsequently by James, and finally by all the apostles (verse 7). The 'finally by all the apostles' presumably refers to the Ascension. The 500 might have happened at Matthew 28:16-20, but the Text refers only to the Eleven, as well as stating that Jesus had indicated the place (and presumably also the time). The reference to doubters presumably means that there were others present, since the Eleven could scarcely still be in doubt. Jesus' half-brothers (verse 10) were probably there, as well as others (recall that Luke 24:33 mentions others besides the apostles). I will assume that the '500' happened later.

9) "Over five hundred brothers at once".

10) James.

11) The Ascension is recorded in Mark 16:9, Luke 24:50-51 and Acts 1:6-11. Mark merely states the fact. Luke gives bare detail, but he offers more information in Acts, which he also wrote.

12) Acts 1:3 has "appearing to them during forty days", and Acts 13:31 has "for many days He was seen", but no specifics are given. However, we may reasonably conclude that those forty days were not empty, there having been further appearances that were not recorded—that is to say, before the Ascension, since we do indeed have some after that event.

13) Stephen—Acts 7:55-56.

14) Saul of Tarsus—Acts 26:13-18, 1 Corinthians 15:8.

15) Ananias—Acts 9:10-15.

16) Paul, more than once—Acts 22:17-21, 23:11, etc.

17) John—Revelation 1:9-13, etc.

And Sovereign Jesus has continued appearing to people down through the ages to this very hour. As He said in Matthew 28:20, "Take note, I am with you every day, until the end of the age". Since that 'end' is still down the road, His promise continues in effect.

Herod and John

To begin, Matthew 14:1-2, Mark 6:14-16 and Luke 9:7-9 are really about Jesus, not John, so I will set them aside. That leaves Matthew 14:3-12 and Mark 6:17-29 for consideration. However, strictly speaking, Matthew 14:6-12 and Mark 6:21-29 are really about Herodias, how she got revenge, so I will start with the remaining verses, Matthew 14:3-5 and Mark 6:17-20.

> Matthew 14:—3 For Herod had laid hold of John and bound him, and put him in prison because of Herodias, his brother Philip's wife. 4 For John would say to him, "It is not lawful for you to have her".[1] 5 And although he wanted to kill him, he feared the crowd, because they counted him as a prophet.

> Mark 6:—17 You see, Herod himself had ordered John arrested, and bound him in prison, on account of Herodias, his brother Philip's wife; because he had married her 18— John had kept saying to Herod, "It isn't lawful for you to have your brother's wife". 19 So Herodias nursed a grudge against him and wanted to kill him;[2] but she could not, 20 because Herod feared John and protected him, knowing him to be a just and holy man. And consulting him he would do many things; indeed, he would hear him with pleasure.

At first glance there appears to be some discrepancy between the two accounts, but let us slow down and take a careful look.

---

[1] The impression one gets is that John took Herod to task several times—a coward he was not.

[2] I suppose that Herodias was ambitious and figured that Herod offered more than did Philip, so she was probably the one who took the initiative; but she had not counted on John being a persistent and vocal 'conscience'.

1) The whole episode revolves around Herodias. Her marriage to Philip presumably had nothing to do with passionate love, as such marriages seldom had. With the passage of time (she had a teenage daughter) she decided that Herod had more to offer than did his brother, and managed to convince Herod to take her on.

2) Enter John the Baptizer: he evidently was on speaking terms with Herod, and had access to him to the extent that he was able to reprimand him repeatedly for what he had done. Now kings generally do not enjoy being reprimanded, and a queen such as Herodias even less. Herod was mad, and Herodias was furious.

3) The evident solution was to get rid of the irritant, so Herod had John arrested, with a view to executing him. But Herod was a puppet king, under the dominion of Rome, and some attention needed to be given to public opinion—it was public opinion that put off the execution: "he feared the crowd, because they counted him as a prophet".

4) Now Herod knew that John was "a just and holy man", and the two had been on talking terms. With the passing of time, Herod calmed down and cooled off. He decided that he did not want to kill John, but because of Herodias he could not release him, either (she kept on insisting that John should be killed). But if you must keep a prophet of God in your prison, you may as well make use of him.

5) Now consider the last half of Mark 6:20—"And consulting him he would do many things; indeed, he would hear him with pleasure." I here follow the best line of transmission, albeit representing only 20% of the Greek manuscripts, that has 'consulting' in the present tense; the rest, followed by all versions, have the verb in the past. Thus the NKJV has: "when he heard him, he did many things". However, and unfortunately, at this point most 'modern' versions garble the account.

The immediately following 'he would do many things/he did many things' is attested by over 99% of the

Greek manuscripts—a mere handful (0.4%), of objectively inferior quality, have 'he was greatly disturbed' or 'very perplexed' (as in NIV, NASB, LB, TEV, etc.). But why then did Herod hear John with pleasure, and why was he 'very sorry' (verse 26)? Those modern versions don't make sense; and just why do they insist on garbling the account on such a totally inadequate basis?

But what sorts of things would Herod take to John for his opinion? I suggest that Herod used John as a sounding board for administrative problems, and since he often followed his advice, he had an unusually good administration, there for a while. That is why he was genuinely sorry to lose John.

6) Alas, Herodias knew how to nurse a grudge, and never gave up looking for a way to kill John. The opportune moment came on Herod's birthday. Herod had doubtless already 'celebrated' more than was good for him before the banquet began, and was no longer thinking clearly. We know the rest of the story. One wonders why God would allow such a servant, as was John, to suffer such an ignominious death; but at least it was instantaneous—in terms of suffering, crucifixion or burning at the stake would have been worse. We have no right to understand everything, and therefore no obligation to explain everything. When you get to heaven you can ask God directly, if you still want to know.

Light for the Blind?—Acts 26:18

Paul was defending himself before King Agrippa. In verses 12 – 18 he described his encounter with the glorified Jesus.

> 12 It was on one of those journeys, as I was going to Damascus with authority and a commission from the chief priests, 13 at midday, O king, as I was on the road, I saw a light from heaven brighter than the sun, blazing around me and those traveling with me. 14 Well we all fell to the ground and I heard a voice speaking to <u>me</u> and saying in

the Hebrew language:[1] "Saul, Saul, why are you persecuting me? It is hard for you to kick against the goads." 15 So I said, "Who are you, Lord?" And He said: "I am Jesus, whom you are persecuting. 16 Now get up and stand on your feet; because I have appeared to you for this purpose, to appoint you as a servant and a witness both of the things you have seen and of the things I will reveal to you, 17 delivering you from 'the people' and the ethnic nations, to which I am sending you: 18 to open their eyes, so as to bring them back from darkness into light and from the authority of Satan to God, so that they may receive forgiveness of sins and an inheritance among those who are sanctified, by the faith into me."

I wish to focus attention on the missionary commission that Paul (he was still Saul) received. Matthew 28:19, Mark 16:15, John 20:21 and Acts 1:8 took place between the resurrection and the ascension, but to commission Paul Jesus returned from Heaven! One other detail deserves special notice—the responsibility that Paul received was primarily concerned with the ethnic nations ("Gentiles" is a translation of the same word that in Matthew 28:19 is rendered "nations"). For these reasons it seems to me that this missionary commission takes on a special importance for us, and the more so for whoever is going to do pioneer transcultural work. So let us consider this commission in more detail.

Paul is sent to the nations (defined ethnically), "to open their eyes, so as to bring them back from darkness into light and from the authority of Satan to God, so that they may receive forgiveness of sins and an inheritance among those who are sanctified, by the faith into Me."

I rendered the second verb as 'bring back' rather than 'turn' or 'convert' because I take that to be the correct nuance of the Text. It gives the impression that someone is in the wrong

---

[1] A conversation between two Jews would naturally be in Hebrew.

place or situation and needs to be brought to the correct one. And now for the main point: the purpose clause introduced by the conjunction 'so that' is subordinated to the verbal phrase dominated by the verb "bring back". In other words, before someone can receive forgiveness of sins, even, he must be freed from the power of Satan! Before a person can be saved someone must do something about Satan's influence upon him.

But I am getting ahead of myself; we need to start at the beginning, "to open their eyes". If their eyes are shut, they are blind. What good is light to a blind person? It should be obvious that the glorified Jesus was not saying that all Gentiles were physically blind; He was referring to spiritual blindness. In Matthew 15:14 He referred to blind guides leading blind people, and He was not speaking of physical blindness, except as an illustration of the spiritual. In Romans 2:19 Paul refers to the spiritually blind. In 2 Corinthians 3:14 he refers to that blindness as a 'veil'. In 2 Corinthians 4:4 Paul spells it out.

In verse 3 he refers to the Gospel being hidden from those who are perishing, or wasting themselves, and then proceeds: "among whom the god of this age has blinded the minds of the unbelieving, so that the light of the Gospel of the glory of Christ, who is the image of God, should not dawn on them." The Text clearly states that Satan, 'the god of this world', is in the business of blinding the minds of unbelievers when they hear the Gospel, so they will not understand, so they will not be convicted, so they will not repent and convert. This is a terrible truth. The enemy has access to our minds, access in the sense that he has the power or ability to invade them, whether by introducing thoughts or by jamming our reasoning. The Lord Jesus had already declared this truth previously, when He explained the parable of the sower. "These are the ones by the wayside where the word is sown; but, as soon as they hear it Satan comes and takes away the word that was planted in their hearts" (Mark 4:15). In the parallel passage in Luke 8:12 Jesus adds the following words: "lest they believe and be saved". Note that the Word is already in the mind or heart of the person, but then Satan comes, invades the mind and 'takes away' that word. I am not sure just how this intrusion by the enemy works, perhaps he causes a mental block of some sort, but the practical effect is that the Word becomes ineffective, as if the person had not even heard it.

It seems obvious to me that whoever does not take this truth into account will be condemning himself to produce little effect in the spiritual realm, to work hard and achieve little. So how can we open people's eyes? We must deal with the cause of the blindness, we must free them from the power of Satan, we must do something about Satan's influence upon them.

The Lord Jesus had already said the same thing in different words during His earthly ministry. We find it in Mark 3:27. "No one can plunder the strong man's goods, invading his house, unless he first bind the strong man; then he may plunder his house." I have used the definite article with the first occurrence of 'strong man' because the Greek text has it, the point being that this particular strong man has already been introduced in the immediate context. 'The strong man' here is Satan. (The Jewish leaders tried to explain Jesus' authority over the demons by saying that He expelled them by the power of Beelzebul, prince of the demons. In His retort Jesus does not waste time with that name but uses the enemy's proper name, Satan.)

So then, the Lord Jesus declares that it is impossible to steal Satan's goods unless we bind him first. (From His use of 'no one' it seems clear that the Lord is enunciating a general principle or truth.) And what might the nature of those 'goods' be? In the context (see Matthew 12:22-24) Jesus had delivered someone from a demon that caused blindness and dumbness, and in their comments the scribes and Pharisees include other instances where Jesus had expelled demons—it seems clear that the 'goods' are people who are subject to Satan's power, in one way or another. Thus we have the same essential truth as that declared in Acts 26:18—we have to do something about Satan's power over a person so that he or she can be saved! So just what can or should we do? Since the point of handcuffs ('bind') is to keep someone from acting, I believe that in so many words, aloud or in thought, we must forbid Satan (who will usually be using demons) from interfering in the minds of our hearers, before we witness, preach or teach. Consider what Sovereign Jesus said in Luke 10:19.

"Take note, I am giving[1] you the authority to trample on snakes and scorpions, and over all the power of the enemy, and nothing at all may harm you." In Matthew 28:18 Sovereign Jesus affirms that He holds "all authority in heaven and on earth", so He is clearly competent to delegate some of that authority to us. Now then, just how does "authority over all the power of the enemy" work, in practice? Authority controls power, but since we have access to God's limitless power (Ephesians 3:20), we should not give Satan the satisfaction of our using his (and he could easily deceive us into doing things we shouldn't). We should use our authority to forbid the use of Satan's power, with reference to specific situations—in my experience, we must be specific. (I have tried binding Satan once for all until the end of the world, but it does not work; presumably because God's plan calls for the enemy's continued activity in this world. We can limit what the enemy does, but not put him completely out of business, or so I deem.) But just how should we go about it?

In the armor described in Ephesians 6 we find "the sword of the Spirit" (verse 17). A sword is a weapon for offense, although it is also used for defense. The Text tells us that this sword is "the ρημα of God"—ρημα, not λογος. It is God's

---

[1] Instead of 'am giving', perhaps 2.5% of the Greek manuscripts, of objectively inferior quality, have 'have given' (as in NIV, NASB, LB, TEV, etc.)—a serious error. Jesus said this perhaps five months before His death and resurrection, addressing the seventy (not just the twelve). The Lord is talking about the future, not the past; a future that includes us!

Word <u>spoken</u>, or applied. Really, what good is a sword left in its sheath? However marvelous our Sword may be (Hebrews 4:12), to produce effect it must come out of the scabbard. The Word needs to be spoken, or written—applied in a specific way.

In the Bible we have many examples where people brought the power of God into action by speaking. Our world began with a creative word from God—spoken (Genesis, 1:3, 6, 9, 11, 14, 20, 24, 26; and see Hebrews 11:3). Moses did a lot of speaking. Elijah spoke (1 Kings 17:1, 18:36, 2 Kings 1:10). Elisha spoke (2 Kings 2:14, 21, 24; 4:16, 43; 6:19). Jesus did a great deal of speaking. Ananias spoke (Acts 9:17). Peter spoke (Acts 9:34, 40). Paul spoke (Acts 13:11; 14:3, 10; 16:18; 20:10; 28:8). In short, we need to speak![1]

I have been asked why Paul himself is not recorded to have forbidden Satan's activity; and if this is so important, why were not the other Apostles told as well. I would say that the other Apostles were indeed told, and three of the Gospels mention it (Matthew 12:29, Mark 3:27, Luke 11:21-2). As for Paul, he did not merely preach and teach, he gave visible demonstrations of God's power (1 Thessalonians 1:5). The first recorded example of his procedure is in Acts 13:6-12. Elymas was presumably demonized, but in any case was being used by Satan to keep Sergius Paulus from the truth. Paul discerned what was involved and took appropriate action, with the result that the proconsul believed, "when he **saw** what had been done". That this was not an isolated case may be seen from Acts 14:3, 16:18, 19:11-20, 2 Corinthians 12:12 and especially Romans 15:18-19. Paul declares that he made the Gentiles obedient "by word and **deed**", "by mighty signs and wonders, by the power of the Spirit of God", and on that basis he claimed to have "fully preached the Gospel of Christ". Which

---

[1] For more on this subject the reader may consult my site: www.prunch.org, under the heading, "Biblical Spiritual Warfare".

leads to the question of how the other Apostles understood their commission.

Paul did not share with the Twelve the advantage of observing the three years of Jesus' ministry at close range. Christ's preaching was inextricably mixed with His healing the sick and expelling demons. He knew exactly what was involved (cf. Luke 13:16). When He sent them out two by two His orders were explicit: "As you go, preach, . . . heal the sick, cleanse lepers, expel demons" (Matthew 10:7-8; cf. Mark 6:7-13 and Luke 9:1-6). In Mark 16:15-18 healing and expelling are expressly included in the Great Commission (I am prepared to demonstrate that verses 9-20 are of necessity the original ending of Mark, and therefore Scripture), and verse 20 affirms that the Lord confirmed their preaching "through the accompanying signs". Hebrews 2:4 repeats that their ministry was characterized by "signs, wonders and various miracles". The Apostles demonstrated the truth of John 14:12, where Jesus affirmed: "he who believes into me, the works that I do he will do also". The Gospel as preached by Jesus and His Apostles was with word and **deed**, miraculous deed, supernatural deed. How about the Gospel we preach?[1]

---

[1] I wonder sometimes if we evangelicals do not regard the Apostles, especially Paul, as virtually divine. Scripture makes clear that the OT writers did not understand the full implications of what they wrote. They were kept from error while writing, but not when interpreting to themselves what they had written. I see no reason for supposing that the NT writers were treated differently. The Sacred Text itself records some of their failures. Why should we assume that Paul and the others had a full grasp of the complete range of options for spiritual warfare? Certainly no detailed procedure or technique is spelled out in the Bible. Why not? I suggest the following. This area of truth is so powerful that if an infallible procedure had been spelled out in an unmistakable way, Satan and his angels would have been wiped out long since. But that would have frustrated the purpose of God in allowing them to continue in operation even though defeated and with their final destination defined. Also, it seems to be God's purpose that our walk with Him not be easy or automatic—He is a rewarder of those who "**diligently** seek" Him (Hebrews 11:6). Further, to wield the power of God is a demanding privilege; it requires clean hands and a pure heart (James 4:8), it demands humility (James 4:6). God does not give up His secrets to the lazy and uncommitted (Proverbs 25:2).

I now return to an analysis of Paul's commission. When attempting to evangelize one or more pagans (non-Christians), there was a sequence of things to be done:

1) Since light is of no use to a blind person, the necessary starting point is to deal with their spiritual blindness, by cancelling the satanic strongholds and blind-spots in their minds (1 John 3:8).

2) "So as to bring them back from darkness into light and from the authority of Satan to God"—the prepositional phrases are parallel and basically synonymous. Having been delivered from the blindness, the person is now ready for light, the light of God's Good News. Once we have repelled the enemy's interference, I believe it is possible to introduce a positive influence, based on Matthew 18:18. I understand the 'binding' to include the repelling of the enemy's interference, and in that event the 'loosing' presumably includes the introduction of a positive influence. I invoke the Spirit of the Truth (John 15:26) and of conviction (John 16:8) to guide and encourage the person to believe into Jesus.

3) "So that they may receive forgiveness of sins and an inheritance among those who are sanctified"—this is the desired result. Strictly speaking, the Text has 'those who have been sanctified', referring to the final result. However, it is well to remember that sanctification is also a process.

4) To receive that desired result, the person must believe into Jesus, 'into', not 'in'—the Text always has 'believe **into** Jesus', the point being that there is a change of position, from being outside to being inside, and commitment is involved.

Are we to handle snakes?—Mark 16:18

In the NKJV, Mark 16:18 reads like this: "they will take up serpents; and if they drink anything deadly, it will by no means hurt them; they will lay hands on the sick, and they will recover."[1]

The NIV renders 'they will pick up snakes with their hands', the 'with their hands' being based on just over 2% of the Greek manuscripts. As we know, there are those who take this translation literally, and believe that they must handle poisonous snakes in obedience to God. I respect their sincerity, but believe they have been misled by a faulty translation.

I would say that this particular statement of the Lord's has been generally misunderstood. The verb in question covers a wide semantic area, one of the uses being to pick up the way a garbage man picks up a bag of trash—he does so to get rid of it (hence 'remove'). I believe Luke 10:19 sheds light on this question. In Luke 10:19 the Lord Jesus said: "Behold, I give [so 98% of the Greek manuscripts] you **the** authority to trample on snakes and scorpions, and over all the power of the enemy, and nothing shall by any means hurt you." The Lord is addressing the Seventy, not the Twelve, and others were doubtless present; further, this was said perhaps four months before His death and resurrection. It follows that this authority is not limited to the apostles, and there is no indication of a time limit. The Lord Jesus affirms that He gives us the authority over all the power of the enemy. In Matthew 28:18 He declares that He holds "all authority . . . in heaven and earth", and so He has the right and the competence to delegate a portion of that authority to us. We may have any number of

---

[1] Since only three Greek MSS (really only two) omit Mark 16:9-20, against at least 1,700 that contain them, there can be no reasonable question as to the genuineness of those verses. For more on this subject please see the respective appendix in any recent edition of my book, *The Identity of the New Testament Text*.

enemies, but <u>the</u> enemy is Satan. The phrase, "all the power", presumably includes his works, followed by their consequences.

Returning to Luke 10:19, the Lord gives us the authority to "trample snakes and scorpions". Well now, to smash the literal insect, a scorpion, you don't need power from on High, just a slipper (if you are fast you can do it barefoot). To trample a snake I prefer a boot, but we can kill literal snakes without supernatural help. It becomes obvious that Jesus was referring to something other than reptiles and insects. I understand Mark 16:18 to be referring to the same reality—Jesus declares that certain signs will accompany the believers (the turn of phrase virtually has the effect of commands): they will expel demons, they will speak strange languages, they will remove 'snakes', they will place hands on the sick. ("If they drink . . ." is not a command; it refers to an eventuality.) But what did the Lord Jesus mean by 'snakes'?

In a list of distinct activities Jesus has already referred to demons, so the 'snakes' must be something else. In Matthew 12:34 Jesus called the Pharisees a 'brood of vipers', and in 23:33, 'snakes, brood of vipers'. In John 8:44, after they claimed God as their father, Jesus said, "You are of your father the devil". And 1 John 3:10 makes clear that Satan has many other 'sons'. In Revelation 20:2 we read: "He seized the dragon, the ancient serpent, who is a slanderer, even Satan, who deceives the whole inhabited earth, and bound him for a thousand years." If Satan is a snake, then his children are also snakes. So then, I take it that our 'snakes' are human beings who chose to serve Satan, who sold themselves to evil. I conclude that the 'snakes' in Luke 10:19 are the same as those in Mark 16:18, but what of the 'scorpions'? Since they also are of the enemy, they may be demons, in which case the term may well include their offspring, the humanoids [see "As were the days of Noah", in chapter V]. I am still working on the question of just how the removal is to be done.

The Natsorean

Every version that I remember seeing misleads the reader by obliterating one of the Lord's titles, a title that the glorified Jesus Himself used when dealing with Saul of Tarsus on the Damascus road. When Saul asked, "Who are you, Lord?", He answered, "I am Jesus the Natsorean, whom you are persecuting" (Acts 22:8). Most versions at this place render 'Jesus of Nazareth', while some have 'Jesus the Nazarene'. For an explanation of why I use 'ts' instead of 'z', please see "'Prophets' in Matthew 2:23", in chapter II.

The familiar 'Nazarene' [Ναζαρηνος] occurs four times: Mark 1:24, 14:67, 16:6 and Luke 4:34. 'Jesus the Nazarene' would appear to be another way of saying 'Jesus of/from Nazareth', and some versions so translate the phrase. Unfortunately, the versions do the same with 'Natsorean' [Ναζωραιος], which I consider to be a serious error. Just looking at the two Greek words, they are obviously different. The Hebrew root is *netser*, 'branch', a reference to Isaiah 11.1 ('Nazareth' is a transliteration of the Hebrew name). Going back to Acts 22:8, why would Jesus waste time with the name of a town? He was dealing with a highly instructed Pharisee; He introduced Himself as David's Branch, the Messiah—a reference that Saul would immediately understand.

'Natsorean' occurs fifteen times: Matthew 2:23, 26:71; Mark 10:47; Luke 18:37, 24:19; John 18:5,7, 19:19; Acts 2:22, 3:6, 4:10, 6:14, 22:8, 24:5 and 26:9. All have the definite article, except the first one—the Natsorean; except that in Acts 24:5 Felix speaks of 'the sect of the Natsoreans'. Speaking of Felix, his use of the term 'sect' is instructive. Aside from Acts 22:8, that I have already discussed, I consider that John 19:19 deserves special comment. The title above the cross read: This is Jesus the Natsorean, the King of the Jews. Pilate had evidently researched Jesus quite well (anyone with a large following is a potential problem); I believe that he knew precisely what he was doing when he used 'Natsorean', just as he knew precisely what he was doing when he put 'the King of the Jews'. For more on the subject of Pilate, please see "Poor Pilate—wrong place, wrong time", above.

Whatever version of the Bible you are using, I would urge you to correct it at the references mentioned above, so you know when a title is being used. 'The Natsorean' needs to be added to any list of the Lord's titles.

Fire loves straw—1 Corinthians 3:13

The context is king of interpretation, so I begin with verses 11-15:

> 11 No one can lay any foundation other than what is laid, which is Jesus Christ.[1] 12 Now if anyone builds on this foundation with gold, silver, precious stones, wood, hay, straw, 13 the work of each will become evident; because the Day will make it clear, because it will be revealed by fire. Yes, the fire will test each one's work, of what sort it is. 14 If the work that anyone built endures, he will receive a reward. 15 If anyone's work is burned up, he will suffer loss; but he himself will be saved, albeit so as through fire.

Paul is talking about the Day of Christ wherein those in Christ will be called to account. The Text plainly states that what we have done will be tested by fire. Someone who spent most of his time living for himself rather than for Christ's Kingdom will be surrounded by nice, dry straw (all that any fire could ask for!). So the angel aims the blowtorch at the straw—the fire is

---

[1] I would say that the primary reference here is to leaders of local congregations, who need to be careful how they 'build' God's 'house'. But I believe it also clearly applies to anyone whose personal life is based on Jesus Christ. Each of us will give an account of how we built our lives on that foundation. Note that we are not offered the option of changing the foundation. Anyone who attempts to do so does not belong to God.

high, hot, but short-lived. The person is left standing in a pile of fine ash, somewhat the worse for the wear.

The price you pay for not living for Christ's kingdom is to lose your life. That is all it costs, just your life! Consider the words of Sovereign Jesus recorded in Luke 9:24-25. Let us begin with verse 23. "If anyone desires to come after me let him deny himself, take up his cross each day and follow me. For whoever wants to save his life will lose it, but whoever loses his life for my sake, he will save it. For what will it profit a man to gain the whole world but waste or forfeit himself?" What does the Lord mean when He speaks of losing one's 'life'? One does not lose one's soul for love of Christ. Nor is the reference to being killed. Rather, Jesus has in mind the life we live, the accumulated results of our living. All that I have done up to this moment plus all that I will yet do until overtaken by death or the rapture of the Church, whichever happens first—that is the 'life' that is at risk (in my own case).

Let us look at our Lord's words a little more closely. There seems to be a contradiction here—if you lose, you save; if you want to save, you lose. How can it work? The following context helps us out. In verse 26 Jesus explains verses 24-25 in terms of His second coming. The parallel passage, Matthew 16:27, is clearer. "For the Son of Man is going to come in the glory of his Father, with his angels, and then he will repay each according to his deeds." Christ was thinking of the day of reckoning. In other words, "we will all stand before the judgment seat of Christ" (Romans 14:10) and "each of us will give account of himself to God" (Romans 14:12). "For we must all appear before the judgment seat of Christ, so that each one may receive his due according to what he has done while in the body, whether good or bad" (2 Corinthians 5:10). I understand that 1 Corinthians 3:11-15 is referring to the same occasion, the day of reckoning. After declaring that Jesus Christ is the only foundation, Paul speaks of different materials that one might use in building on it: "gold, silver, precious stones" or "wood, hay, straw". The point is, our deeds will be tested by fire. If fire has any effect upon gold or silver it is only to purify them, but its effect on hay and straw is devastating! Okay, so what?

Let us go back to the beginning. God created the human being for His glory; to reflect it and contribute to it. I suppose we may understand Psalm 19:1 and Isaiah 43:7 in this way, at least by extension. But Adam lost this capacity when he rebelled against God. For this reason the sentence that weighs against our race is that we "fall short of the glory of God" (Romans 3:23). But the Son came into the world to restore our lost potential. Ephesians 1:12 and 14 tell us that the object of the plan of salvation is "the praise of His glory" (see also 2 Corinthians 1:20). And 1 Corinthians 10:31 puts it into a **command**: "Whether you eat or drink, or whatever you do, do all to the glory of God." Now then, the point of all this is not to 'ruin' our lives, to take all the 'fun' out of them (as many seem to think). God is not being arrogant, unreasonable, too demanding. Quite the contrary—He is just trying to save us from throwing away our lives. Surely, because the glory of God is eternal (Psalm 104:31), and when I do something for His glory that something is transformed and acquires eternal value—it becomes "gold, silver, precious stones". Works done for the glory of God will go through the fire without harm. On the other hand, what is done with a view to our own ambitions and ideas is "straw". We all know what fire does to straw!

So there it is. To be a slave of Christ means to live with reference to the Kingdom; it means to do everything for the glory of God. In this way the slave 'saves' his life because he will be building it with 'gold and silver', which will pass through the fire at the judgment seat of Christ without loss. In contrast, the believer who refuses to be a slave of Jesus builds his life with 'hay and straw', which will be consumed by the fire—and so he 'loses' his life; he lived in vain; the potential that his life represented was wasted, thrown away. What a tragedy!

When did Jesus leave Annas?—John 18:24

After Jesus was taken prisoner in the Garden, only John mentions that He was taken first to Annas; all the others only mention His being taken to Caiaphas, where the recorded proceedings took place, although of the three only Matthew actually names him (Matthew 26:57, Mark 14:53, Luke 22:54).

So far, so good, but the difficulty begins with John 18:15, that takes up Peter's denials without further ado; but Peter's denials took place at Caiaphas' house, not Annas'. Then verses 19-23 have the high priest questioning Jesus, still at Caiaphas'. Then comes verse 24: NKJV reads, "Then Annas sent Him bound to Caiaphas the high priest"; NIV reads, "Then Annas sent him, still bound, to Caiaphas the high priest" (but a footnote offers, "Now Annas had sent him"); TEV reads, "So Annas sent him, still bound, to Caiaphas the High Priest"; while NASB reads, "Annas therefore sent Him bound to Caiaphas the high priest". All four of these versions have John 18:15-23 occurring in Annas' house, rather than that of Caiaphas—the NIV footnote points to the correct rendering.

It would appear that all four of the versions follow the so-called 'critical' (read 'eclectic') text, that follows some 9% of the Greek manuscripts in adding a conjunction, 'then' or 'therefore' (ουν), after the initial verb, thereby creating the 'problem'. Following the 90%, including the best line of transmission, I render, "(Annas had sent Him bound to Caiaphas the high priest.)". The use of parenthetical comments, or historical/cultural asides, is standard procedure for John; for a partial list see: 1:44, 2:6, 4:2,9,44, 6:4,64, 7:50, 9:14, 11:2,18-19,30-31, 12:1,6,16, 13:2,11,28-29 (there are at least a dozen more). I take it that verse 24 here is just one more instance; it is as if at this point John realizes that the reader could think that the proceedings were still going on at Annas' house. 8:25 resumes with Peter's denials. Following the correct Text, and the correct understanding thereof, John's record is not at variance with that of the other three Gospels.

Where is Mt. Sinai?

I invite attention to Galatians 4:25, that declares that Mt. Sinai is in Arabia: I do not know Paul's definition of 'Arabia', but what the maps call 'Mt. Sinai' probably is not the real one;[1] consider: When Moses fled from Pharaoh he stopped in Midian (Exodus 2:15). Midian lies on the east side of the eastern 'rabbit-ear' of the Red Sea (the Gulf of Aqaba), in present day Saudi Arabia. It has never been part of the so-called 'Sinai Peninsula'. It was at "Horeb, the mountain of God" that Moses saw the 'burning bush' (Exodus 3:1), and in verse 12 God tells Moses: "when you have brought the people out of Egypt, you shall serve God on this mountain". Mt. Horeb has always been in Midian. (Present day Saudi Arabia calls it 'el Lowz', and has it fenced off.) As God continues with Moses' commission, He specifies "three days' journey into the wilderness" (verse 18). According to Exodus 4:27 Aaron met Moses at "the mountain of God" (Horeb, in Midian), and they went together to Egypt.

When the people left Egypt, God led them on a forced march; notice the "so as to go by day and night" (Exodus 13:21). Three days of forced march (Exodus 3:18) would have gotten them close to Ezion Geber (present day Elath), and just another two days would have put them well into Midian. But then God told them to "turn back" and "encamp by the sea, directly opposite Baal Zephon" (Exodus 14:2). To do this they had to leave the established route from Egypt to Arabia, and head south into the wilderness, and this led Pharaoh to conclude that they had lost their way (obviously he would have spies following them, mounted on good horses, to keep him informed). It would have been simply impossible for them to lose their way between Goshen and the western arm of the

---

[1] The difficulty here is not in the Text itself, but in the circumstance that almost all modern maps, whether in Bibles or elsewhere, place Mt. Sinai in the peninsula between the two gulfs, Suez and Aqaba; so much so that the peninsula itself is even so named. But such a location for the mount makes the Biblical account out to be ridiculous, as I explain below, and an inspired Text should not be ridiculous.

Red Sea (the Gulf of Suez), but this is what those who place Mt. Sinai in today's 'Sinai Peninsula' are obliged to say—an evident stupidity. The Israelites would have hunted and explored all over that area, down through the years. (And why the chariots? Pharaoh could have surrounded them with foot soldiers.)

God led them down a ravine called 'Wadi Watir' which comes out on a surprisingly large beach called 'Nuweiba' (it is the only beach on that gulf large enough to accommodate that crowd of people and animals). Most of the Gulf of Aqaba is many hundreds of feet deep, with sheer sides, but precisely at Nuweiba there is a land bridge not far below the surface that goes from shore to shore, the width of the gulf at that point being close to 10 miles—the width of the land bridge is several hundred yards, so there was an ample 'causeway' for the crossing. The ravine that opens out on Nuweiba is narrow, with steep sides, so when God moved the pillar of cloud to the mouth of the ravine, Pharaoh and his chariots were blocked. They could not pass the pillar, they could not climb the sides of the ravine with chariots, and with over six hundred chariots in a narrow ravine they would have a proper 'gridlock' (lots of unhappy horses!). I suppose that God removed the pillar of cloud while part of the crowd was still on the land bridge, which encouraged Pharaoh to chase after them; and we know the rest of the story. If God let them get out to the middle, they would be five miles from either shore, too far for most people to swim.[1] I take it that God's purpose was to destroy the Egyptian army so it could not be a threat to Israel in the early years.

---

[1] In our day chariot pieces have been discovered along that land bridge.

Did the cross kill Jesus?—John 10:18 X Mark 15:39, John 19:30, Matthew 27:50, Luke 23:46

In the NKJV, John 10:17-18 reads like this: "Therefore My Father loves Me, because I lay down My life that I may take it again. No one takes it from me, but I lay it down of Myself. I have power to lay it down, and I have power to take it again. This command I have received from My Father." Please notice: "**No one takes it from me**". That includes Pilate, etc. In Matthew 27:50 and John 19:30 the Text states that Jesus "dismissed His spirit". Now consider Mark 15:39. "So when the centurion, who stood opposite Him, saw that He cried out like this and breathed His last, he said, 'Truly this Man was the Son of God!'" Now what could convince a hardened Roman centurion? He had doubtless witnessed no end of crucifixions; he knew that the victim died of asphyxiation. Hanging from one's hands, the diaphragm is pressed against the lungs, and the victim can't breathe. Nailing the feet was a sadistic procedure, to prolong the agony—in spite of the pain, the victim would push up so he could get a breath, until finally too worn out to do so. (That is why the Pharisees requested Pilate to have the legs broken; then they died within minutes.) Now then, someone who is dying asphyxiated does not give a tremendous shout; but ordinary people cannot just tell their spirit to leave. So when that centurion observed that Jesus gave a tremendous shout and then immediately died, he drew the obvious conclusion: he was looking at a supernatural being. The cross did not kill Jesus; He gave His life voluntarily, for you and me. Thank you, Lord!

'Censer', or 'altar of incense'?—Hebrews 9:4

What concerns us here is the Greek word, θυμιατηριον, that occurs only here in the NT. In the LXX the meaning of the word is 'censer', and that is plainly the intended meaning here. But unfortunately modern versions like NIV, TEV, LB, NASB, etc.

render 'altar of incense', thus setting up a contradiction with the Old Testament. [What could have motivated such a perverse proceeding?] According to Exodus 30:6 the altar of incense was placed in front of the curtain leading into the Holy of Holies, and so it was in the Holy Place, not the Holy of Holies. The only reference to this particular censer appears to be in Leviticus 16:12, where it was to be used behind the second curtain to hide the Ark with smoke. Since that censer would only be used once a year (on the day of atonement), it may well have been stored just behind a corner of the second curtain (where the high priest could retrieve it without looking in) and thus the author of Hebrews would be correct in saying that the <u>censer</u> was behind the second curtain, whereas the altar was in front of it. In any event, evidently that censer was **used** only within the Holy of Holies, and so it would be appropriate to say that the area 'had' a golden censer.

'Jesus', or 'Joshua'?—Hebrews 4:8

Beyond question, the Greek Text has 'Jesus', as in the AV, but most modern versions put 'Joshua'. I suppose that 'Jesus' was judged to be an anachronism, and so 'Joshua' was elected to relieve the situation. To be sure, the Septuagint we know uniformly spells 'Joshua' as Ιησους (Jesus) [as a linguist I wonder why the translators transliterated 'Iehoshua' as 'Iesus'], and probably in consequence, in Acts 7:45 Luke refers to Joshua as 'Iesus' [it was not his purpose to correct the LXX]. However, looking carefully at the context in Psalm 95:7-11, Joshua just does not fit. Consider: it is presumably Jehovah the Son who is speaking ("Jehovah our Maker", verse 6), and since the reference is to those who fell in the wilderness during the forty years, Joshua cannot be in view. Not only that, I invite attention to Joshua 21:43-45 and 23:1, where the Text says that Joshua did in fact give them rest. So whom are you going to believe? Of course the Text is referring to physical rest, not spiritual, since neither Joshua nor anyone else could be responsible for a people's spiritual rest. Ezekiel chapter 18 is very clear to the effect that each individual is responsible for his own eternal destiny. God has no grandchildren, only sons and daughters. In Mathew 23:8-10 Sovereign Jesus forbids any attempt to dominate someone else's faith or conscience. This is consistent with His statement in John 4:23-24. The worship that the Father wants cannot be forced, imposed, controlled or faked.

In relief of the notion of 'anachronism' I offer the following: 1) in John 12:41 John affirms that Isaiah saw Jesus (it was Jehovah the Son on the throne); 2) in 1 Corinthians 10:4 Paul affirms that the Rock that provided water was Christ; 3) in Hebrews 11:26 the same author [as I believe] has Moses choosing "the reproach of Christ"; 4) in 1 Peter 1:19-20 Peter affirms that the shed blood of God's Lamb, Jesus, was foreknown before Creation—but blood requires a body, and the Lamb's body was that of Jesus; so Jesus, as Jesus, was known before Creation. Returning to Hebrews 4:8, it was precisely Jesus, Jehovah the Son, who did not allow that generation to enter the 'rest'.

'Saved in childbearing'—1 Timothy 2:15

In the NKJV, 1 Timothy 2:14-15 reads like this: "And Adam was not deceived, but the woman being deceived, fell into transgression. Nevertheless she will be saved in childbearing if they continue in faith, love, and holiness, with self-control." We begin with "she will be saved"; 'she' is a pronoun, that stands for a noun, and in the context the reference is clearly to Eve. So how is Eve to be saved? (To render 'preserved' is basically meaningless.) Neither Eve nor any other woman is saved by bearing a child. In the Greek Text we find 'childbirth', a noun, not a verb. Further, there is a definite article with the noun, so it is 'the childbirth'. There is only one childbirth that could result in salvation for Eve, and the rest of us, the birth of the Messiah.

Here is my translation of verses 14-15: "Also, Adam was not deceived; rather, the woman, being deceived, became a transgressor. However, she will be saved through the Childbirth—if they continue in faith, love and holiness, with self-control." Of course Eve bore Seth, thus beginning the line that culminated in the Messiah (Genesis 3:15).

In the middle of verse 15, and of the sentence, Paul breaks the rules of grammar and switches from 'she' to 'they'—what is true of Eve is applied to all women. Well, strictly speaking, since 'they' has no antecedent I suppose it could include men as well, everybody (unless someone wants to argue that women are saved on a different basis than men [which I think would run afoul of other passages]). Still, the paragraph is about women. Any sisters in Christ who have been troubled by this verse, thinking that they must bear a child, may relax on that score.

Did Jesus hide?—John 8:59

In the NKJV, John 8:59 reads like this: "Then they took up stones to throw at Him; but Jesus hid Himself and went out of the temple, going through the midst of them, and so passed by." My translation reads like this: "Then they picked up stones to throw at Him;[1] but Jesus was concealed and went out of the temple, going through the middle of them; yes, that is how He got away!" The familiar "hid Himself" is not the best rendering here. Jesus did not try to hide behind a pillar, or whatever. He was surrounded by angry Jews with stones in their hands. Obviously they would have seen Him and started stoning. He became invisible and simply walked out, passing right through the middle of them. About half a percent of the Greek manuscripts, of objectively inferior quality (demonstrably so), omit "going through the middle of them; yes, that is

---

[1] Since certain situations demanded a stoning, there were doubtless piles of ammunition placed strategically around the temple premises.

how He got away" (as in NIV, NASB, LB, TEV, etc.). The 99.5% are doubtless correct, and supply an important detail.

Did they hear the Voice, or not?—Acts 9:7 X Acts 22:9

In the NKJV, Acts 9:7 reads like this: "And the men who journeyed with him stood speechless, hearing a voice but seeing no one." And Acts 22:9 reads like this: "And those who were with me indeed saw the light and were afraid, but they did not hear the voice of him who spoke to me." Comparing the two accounts, we seem to have a discrepancy: did they hear the Voice, or didn't they? Comparing the verses in the Greek Text, we discover that the verb, 'hear', and the noun, 'voice', are the same in both. Looking more closely, however, we notice that in 9:7 the noun is in the Genitive case, while in 22:9 it is in the Accusative. We have here a subtlety of Greek grammar: in the Genitive case 'voice' refers to sound, while in the Accusative case it refers to meaning, to the words. Saul's companions heard the Voice, but were not allowed to understand the words—only Saul understood the words. A similar thing happened in John 12:28-29; the people heard the sound (sufficiently impressive that they called it thunder), but only Jesus understood the words.

Buy a ticket to Heaven?—Luke 16:9

In the NKJV, Luke 16:9 reads like this: "And I say to you, make friends for yourselves by unrighteous mammon, that when you fail, they may receive you into an everlasting home [literally, 'the eternal dwellings']." Within the context the Lord is clearly using irony, or sarcasm. In the immediately preceding verse the owner's 'commendation' of the stupid steward is obviously sarcastic, since the steward was sacked. And verse 14 below indicates that what Jesus said was for the benefit of the Pharisees, who were greedy. The use of sarcasm is not rare in the Bible. Getting into the eternal dwellings does not depend on 'buying' friends down here; it depends on pleasing the Owner up there. And who says someone who can be bought with 'unrighteous mammon' is going to Heaven? He would have to get there first in order to 'receive' the buyer. The whole 'scene' is patently ridiculous. Just by the way, verse 13 declares a terribly important truth. To embrace the world's value system (humanism, relativism, materialism) is to reject God. Materialistic 'Christians' are really serving mammon ('mammon' includes more than just money).

Buy cleansing? Luke 11:41

In the NKJV, Luke 11:41 reads like this: "But rather give alms of such things as you have; then indeed all things are clean to you." My translation reads like this: "Nevertheless, give what is possible as alms; then indeed all things are clean to you." At first glance this statement seems difficult, but because they were filled with greed, for them to give away as much as possible would represent a major change in their values. Zacchaeus offers a case in point: the Lord Himself declared that he was saved (Luke 19:8-9).

Do we command God?—Matthew 18:18

In the NKJV, Matthew 18:18 reads like this: "Assuredly, I say to you, whatever you bind on earth will be bound in heaven, and whatever you loose on earth will be loosed in heaven." The normal meaning of this translation is that Heaven has to follow our lead (is it not?), and there is no lack of religious communities that teach this. But really now, what possible competence might human beings have to tell God what to do? We may ask, but not command. The difficulty arises from an inaccurate translation. The tense of the Greek verb phrase here is a periphrastic future perfect, passive voice (so also in Matthew 16:18). Thus, "will have been bound/loosed" not "will be bound/loosed". We are not telling God what to do; we are to apply down here that which He has already done in heaven. (What had been just for Peter is now given to all the disciples.)

In John 5:19 the Lord Jesus stated that He could only do what He saw the Father doing. Our inability to see what the Father is doing is probably one of our worst spiritual problems—it condemns us to waste a lot of time and energy trying to do things that we shouldn't. In practical terms, when I 'bind' something and nothing happens, I conclude that it had not been 'bound' in Heaven. I tried to do something that the Father was not doing.

'Size' of faith?—Luke 17:6, Matthew 17:20

In the NKJV, Luke 17:6 reads like this: "If you have faith as a mustard seed, you can say to this mulberry tree, 'Be pulled up by the roots and be planted in the sea,' and it would obey you." Perhaps because of the parables just discussed, I do not remember ever hearing any other interpretation for this than the size of the faith. (The same holds for Matthew 17:20.) But that usually left me disgruntled: surely my faith was bigger than a seed, but I was never able to make a tree or hill obey me! But looking at the Text again, might the intended meaning of 'as a mustard seed' be different? Is not the phrase ambiguous? Could the verb 'has' be implied? Well then, what kind of 'faith' might a mustard seed have? Albeit so small, it reacts without question to the climactic circumstances, and grows to remarkable proportions. If we reacted similarly, without question, to the Holy Spirit's promptings, our spiritual 'climactic circumstances', we should indeed move mountains, literally. Or to put it another way, a seed has the faith to die, like the Lord Jesus said in John 12:24: "unless a grain of wheat falls into the ground and dies, it remains alone". In 1 Corinthians 15:31 Paul said that he died daily. How so? Obviously he did not die physically; he died to himself, his own ideas and ambitions, so as to embrace God's will. Dying to self is a pre-requisite for moving mountains, because then we will only attempt to do what we see the Father doing (John 5:19).

'Valley', or 'ravine'?—Luke 3:5

In the NKJV, Luke 3:4-5 reads like this: "The voice of one crying in the wilderness: 'Prepare the way of the Lord; make His paths straight. Every valley shall be filled and every mountain and hill brought low; the crooked places shall be made straight and the rough ways smooth; . . .'" Does this mean that the surface of the earth will be flattened out? My translation reads like this: "A voice calling out: 'Prepare the way of the Lord in the wilderness, make His paths straight. 5 Every ravine will be filled up, and every mountain and hill will be leveled; the crooked parts of the roads will be straightened out, and the rough parts will be smoothed out; . . .'" The reference is to Isaiah 40:3. Hebrew poetry, and prose, makes heavy use of parallel or synonymous statements. From the context in Isaiah it seems clear that "in the wilderness" goes with the verb "make straight", not "call out". But why a straight road in the wilderness? Any road facilitates the movement of people and goods, but a straight road through accidented terrain is a ma-jor asset, and Jerusalem is surrounded by accidented terrain. I render 'ravine' according to the normal meaning of the Greek word here; 'ravine' is also one of the normal meanings of the corresponding Hebrew word in Isaiah. Actually, Isaiah 40:3-4 describes the construction of a modern super highway. Luke 3:5 describes what happens where the highway passes, not all over the place.

Peter's mother-in-law—Matthew 8:14-15 X Mark 1:29-31, Luke 4:38-39

For most of my adult life, I assumed that Jesus healed Peter's mother-in-law only once, until one day it occurred to me that some of the details do not match. Consider: although the details of the actual healing are slightly different in the three accounts, they could be harmonized to come out with a single episode; it is the context that differs. Mark and Luke have the same context; the healing they record took place not long after the ministry in Samaria (John chapter four), but certainly before the 'Sermon on the Mount' recorded by Matthew. The context for the healing in Matthew is quite different, and happened after that 'Sermon'. As recorded by Matthew, Mark and Luke, I would say that the events occurring between the two healings occupy the following stretches of Text: Matthew 4:23-8:13, Mark 1:32-45 and Luke 4:40-5:15. I see a practical application to this: just because God heals you one time does not mean that you will never get sick again (even with the same problem).

Acts 10:30—"this very hour"

The question is: to which day and to what hour was Cornelius referring?

We need to try to feel the atmosphere of the situation. Cornelius is a gentile, but he REALLY wants to know God; yet he 'knows' that Jehovah has a thing with the Jews and is not too big on Gentiles. But he is convinced that Jehovah is the true God and is doing his very best to please Him. So one day God gives him a special dispensation of grace; He sends an angel! Was Cornelius excited, or was he excited!! Like, **wow**. So he sends his messengers hotfooting it to Joppa (some 60 km), and they do it in less than 24 hours. So what does Cornelius do while he waits? He prays and <u>fasts</u>. Surely, he was already a

man of prayer (v. 2) so how is he going to show his appreciation to God for the special favor? He fasts—now that he has
God's attention, marvel of marvels, he wants to stay tuned in
so as not to miss anything. And after allowing for the minimum time necessary for the roundtrip, he is at the door looking down the road. This man is **serious**.

Enter Peter. He lays on the bit about Jews not contaminating
themselves with Gentiles, but God told him to come, and so
what does Cornelius want. Now it is his turn—he is looking at
a Jew who is not exactly oozing enthusiasm at being there, but
he is Jehovah's messenger and the centurion understands
about rank and authority; so he plays the only cards he has:
his own sincerity and seriousness, and God's revealed will. "I
have been fasting during four days until this very hour" (the
first card) and "the ninth hour . . . ." (the second card).

To me, ταυτης της ωρας is emphatic, "this very hour".
νηστευων και is attested by 95.2% of the Greek manuscripts,
including P^{50} and D, among the oldest extant, not to mention
the old Latin and Syriac versions (another 1.5% have just
νηστευων). So we have a periphrastic verb phrase,
ημην νηστευων, which emphasizes the continuous aspect of
the action. απο and μεχρι define the time span, "from . . .
until". Putting it all together we have, "I have been fasting
during four days until this very hour."

About the sequence, we observe the following:

v. 3—1st day: Cornelius sees angel, about 3 p.m., and sends
messengers forthwith;

v. 9—2nd day: Peter has vision, after 12 noon, and messengers
arrive (and are lodged for the night);

v. 23—3rd day: Peter and company leave Joppa;

v. 24—4th day: they enter Caesarea (probably before noon).

So by western reckoning we have not quite three full days, but by Hebrew and Brazilian reckoning we have a situation that involves four days.

The messengers, under urgent orders, did the 60 km in under 24 hours (whether they went all night, we don't know, but they were probably obviously tired when they showed up at Peter's gate). Peter was not about to be stampeded into action; he had to eat, sort things out in his mind, talk it over with the others—since they decided to send a committee, preparations had to be made. So they set out the next day, but they are dignified Jews and are not going to run—they set a steady pace and probably make some 45 km before stopping for the night. The remaining 15 km they knock off before noon the next day. So, the "this very hour" refers to the time of Peter's arrival, not the time that the angel appeared to Cornelius.

Deuteronomy 32:8

"When the Most High divided their inheritance to the nations, when He separated the sons of Adam, He set the boundaries of the peoples according to the number of the children of Israel" (as in the NKJV). In recent decades versions have appeared replacing the last word, 'Israel', with 'God', either in the text itself or in a footnote, or both. To understand what is going on, we must look at the evidence:

'sons/children of Israel'—Masoretic Hebrew Text, Samaritan Pentateuch, all ancient versions except the Septuagint (LXX)

'angels of God'—LXX

'sons/children of God/gods—Dead Sea Scrolls (DSS); so alleged by the footnotes mentioned above

Of course the LXX has been around for a long time, but few had the courage to follow it in Deuteronomy 32:8 until the advent of the DSS, so to them I now turn.

Those who have given any attention to the DSS know that for Deuteronomy there are only fragments, most being mere scraps with a few letters on them. Of these, two have been alleged to contain bits of 32:8—4QDeut-j and 4QpaleoDeut-r. 4QpaleoDeut-r stands for a group of scraps (a. 20), one of which is said to contain bits of 32:6-8. Upon inspection, the end of verse 8 is not there, so this scrap is irrelevant to the question in hand.

4QDeut-j is a fragment containing a few letters spread over three lines: the first line has parts of three letters; the second line has five or six letters; the third line has nine letters, being *bene elohim*, 'sons of gods'. So far as I have been able to confirm, this is the sole basis for the claim that the DSS have 'sons/children of God' in Deuteronomy 32:8. (If anyone knows of something that I have missed, please send it to me.) But wait just a minute please, on what basis can anyone responsibly claim that 4QDeut-j is an honest copy of the biblical book, Deuteronomy? The Essenes had their own ideas about such things, and were not averse to writing in defense of their ideas. The scrap is scarcely sufficient for a clear, demonstrable identification. Indeed, the editors themselves say that it is from an "excerpted" document. Not only that, the scrap definitely does **not** have the biblical *bene ha-Elohim* found in Genesis 6:2 and 4, and Job 1:6, 2:1 and 38:7. **I deny that the DSS furnish any valid evidence against the reading of the Masoretic Text in this place**.

Now I wish to say a few words about the LXX here. The LXX that we know and use is based on three Alexandrian manuscripts from centuries after Christ: Alexandrinus, Sinaiticus and Vaticanus. With reference to the New Testament, the contribution of those three MSS has been mainly negative, and especially so on significant doctrinal questions. What possible basis could anyone have for imagining that the editors responsible for the NT in those MSS would not do similar damage to the Old Testament? If they did not like or understand 'sons of Israel', they were perfectly capable of changing it to 'angels of God'. None of which should encourage us to follow them.

Having said all of the above, we should not be unduly critical of those who have difficulty understanding this verse. How can the inheritance of the nations depend on the number of Israelites [or on the number of angels, for that matter]? I don't know; but God does! Consider the following texts:

1 Peter 1:19-20: "but with the precious blood of Christ, as of a faultless and pure lamb; who was foreknown indeed before the foundation of the world, but was revealed in these last times for your sake." God's Lamb, with blood shed, was so known before the creation of our race and planet. You cannot have blood without a body, so the incarnation and the whole Plan of redemption was in place before the Creation.

Ephesians 1:4: "just as He chose us in Him before the foundation of the world, that we should be holy and blameless before Him, in love." This one is difficult for our poor little finite minds to handle. I, Wilbur Pickering, was chosen before the world was made, so God knows who I am, and all about me. Our Good Shepherd calls us by name (John 10:3). If God knew all about me before Creation, then obviously He knew all about the "sons of Israel" also, so Deuteronomy 32:8 should present no difficulty to our understanding.

2 Timothy 1:9: "the One who saved us and called us with a holy calling, not because of our works but because of His own purpose and grace, which was given to us in Christ Jesus before time began." Repeat the comment above. Note that 'time' had a beginning.

Titus 1:2: "in hope of eternal life—which life God, who cannot lie, promised before the ages of time." Repeat the comment above.

Acts 15:18: "All His works are known to God from eternity." Although perhaps 5% of the Greek manuscripts omit this verse (as in most modern versions), the 95%, including the best line of transmission, are certainly correct. Of what relevance is 'time' to an eternal Being? It may be that 'time' and 'space' are concepts that are limited to our planet and our solar system. (Without time and space, how can you calculate speed or distance, or determine the size and age of the universe?) God knew all about the "nations" and the "sons of Israel" before Creation.

Matthew 25:34: "Then the King will say to those on His right: 'Come, you blessed of my Father, inherit the kingdom that was prepared for you at the foundation of the world." More of the same.

Hebrews 4:3: "His works were certainly finished from the foundation of the world." More texts could be added to this list, but I have given enough to make the point: our notions of 'time' do not place any limit upon the eternal God. The Text is perfectly clear; God knows what is going to happen long before it actually does. Our tiny, limited, finite minds have trouble understanding this, but that does not alter the fact. It should be equally obvious that we are totally incompetent to 'improve' upon a divinely inspired Text.

Vast segments of Christianity, beginning in early centuries, have been anti-Semitic, at least theologically. They consider that the Church replaced Israel as God's people, and so on. I wonder if that anti-Semitism might have something to do with the haste with which some have jumped on the 'sons of God' band-wagon. But whatever one's personal predilections, surely questions of the Text should be resolved on the basis of objective evidence.

Chapter II: DIFFICULTIES?

The purpose of this section is to take up passages in the Sacred Text that appear to present us with a genuine difficulty, a difficulty that arises from the language of the Text itself. Again, the context has not received the careful attention it requires, except that here the historical and geographic contexts may also enter in.

'Cainan' #2—Luke 3:36 X Genesis 11:12

Luke 3: "35 of Serug, of Reu, of Peleg, of Eber, of Shela, 36 of Cainan, of Arphaxad, of Shem, of Noah, of Lamech,"

There are several spelling variations that together are attested by almost 1% of the MSS; 99% have Καιναν. Apparently only two omit, P[75v] and D, but no printed text follows their lead. So there is no reasonable doubt that Luke in fact wrote that Shelah was fathered by Cainan, not Arphaxad. This Cainan has been widely used to justify treating the genealogies in Genesis like accordions—if one name was demonstrably left out in the Genesis account, then who knows how many others were also left out. This Cainan is also used to deny the validity of constructing a strict chronology based on the time spans given in the genealogies.

But where did Luke get this information? The LXX contains Cainan in Genesis 11:12, but is so different from the Massoretic text here that it looks like fiction. Recall that the LXX we know is based on codices Vaticanus, Sinaiticus and Alexandrinus, produced centuries after Luke. It is more likely that our LXX is based on Luke than vice versa. Where then did Luke get it? I understand that Luke obtained the information about this Cainan from records existing in his day, and being correct information was led by the Holy Spirit to include it in his Gospel. Just like Jude, who quoted Enoch—Enoch's prophecy must have been in existence in Jude's day, but we have no copy in

Hebrew today (though Jews are reported to have used one so recently as the 13th century A.D.); similarly we have no copy of Luke's source.[1]

This brief note was inspired by the discussion of the subject given by Dr. Floyd N. Jones in *Chronology of the Old Testament*[2] (which book comes close to solving all the alleged numerical discrepancies in the OT, at least as I see it). However, the explanation that follows is original with me (if anyone else has proposed it, I am unaware). Let us recall the exact wording of Genesis 11:12-13. "Arphaxad lived thirty-five years and begot Salah; after he begot Salah, Arphaxad lived four hundred and three years, and begot sons and daughters."

The verb 'begot' requires that Salah be a blood descendent of Arphaxad, not adopted. He could be a grandson, the son of a son of Arphaxad, or even a great-grandson, etc., except that in this case the time frame only has room for one intervening generation. The plain meaning of the formula in the Text, 'W lived X years and begot Y; after W begot Y he lived Z years,' is

---

[1] Let us recall Luke's stated purpose in writing: "It seemed good to me also, most excellent Theophilus, having taken careful note of everything from Above, to write to you with precision and in sequence, so that you may know the certainty of the things in which you were instructed" (Luke 1:**3**-4). Given his stated purpose in writing, Luke's account needs to be historically accurate (cf. 2:2 and 3:1). So then, I take it that the Holy Spirit guided Luke to include Cainan #2; I will argue the same for Joram below. While I am on this tack, my solution to the 'Jeremiah' problem in Matthew 27:9-10 is similar. Daniel (9:2) refers to "the books" (plural) in connection with Jeremiah the prophet. So I assume that Matthew had access to other writings of Jeremiah, of which no copy survives.

[2] *Chronology of the Old Testament: A Return to the Basics* (Floyd Nolen Jones, The Woodlands, TX: Kings Word Press, 1999, pp. 29-36). (This is the 14th edition, revised and enlarged—the 1st came out in 1993.) I imagine that many readers may feel uncomfortable with the author's very dogmatic way of expressing himself, but I would urge them to filter out the rhetorical style and concentrate on the substantial arguments, that are of extraordinary value. For example, his solution to the conundrum of the reigns of the kings on the two sides of the divided monarchy is simply brilliant, and to my mind obviously correct, leaving no loose ends. (In this connection, he debunks the claims of Edwin R. Thiele and William F. Albright.)

that W was X years old when Y was born, is it not?[1] I take the clear meaning of the Hebrew Text to be that Arphaxad was 35 years old when Salah was born, whatever we may decide to do about 'Cainan'.

Let us try to imagine the situation in the years immediately following the Flood. After the Flood the 'name of the game' was to replenish the earth. Indeed, the divine command was: "Be fruitful and multiply" (Gen. 9:1). So, whom could Noah's grandsons marry? Obviously their cousins, Noah's grand-daughters. There would be an urgency to reproduce—thus, the girls would be married off at puberty, and the boys would not be wasting around either. The women would be giving birth as often as they possibly could. Really, the absolute top priority would be to increase the number of people.

Arphaxad was born two years after the flood, but his wife could have been born a year or two earlier. (The Sacred Text is clear to the effect that only eight souls entered the ark, but some of the women could have conceived during the Flood.) Thus, Arphaxad could have fathered "Cainan" when he was 17/18. Similarly, Cainan could have fathered Salah when he was 17/18. In this way Arphaxad could be said to have "begotten" Salah when he was 35. Cainan could have died early or been passed over in Genesis because the time span did not constitute a 'generation', or both. Or, as things got back to normal, culturally speaking, the haste with which Arphaxad and Cainan procreated might have been viewed as unseemly. The expedient of omitting Cainan would make the account more 'normal' while preserving precision as to the elapsed time.

But Luke would be correct in saying that Salah was "of" Cainan who was "of" Arphaxad. Salah was Arphaxad's grandson. In

---

[1] It follows that this formula destroys the 'accordion' gambit. There were precisely 130 years between Adam and Seth, 105 between Seth and Enosh, 90 between Enosh and Cainan #1, etc., etc.

any case, the Messianic line was passed on by Salah. Without Luke's record I, for one, would never have stopped to consider what must have happened immediately following the Flood—the absolute priority must have been to increase the number of people.

How long was Jesus in the tomb?

Many books and articles have been written about this question. The principal difficulty derives from Jesus' own use of several different expressions to describe that time. Referring to the time period between His death and resurrection He Himself said—"the third day", "after three days" and "three days and three nights". A careful look at all the relevant passages makes clear that the three phrases are not equal candidates. Consider:

There is only one instance of 'three days and three nights', to be found in Matthew 12:40. Jesus cites the experience of Jonah (Jonah 1:17) and says that He will have a similar experience. That we are in the presence of a Hebrew idiom will become apparent from what follows.

There are just two instances of 'after three days', to be found in Mark 8:31 and Matthew 27:63. In Mark Jesus is cited in an indirect quote, as Jesus tells the disciples what is going to happen to Him. In Matthew Jesus is quoted by the Jewish leaders as they ask Pilate to guard the tomb; but notice that in verse 64 they go on to say, "until the third day", so the two phrases would appear to be synonymous.

As for 'the third day', there are eleven direct instances, plus three related ones. Proper hermeneutic procedure requires that we interpret the few in terms of the many, and not the reverse. In Matthew 16:21, 17:23, 20:19; Mark 9:31, 10:34;[1]

---

[1] In Mark 10:34 the eclectic text currently in vogue reads 'after three days', following a mere 0.7% of the extant Greek manuscripts, which manuscripts are of objectively inferior quality, demonstrably so.

Luke 9:22, 18:33, Jesus is telling the disciples what is going to happen to Him. In Luke 24:7 the angel quotes Jesus to the women at the empty tomb. In Luke 24:46 the resurrected Jesus is speaking with the disciples. In Acts 10:40 Peter is preaching to Cornelius. In 1 Corinthians 15:4 Paul makes a statement. Those are the eleven direct instances. In Luke 24:21 Cleopas says to Jesus, "today is the third day since these things happened"—the 'these things' refers to the crucifixion, and the 'today' includes the resurrection, since he cites the women. In John 2:19 Jesus says, "destroy this temple, and in three days I will raise it". In Luke 13:32 Jesus sends a message to Herod, "the third day I will be perfected". Those are the three related instances, for a total of fourteen. Well, the last one is marginal, so make it thirteen.

I suppose that all human cultures have the tendency to think that their way of seeing things is right, and all others wrong. But what to do when conflicts arise? When attempting to understand a given event, it is the culture within which it happened that must be respected. Jews and Brazilians handle time differently than do 'Westerners' in general. Here in Brazil, after church, we often say, "I'll see you in eight days", which means the next Sunday. The day in which you are is included in the number. We have biblical basis; consider John 20:26. "Well, after eight days His disciples were inside again, and Thomas with them." 'Eight days' from when? "Then at evening on that first day of the week, the doors being locked where the disciples were assembled, for fear of the Jews, Jesus came and stood in the middle" (John 20:19). The 'first day of the week' is Sunday; the use of "that" indicates that it was Resurrection Sunday. With few exceptions, the Church Universal has always understood that Jesus arose on a Sunday, as the Text plainly indicates. In John 20:26 "after eight days" means the next Sunday. To the 'western' mind, the use of 'after' is misleading; 'after eight days' would place one in the ninth day. But we are in the presence of a Hebrew idiom, wherein 'after eight days' = 'the eighth day'. This is plainly indicated in Matthew 27:63-64, where 'after three days' = 'until the third day'. But as already noted, the beginning day is included in the number; so 'after eight days' = 'the eighth day' = seven consecutive solar days of elapsed time (although the first and last solar day may not be a full 24 hours).

Now consider Luke 23:53-24:1. "Then he took it down, wrapped it in linen, and placed it in a tomb cut out of rock, where no one had ever been laid. 54 It was a Preparation day; the Sabbath was drawing near. 55 The women who had come with Him from Galilee followed along, and they saw the tomb and how His body was placed there. 56 Then they returned and prepared spices and perfumes. But they rested on the Sabbath according to the commandment. 1 Then on the first day of the week, at early dawn, they went to the tomb carrying the spices that they had prepared, along with some others." After the women observed the burial, they rested for one day—Sabbath is singular. They took their spices to the tomb on Sunday. It follows that Jesus was buried on Friday. Jesus was in the tomb for part of Friday, all of Saturday, and part of Sunday—He rose 'the third day'.

Mark 14:1 may also be of interest. "It was two days before the Passover and the Unleavened Bread." According to a careful analysis of the sequence of events that made up the last week, at this point it was late Tuesday afternoon, probably after 6:00 p.m.—adding two days takes us to 6:00 p.m. on Thursday, but the proceedings in the upper room began after 6:00 p.m. on that Thursday, which to the Jews was already Friday. Therefore Jesus died on a Friday. We take it that "3 days and 3 nights" was an idiomatic expression that could refer to three solar days represented by some part of each, but in sequence—in this case: Friday, Saturday and Sunday.

Harmonizing the accounts of the 'temptation'

The 'temptation of Jesus' is mentioned by three of the Gospels. Mark is very brief (1:12-13); he has the Holy Spirit 'driving' Jesus into the wilderness, rather than the 'leading' of the other two; also, he is the only one who mentions the animals. Mathew and Luke give more detailed accounts, with some discrepancies, which give rise to this note.

Matthew has, "into the wilderness to be tempted by the devil". Luke has, "into the wilderness, being tempted for forty days by the devil". We have no record of what Satan did during the forty days. That which <u>is</u> recorded happened at the end. Both Matthew and Luke agree that Jesus ate nothing during the 40 days, that at the end He was hungry, and that at that point Satan presented himself. They both record the same three tests, but in a different order, and it is this difference that requires special comment. The descriptions of the tests are not identical, but can easily be harmonized. At the end, Matthew has, "then the devil left Him, and angels came and ministered to Him". (Mark also mentions the angels.) Luke has: "When the devil had ended every temptation, he departed from Him until an opportune time." The two statements complement each other.

I will now consider the three tests. Both begin with 'bread', but Matthew has "these stones", while Luke has 'this stone'. I assume that both are correct. Satan started with 'these stones' and then singled out one that looked just like a loaf and said 'this one'. Both have Jesus responding with Deuteronomy 8:3. (Unfortunately, in Luke 4:4, less than half a percent of the extant Greek manuscripts, of objectively inferior quality, omit "but by every word of God", to be followed by most modern versions.)

For the second test, Matthew has the temple, while Luke has the high mountain, the third test being the reverse. So who has the correct sequence? Luke introduces both his second and third tests with the conjunction 'and', as if they were like separate blocks in a row. Matthew introduces his second test with a temporal adverb of sequence, 'then'; he introduces the third with another adverb, 'again', one of whose uses is sequence. Since Matthew overtly states the sequence, I conclude that his order is the correct one—Luke was not concerned to give the sequence; he handles the 'temple' almost like an afterthought (the introductory conjunction could be rendered 'also'). Matthew's order is also the logical sequence; there is a progression in the severity or importance of the tests.

The actual description of the temple test given by both is almost identical. Matthew says "holy city" while Luke says "Jerusalem". Satan cites Psalm 91:11-12, and Jesus responds with Deuteronomy 6:16. As for the high mountain test, Luke has a fuller description than does Matthew, but they are in harmony. In Matthew 4:10 some 12% of the Greek manuscripts omit "behind me", as in most versions; in Luke 4:8 the whole "Get behind me, Satan!" is omitted by perhaps 3.5% of the Greek manuscripts (of inferior quality), to be followed by most modern versions. (Strange to relate, in Luke 4:5 just three known Greek manuscripts, of objectively inferior quality [against over 1,700, almost all of which are better than the three], omit "up on a high mountain the devil", to be followed by most modern versions, except that some keep 'the devil'.)

To conclude, each of the three accounts supplies some information not found in the others, but they harmonize, being complementary. The one apparent discrepancy, the order of tests two and three, has a reasonable solution.

'Prophets' in Matthew 3:23

"And upon arriving he settled in a town called Natsareth [Branch-town], so that what was spoken through the prophets should be fulfilled, that He would be called a Natsorean [Branch-man]."

We know from Luke that Natsareth was Joseph's home—his house and business were waiting for him (although he had been gone for quite a while). The name of the town in Hebrew is based on the consonants נצר (*resh, tsadde, nun*), but since Hebrew is read from right to left, for us the order is reversed = n, ts, r. This word root means 'branch'. Greek has the equivalent for 'ps' and 'ks', but not for 'ts', so the transliteration used a 'dz' (*zeta*), which is the voiced counterpart of 'ts'. But when the Greek was transliterated into English it came out as 'z'! But Hebrew has a 'z', ז (*zayin*), so in transliterating back into Hebrew people assumed the consonants נזר, replacing the correct *tsadde* with *zayin*. This technical information is necessary as background for what follows.

Neither 'Nazareth' nor 'Nazarene', spelled with a *zayin*, is to be found in the Old Testament, but there is a prophetic reference to Messiah as the Branch, *netser*—Isaiah 11:1—and several to the related word, *tsemach*—Isaiah 4:2, Jeremiah 23:5, 33:15; Zechariah 3:8, 6:12. So Matthew is quite right—the prophets (plural, being at least three) referred to Christ as the Branch. Since Jesus was a man, He would be the 'Branch-man', from 'Branch-town'. Which brings us to the word 'natsorean'. The familiar 'Nazarene' (Ναζαρηνος) [Natsarene] occurs in Mark 1:24, 14:67, 16:6 and Luke 4:34, but here in Matthew 2:23 and in fourteen other places, including Acts 22:8 where the glorified Jesus calls <u>Himself</u> that, the word is 'Natsorean' (Ναζωραιος), which is quite different. (Actually, in Acts 22:8 Jesus introduced Himself to Saul as '<u>the</u> Natsorean', which strict Pharisee Saul would understand as a reference to the Messiah.) I have been given to understand that the Natsareth of Jesus' day had been founded some 100 years before by a Branch family who called it Branch town; they were very much aware of the prophecies about the Branch and fully expected the Messiah to be born from among them—they called themselves Branch-people (Natsoreans). Of course everyone else thought it was a big joke and tended to look down on them. "Can anything good . . . ?"

The difficulty in this case is caused by differing phonologies; the sounds of Hebrew do not match those of Greek, or of English. Since proper names are often just transliterated, as in this case, and a translator will normally follow the phonology of the target language, what happened here was straightforward, without malice. We would have felt no inconvenience had Matthew not appealed to "the prophets". It is the false transliteration going back to Hebrew, from either Greek or English, that creates the seeming difficulty.

Before, or after?—2 Thessalonians 2:2 X 2:7-8

In Matthew 24:44 we read, "Therefore you also be ready, because the Son of the Man is coming at an hour that you do not suppose." I take it that for there to be the element of surprise the Rapture of the Church must occur before the "abomination of desolation". When the Antichrist takes his place in the Holy of Holies and declares himself to be god there will be precisely 1,290 days until the return of Christ to the earth. "An hour that you do not suppose" presumably requires a pre-'abomination' rapture—if the rapture is pre-wrath but post-abomination, only a fool will be taken by surprise, unless the Rapture happens immediately after the 'abomination' (2 Thessalonians 2:3-4).

We may begin with 2 Thessalonians 2:2. Some 15% of the Greek manuscripts have 'day of the Lord' (as in NIV, NASB, LB, TEV, etc.); the 85% that have 'day of Christ' (including the best line of transmission) are doubtless correct. I remember one day in a Greek exegesis class, the professor stated that one reason he preferred the 'critical' text (that reads 'Lord' here) is that it fit better with his view of eschatology—the 'Day of Christ' is usually associated with the Rapture and blessing of the saints, while the 'Day of the Lord' is usually associated with heavy judgment upon the world and unrepentant Israel, including the outpouring of wrath just before and after the Second Coming of Christ, when He returns in glory to establish His Millennial Reign, His Messianic Kingdom. The perceived difficulty here would appear to be that while verses 1, 6 and 7 evidently relate to the Rapture, verses 3-4 and 8-10 evidently relate to the Great Tribulation and the Second Coming. What to do? Look carefully at the Text. In verse 2, why would the Thessalonian believers be "disturbed"? Someone was teaching that the Rapture had already happened and they had been left behind—I would be disturbed too! So 'day of Christ' is precisely correct with reference to the content of verses 1 and 2. The trouble comes in verse 3 because a clause is elided; as an aid to the reader translations usually supply a clause, preferably in italics, to show that it is an addition, as in NKJV—"*that Day will not come*". But that would put the Rapture <u>after</u> the revelation of the man of sin and the 'abomination of desolation'— definitely not congenial to certain eschatological systems. An easy 'solution' would be to change 'Christ' to 'Lord' in verse 2, but that would put the Rapture within the 'day of the Lord'— also not congenial. I submit that fine-tuning our view of eschatology is preferable to tampering with the Text.

If the 'Restrainer' in verses 6-8 is the Holy Spirit, then the Rapture happens before the 'abomination', and may be viewed as its 'trigger'. I translate verse 7 as follows: "For the mystery of the lawlessness is already at work; only He who now restrains *will do so* until He removes Himself." Perhaps more literally, 'gets Himself out of the middle' (the verb γινομαι is inherently middle in voice). I would say that the Holy Spirit is the only one who satisfies the description. But if the 'Day of Christ' includes the Rapture, then verse 3 would appear to place the Rapture <u>after</u> the 'abomination'. So where does that leave us? Although my own training was strongly 'pre-trib', I have moved to a 'meso-trib' position. If the Rapture follows immediately upon the 'abomination', then the 'surprise' factor remains untouched. If the 'abomination' and the Rapture happen within minutes of each other, then from God's point of view they form a single 'package', and the actual sequence is not important—for all practical purposes they happen at the same time.

Jeremiah?—Matthew 27:9-10

In the NKJV, Matthew 27:9-10 reads like this: "Then was fulfilled what was spoken by Jeremiah the prophet, saying, *And they took the thirty pieces of silver, the value of Him who was priced, whom they of the children of Israel priced, and gave them for the potter's field, as the LORD directed me*." The difficulty comes when we try to find this material in our canonical Jeremiah. Cross-references send us to Jeremiah 32:6-9, or 18:1-4, or 19:1-3, but upon inspection they just do not match. In Zechariah 11:12-13 we find a general approximation, but it is not precise—and of course Zechariah is not Jeremiah. Evidently there are Hebrew manuscripts that begin the scroll containing the prophets (major and minor) with Jeremiah, and it has been argued that Matthew used 'Jeremiah' to refer to the contents of the entire scroll. I suppose that could be a possibility, but I prefer to appeal to Daniel 9:2. "In the first year of his reign [Darius] I, Daniel, understood by the books the number of the years *specified* by the word of the LORD through Jeremiah the prophet, . . ." Note that 'books' is plural. Why should any of us assume that men like Jeremiah, or Isaiah, wrote only what is in our canon? (I myself have written a great deal that has never been published.) Daniel clearly wrote 'book̲s', presumably referring to Jeremiah. I conclude that such extra-canonical books were still known in Matthew's day, and that he refers to one of them. I am aware that the distinction cannot be insisted upon, but Matthew did use 'spoken' rather than 'written'.

How did Judas die?—Matthew 27:5-8 X Acts 1:18-19

In the NKJV, according to Matthew, he "went and hanged himself", while according to Acts, "falling headlong he burst open in the middle and all his entrails gushed out". From the context it is clear that this happened at the field that he purchased, posthumously. For a successful hanging, there must be enough altitude so that when the end of the rope is reached the victim is still in the air. But to fall headlong there has to be a cliff, and you would have to dive off. Putting the two accounts together we may understand that there must have been a tree near the edge of the cliff, with a branch reaching out beyond the edge; Judas tied a cord around that branch and his neck and jumped —either the cord or the branch broke, and the impact was sufficient to split him open. Matthew states that it was actually the chief priests who bought the field, using the money that Judas had thrown on the temple floor; so Judas made the purchase posthumously.

Did the centurion leave his house?—Luke 7:1-10 X Matthew 8:5-13

It has often been supposed that these are parallel accounts of the same incident. To be sure, both involve a centurion, in Capernaum, a sick servant, and the statement of the centurion along with the Lord's reaction are very similar. But other details simply do not match. Evidently the Romans had an army base in Capernaum, with a centurion as commanding officer, who could be rotated. [Where do you suppose Peter sold most of his fish? And what language did he use?] Looking at the sequence of events in both Matthew and Luke, I would say that the incident recorded by Matthew happened first, and a number of months before the one recorded by Luke. Of course an incident like that would become part of the 'folklore' of the base. I assume that the centurions were different, but they certainly knew each other, so the second one knew every detail of the first incident. When his turn came, he used a different strategy to make his appeal (he was asking for a second favor), but then repeated the statement that had impressed Jesus so favorably. So, the first centurion left his house, but the second did not.

'Staff', or 'bed'?—Hebrews 11:21 X Genesis 47:31

In the NKJV, Hebrews 11:21 reads like this: "By faith Jacob, when he was dying, blessed each of the sons of Joseph, and worshipped, *leaning* on the top of his staff." It has been alleged that this statement disagrees with Genesis 47:31, that has Jacob leaning on the head of the bed (following the Massoretic Text), rather than the top of his staff. However, close attention to the contexts indicates that Hebrews 11:21 and Genesis 47:31 refer to different occasions, so there is no need to imagine a discrepancy. That said, it may be of interest to note the following. The Hebrew words for 'bed' and 'staff' are spelled with the same three consonants, the difference being in the vowels, that were not written. Thus the Original Hebrew Text was ambiguous here. When the Massoretes added vowel pointing to the Hebrew Text, many centuries after Christ, they chose 'bed'. Long before, the Septuagint had chosen 'staff'.

The 'smallest' seed?—Mark 4:31-32, Matthew 13:32

In the NKJV, Mark 4:31-32 reads like this: "It is like a mustard seed which, when it is sown on the ground, is smaller than all the seeds on earth; but when it is sown, it grows up and becomes greater than all herbs, and shoots out large branches, so that the birds of the air may nest under its shade."

The rendering 'the smallest seed in the world/earth' is unfortunate and misleading. The Text has 'of those on the ground', repeating the phrase above it, only eliding the verb. The Lord was not making a global botanical statement, as the next verse makes clear—He was referring to vegetables planted in a garden in His day and in that area, and of such herbs mustard had the smallest seed. To object that tobacco and orchid seeds are smaller is beside the point. My translation reads like this: "It is like a mustard seed, that when it is sown on the ground is the smallest of all such seeds, yet when it is sown, it grows up and becomes larger than all the garden herbs and produces big branches, so that the birds of the air are able to rest in its shade." The verb I have rendered 'to rest' is a compound form. The noun root refers to a temporary shelter, like a tent or a hut. The verbal form means to make use of such a shelter. Here the preposition *kata* is prefixed to the verb, emphasizing, as I suppose, the temporariness. The Text says that the birds can use the <u>shade</u>, not the branches. But shade moves with the sun, and with the wind—how can you build a nest in something that keeps moving around (the Text actually says 'under its shade')? My comments also serve for Matthew 13:32, except that there the birds are resting in the 'branches', rather than the shade. The verb is the same, and I handle it the same way, 'rest' rather than 'nest', although 'nest' is possible.

'This is', or 'You are'?—Matthew 3:17 X Mark 1:11, Luke 3:22

In the NKJV, Matthew 3:17 reads like this: "And suddenly a voice came from heaven, saying, 'This is My beloved Son, in whom I am well pleased'." And Mark 1:11 reads like this: "Then a voice came from heaven, 'You are My beloved Son, in whom I am well pleased'." Luke also has "You are". So what did the Voice actually say? In a manner similar to what happened on the Day of Pentecost, I conclude that each hearer received his own interpretation, or message. Matthew records the event from John's perspective: he heard, "This is . . ." Mark and Luke record the event from Jesus' perspective: He heard, "You are   . . ." At Pentecost, with over a dozen languages being spoken at once, even if one of them was yours, it would require a personal miracle in your ear to enable you to extract your message from the welter of sound.

Who said what?—Matthew 27:48-49 X Mark 15:36 X John 19:29-30 (Luke 23:36)

I take it that the action in John 19:29, as well as Luke 23:36, was carried out by soldiers, and should not be confused with that recorded in Matthew and Mark, although all four refer to offering Jesus sour wine to drink (since Jesus was on the cross for some six hours, there was time for several drinks). The seeming discrepancy I wish to address is in Matthew and Mark. In the NKJV, Matthew 27:48-49 reads like this: "Immediately one of them ran and took a sponge, filled it with sour wine and put it on a reed, and offered it to Him to drink. The rest said, 'Let Him alone; let us see if Elijah will come to save Him'." A single man offers the drink, but the rest say, "Let Him alone, . . ." And Mark 15:36 reads like this: "Then someone ran and filled a sponge full of sour wine, put it on a reed, and offered it to Him to drink, saying, 'Let Him alone; . . .'" A single man offers the drink, and **he** says, "Let Him alone, . . ." I would not be surprised if the man involved here was John Mark himself. But whoever he was, if he knew Hebrew he knew perfectly well that Jesus was not calling Elijah, so he sarcastically repeats their statement, in disgust. I deny any discrepancy.

Bethsaida, or Tiberias?—Luke X John

The question is: just where did the feeding of the 5,000 men take place? Matthew 14:13 and Mark 6:32 merely say that it was in a deserted spot, without identification. But Luke 9:10 says it was in "a deserted place belonging to a town named Bethsaida",[1] while John 6:23 informs us that the spot was near

---

[1] Lamentably, the eclectic Greek text currently in vogue, following a mere half of one percent of the Greek manuscripts (and that half made up of objectively infe-

the town of Tiberias. Well now, Tiberias was located on the west side of the Sea, a mile or two above the place where the Jordan River leaves the Sea. But Bethsaida was at the top of the Sea, a little to the east of where the Jordan enters the Sea. What to do?

We may deduce from Mark 6:31 and John 6:17 and 24 that Jesus and His disciples started out from Capernaum, where Jesus had His base of operations. It happens that Capernaum, like Bethsaida, was situated at the top of the Sea, but a little to the west of the entrance of the Jordan. To go from Capernaum to Bethsaida by boat one would not get far from the shore. But John 6:1 says that Jesus "went over the Sea of Galilee", and that agrees better with Tiberias, since there is a large bay between Capernaum and Tiberias, although they are both on the west side of the Sea—they crossed close to ten miles of water. Further, after the feast, Matthew 14:22 says they went by boat "to the other side", and verse 24 has them "in the middle of the Sea"; while Mark 6:45 says that they went by boat "to the other side, to Bethsaida", and verse 47 has them "in the middle of the Sea"; and John 6:17 says that they "started to cross the Sea toward Capernaum", and verse 19 that "they had rowed some three or four miles".

Well now, to stay close to the shore is one thing, to go over the Sea is another. Further, if they were already in or near Bethsaida, how could they cross the Sea in order to get there (Mark 6:45)? It becomes clear that the miracle in fact took place near Tiberias, as John affirms. But that raises another difficulty: how could a property near Tiberias 'belong' to Bethsaida (Luke 9:10)? Either it had been deeded to the town

---

rior ones), says that they went "to a town named Bethsaida". This is an obvious perversity because two verses later the same text has them in a deserted place. So the editors of that text make Luke contradict himself, as well as contradicting the other three Gospels, since all agree that the place was deserted. Unfortunately, this perversity is duly reproduced by NIV, NASB, TEV, etc.

somehow, or, more likely, it belonged to a family that lived in Bethsaida. My reason for saying this is based on the Text.

John 6:17 says that they "started toward Capernaum", while Mark 6:45 says that they went "to Bethsaida". Since the two towns were a short distance apart, at the beginning of the crossing the direction would be virtually the same. I understand that they did indeed go to Bethsaida, but spent very little time there, going from there directly to Genesaret. Indeed, the day after the miracle Jesus was already back in Capernaum (John 6:24-25). But just why did they make that side trip to Bethsaida (Genesaret lies just south of Capernaum)? I imagine the following: a property near Tiberias, but belonging to someone in Bethsaida, would likely be deserted, a great place for a picnic. I suppose that Jesus had permission to use the place, when He wanted to get away, but no one had foreseen a crowd of perhaps 15,000 (5,000 men plus women and children). Please pardon the unpleasant consideration, but what effect would a crowd that size have on the hygiene and appearance of the place? I conclude that Jesus felt obligated to give a report to the owner, in Bethsaida.

While we are here, allow me to call attention to another miracle Jesus performed, that you will not find in the usual lists. As already noted, Matthew 14:24 and Mark 6:46 say that they were in the middle of the Sea, but John 6:19 is more precise, saying that they had gone perhaps four miles. It happens that a crossing from Tiberias to Bethsaida would involve about eight miles. And now, attention please to John 6:21, "Then they wanted to receive Him into the boat, and immediately the boat was at the land to which they were going". If the total distance was eight miles, and they had only managed half of it, then Jesus transported the boat four miles instantly. Now that was a fair sized miracle, to transport a boat four miles in an instant! You will not find this miracle in most lists, because few people take the time to give a detailed examination to the Sacred Text.

1 Samuel 13:1 and the Preservation of the Hebrew Text

When I was a new student in my ThM program, one of the prime movers in the Majority Text vineyard was in his last year, and we worked together in the Seminary kitchen. Our tongues wagged about as fast as our hands moved; we did a lot of talking, mostly about things text-critical and theological. In those pristine years, he was a firm believer in the divine preservation of both the Hebrew and Greek Testaments, to the letter. In due time I came to Brazil as a missionary, and he continued in his teaching career. Every furlough (back then field terms were usually five years) I would touch base with him and compare notes. On one of those occasions (I forget which one), when the subject of divine preservation came up, he opened a Bible to 1 Samuel 13:1 and affirmed that the original wording of that verse had been irretrievably lost—bye-bye preservation.

Well now, what he did to me, someone else had done to him, and so on into the night. I rather imagine that this verse has come to represent a difficulty in the thinking of not a few people who would like to believe in the divine preservation of the Text, but . . . . Since I still believed in preservation at that time (and continue to do so), his gesture gave me pause—could he possibly be correct? So I sat down and studied the situation (including an inquiry to the local synagogue). Here is my conclusion.

The NKJV renders 1 Samuel 13:1-2 like this: "Saul reigned one year; and when he had reigned two years over Israel, Saul chose for himself three thousand men of Israel. Two thousand were with Saul in Michmash and in the mountains of Bethel, and a thousand were with Jonathan in Gibeah of Benjamin. The rest of the people he sent away, every man to his tent." In the NIV the first verse is quite different: "Saul was ⌐ thirty ⌐ years old when he became king, and he reigned over Israel ⌐

forty- ⌐ two years." A footnote informs the reader that the bracketed words are not in the Hebrew Text. An uninitiated layperson who compares the two could easily conclude that they are translating completely different texts, but such is not the case. The Hebrew text is one, without variants—the problem lies in the interpretation.

An interlinear, morpheme by morpheme, rendering of the first verse looks like this: "Son-of-a-year Saul in-his-reigning and-two years he-reigned over-Israel" (except, of course, that Hebrew is read from right to left). The confusion arises in that this became a formula used in the summary statement about a king's reign: a son of X years was Y in his reigning (= when he began to reign), and he reigned Z years . . . The formula usually occurs at the end of a king's history, but sometimes at the beginning. Of course, any attempt to apply the formula in 1 Samuel 13:1 is ridiculous. Obviously Saul could not have been one year old when he began to reign, and just as obviously he reigned more than two years. Unfortunately, NIV and others have insisted on imposing the formula on this verse, inventing the 'thirty' and 'forty-' so as not to have complete nonsense. (This also has the unfortunate effect of contradicting Acts 13:21, that affirms that Saul reigned 40 years, not 42.) I suppose they have convinced themselves that the original numbers have disappeared from the Text, having been irretrievably lost during the process of transmission.

But let us look carefully at the context of 13:1. To begin, Saul being the very first king of Israel, such a formula would not yet be in use—there had been no occasion to write of the beginning and length of reigns. Then, in the context this is not the place for a summary statement; it is neither the beginning nor the end of the history of Saul's reign. In 1 Samuel 10:24 he was publicly installed as king—since he was the first, there was no precedent, no established procedure. In Chapter 11 Saul defeats the Ammonites and is confirmed in the kingship (verse 15). In chapter 12 Samuel defends his ministry and gives a lesson in history. Chapter 13 resumes Saul's story and starts by saying when he established a standing army—in the second year of his reign. I invite special attention to the concluding statement of verse two, "The rest of the people he sent away, every man to his tent." To be 'sent away' they had to be there. Be where? In Gilgal (11:15), where Samuel's discourse (chapter 12) also took place, as part of the occasion. According to 11:9, Saul had mobilized 330,000 men against the Ammonites, and I imagine that most of them had accompanied Samuel and Saul to Gilgal. So 13:1-2 is a continuation of what happened at Gilgal, and verse one **CANNOT** be a summary statement about Saul's total reign. Of the 330,000 that had been mobilized against Ammon, Saul chose 3,000 to be a standing army and sent the rest home. Perhaps the lack of a standing army had encouraged the Ammonites to get frisky; the news that Israel now had one would serve as a deterrent.

I take the point of 13:1 to be that Saul had a full year behind him, so these events at Gilgal took place during his second year. Hebrew is not my forte, but I would paraphrase our verse something like this, "Saul had reigned for a full year over Israel, and it was during his second year that he chose for himself three thousand men . . . ."

I reject as unfounded the allegation that some of the original wording of 1 Samuel 13:1 has been lost. The NIV does a considerable disservice to the Kingdom of God here.

Four hundred years—Acts 7:6

Almost all of chapter 7 is occupied with Stephen's trial and defense, although it closes with his death. The high priest knows it is all a farce, but he pretends astonishment. Stephen knows he is in a kangaroo court, so he wastes no time with the ridiculous charge; he delivers a prophetic, and condemnatory, sermon. His history lesson begins with Abraham's incomplete obedience, but what concerns us here is verse 6.

7:1 Then the high priest said, "Can these things be so?" 2 So he said: "Men, brothers and fathers, listen: The God of glory appeared to our father Abraham when he was in Mesopotamia, before he resided in Haran, 3 and said to him, 'Leave your country and your relatives, and come into a land that I will show you'. 4 Then he left the land of the Chaldeans and resided in Haran.[1] From there, after his father died,[2] *God* moved him to this land in which you now live; 5 yet He did not give him an inheritance in it, not even a footstep. He promised to give it to him for a possession, that is, to his seed after him, though he had no child.[3] 6 Further, God spoke like this: that his offspring would be aliens in a foreign land—and that they would be enslaved and oppressed—four hundred years.

To begin, it will be observed that my rendering of verse 6 differs from every version that I remember seeing. For example, the NKJV has: "But God spoke in this way: that his descendants would dwell in a foreign land, and that they would bring them into bondage and oppress them four hundred years." The NIV has: "God spoke to him in this way: 'Your descendants will be strangers in a country not their own, and they will be enslaved and mistreated four hundred years'." And so on— the impression that all these versions give is that the descendants would spend 400 years in a single country, namely Egypt. But such an impression lands us in a quandary: 400 years in

---

[1] But he took his father and a nephew along, and Haran was not that land. 'Our father Abraham'—the Jews began their history with Abraham, who started out with incomplete obedience.

[2] There went fifteen years of his life. And he took his nephew Lot along, who would be a **big** headache (he fathered the Moabites and the Ammonites—not good news—under circumstances that would not have happened had he been left in Haran).

[3] Abraham was 100 when he begot Isaac, who was 60 when he begot Jacob and Esau. Abraham died at 175, so lived to see his two grandsons. But before Isaac there was Ishmael . . . .

Egypt does not fit with the clear chronological statements found elsewhere in the biblical Text.

Stephen cites Genesis 15:13, which should be understood as a chiasmus, a frequent structure in the Bible:

- a. his offspring would be aliens in a foreign land
    - b. and they would be enslaved
    - b. and oppressed
- a. four hundred years.

A careful comparison of the relevant texts shows that the 400 years includes from the weaning of Isaac to the Exodus (1891 to 1491 BC). Since Jacob moved to Egypt in 1706, Abraham's descendants were aliens in Canaan for 185 years; then they were aliens in Egypt, where they came to be enslaved, for 215 years. (The Exodus was 144 years after Joseph's death, so the period of slave labor was presumably somewhat less, perhaps around 100 years.)

For a detailed discussion and defense of the dates and time frames given above the interested reader is referred to a book that I consider to be one of a kind: *Chronology of the Old Testament: A Return to the Basics*, by Floyd Nolen Jones, ThD, PhD. The first edition appeared in 1993; I have in hand the 14th edition, published in 1999 by KingsWord Press, The Woodlands, Texas. The relevant discussion is on pages 58-61, but I venture to suggest that anyone who reads the whole book will consider that it was time well spent.

Chapter III: DISCREPANCIES?

The purpose of this section is to take up passages in the Sacred Text that have been alleged to present us with actual discrepancies, discrepancies that arise from the language of the Text itself. Again, the context has not received the careful attention it requires, except that here the historical and geographic contexts may also enter in.

How Often Did Jesus Say Peter Would Deny Him?

The question can be understood in two different senses, and I wish to explore them both. How often was Peter to deny the Lord, and how often did the Lord warn him? I will consider the second question first. Each Gospel records a warning—the relevant passages are Matthew 26:30-35, Mark 14:26-31, Luke 22:31-34, 39 and John 13:36-38, 18:1. For reasons that will presently become apparent I will start to discuss the passages in reverse order.

How Many Warnings?

First, John 13:36-38:

> 36 Simon Peter says to Him, "Lord, where are you going?" Jesus answered him, "Where I am going you cannot follow me now, but later you will follow me". 37 Peter says to Him: "Lord, why can't I follow you now? I will lay down my life for your sake!" 38 Jesus answered him: "You will lay down your life for my sake? Most assuredly I say to you, no rooster can crow until you have denied me three times!"[1]

---

[1] The emphasis here is on the obligatory absence of any cockcrow until Peter has denied [at least] three times. There is no definite article with 'rooster', so it is "a rooster"; the negative is double, therefore emphatic, "absolutely not". If you have lived where there were a number of roosters, you know that one or another

Notice the distinctive context that leads into our Lord's warning. Notice also the emphatic nature of His declaration—by employing a double negative (in the Greek text) He leaves no question but that three denials will take place before the first rooster crows from that moment on. Notice finally where and when this exchange took place. They were in the upper room where they had gathered to observe the Passover. Evidently this conversation between the Lord and Peter came comparatively early in the proceedings, because it was followed by the contents of chapters 14, 15, 16 and 17 before they left the room and went to the garden on the Mount of Olives (18:1).

Second, Luke 22:31-34:

> 31 Then the Lord said, "Simon, Simon, indeed Satan has asked for you (pl) that he may sift you as wheat, 32 but I have prayed for you (sg) that your faith should not fail, and when you have returned to me strengthen your brothers." 33 But he said to Him, "Lord, I am ready to go with you both to prison and to death!" 34 So He said, "I tell you, Peter, no rooster can crow <u>this day</u> before you will deny three times that you know me!"

Notice again the distinctive context that leads into our Lord's warning. It is clearly different from that given in John 13. Notice also that there seems to be an increase in the intensity of their exchange. There is a note of reproach in Peter's speech, and the use of Peter's name gives a stern note to the Lord's response. The addition of "today" (compared to John 13) and

---

can sound off at any time, and some one of them will crow almost on the hour throughout the night, while at dawn they put on a chorus. It was probably somewhere around 9 p.m. when Jesus issued this warning, and Peter's first denial probably happened at least five hours later. For not a single rooster to crow anywhere within earshot during that time required supernatural intervention—which is why I render "no rooster can crow" (if an angel can close lions' mouths [Dan. 6:22], closing roosters' beaks would be a cakewalk).

the shifting of "thrice" to an emphatic position (in the Greek text—again as compared to John) contribute to the feeling of heightened intensity. Also, now Peter will deny that he even knows Him. Note finally where and when this exchange took place. They were still in the upper room, but this conversation evidently came near the end of the proceedings, because only the contents of verses 35-38 intervened before they left the room and went to the Mount of Olives (22:39). Of course, more may have actually happened than is recorded in 22:35-38, but it seems clear that the warning recorded in Luke is not the same as the one recorded in John, and that the one in John happened first.

I find a comparison of the two warnings in Greek to be impressive and convincing:

John 13:38: ~~Την ψυχην σου υπερ εμου θησεις? Αμην, αμην λεγω σοι, ου μη αλεκτωρ φωνηση εως ου απαρνηση με τρις. VV

Luke 22:34: ~~Λεγω σοι, Πετρε, ου μη φωνηση σημερον αλεκτωρ πριν η τρις απαρνηση μη ειδεναι με) VV

Really, there is no comparison; they are obviously different (even taking into account that they probably spoke Hebrew, so we are looking at a translation). As in John, here again we have a plain affirmation that three denials [at least] will take place before the first rooster crows.

Third, Matthew 26:30-35:

> 30 And after hymn-singing they went out to the Mount of Olives. 31 Then Jesus says to them, "All of you will be caused to stumble because of me this night, for it is written: 'I will strike the Shepherd and the sheep of the flock will be scattered'. 32 But after I am raised I will go before you to Galilee." 33 Peter answered and said to Him, "Even if everyone *else* is caused to stumble because of you, I will never be caused to stumble!" 34 Je-

sus said to him, "Assuredly I say to you that this night, before *any* rooster crows, you will deny me <u>three</u> times!" 35 Peter says to Him, "Even if I have to die with you, I will **not** deny you!" All the *other* disciples said the same.

Notice that this exchange took place after they had left the upper room and were on their way to the Garden of Gethsemane. Again the context is distinct from that in Luke or John—here the Lord begins by warning all the disciples. Peter counters by contradicting Him. The Lord's reiterated specific warning to Peter contains no new elements except that now it is "this very night". Peter contradicts again, using a double negative for emphasis—he 'has his back up' and is starting to get impertinent. It seems clear that Matthew records a third warning to Peter, subsequent to those in Luke and John.

Fourth, Mark 14:26-31:

> 26 And after hymn-singing they went out to the Mount of Olives. 27 And Jesus says to them, "All of you will be caused to stumble because of me this night, for it is written: 'I will strike the Shepherd and the sheep will be scattered'. 28 But after I am raised I will go before you to Galilee." 29 But Peter said to Him, "Even if all are caused to stumble, yet I will not be!" 30 And Jesus says to him, "Assuredly I say to you that you, today, even this night, before a rooster crows <u>twice</u>, you will deny me three times!" 31 But he spoke the more vehemently, "If I have to die with you, I will certainly not deny you!" And they all said the same.

The first four verses are virtually identical with the parallel passage in Matthew, so we evidently have the same time and place in both. But now we come to verse 30, the despair of those who defend scriptural inerrancy and the delight of their opponents. Our Lord's statement here differs in several ways from that in Matthew 26:34 but the main problem is the word "twice". What are we to say: Are Matthew 26:34 and Mark 14:30 contradictory accounts of the same warning?

Before settling for that explanation, the precise turn of phrase in Mark 14:30 invites our attention. I believe it will help to see a word for word rendering of what Jesus said. "Assuredly I say to you that <u>you</u>, today, this very night, before twice a rooster crows, thrice you will deny me." The Lord's declaration here seems quite sharp. There is extraordinary emphasis on the second "you". "Twice" is also heavily emphasized. How are we to account for such severity? Peter's effort in verse 29 scarcely seems to merit such a reaction—the reaction recorded in Matthew 26:34 seems much more appropriate. And what shall we say to Mark 14:31? Peter's words here are virtually identical to those in Matthew 26:35 but they are introduced by "but he spoke the more vehemently". Why the vehement reiteration?

I suggest that the solution is to read the following sequence. Matthew 26:30-35[a] then Mark 14:30-31:

> Jesus: "All of you will be caused to stumble because of me this night . . ."
> Peter: "Though all are caused to stumble because of you, I will never be caused to stumble."
> Jesus: "Assuredly I say to you that this night, before any rooster crows, you will deny me <u>three</u> times."
> Peter: "Even if I have to die with you I will certainly not deny you!"
> Jesus: "Assuredly I say to you that <u>you</u>, today, this very night, before a rooster crows <u>twice</u>, you will deny me three times."
> Peter, more vehemently: "If I have to die with you, I will certainly not deny you!"

In other words, Mark omitted the exchange recorded in Matthew 26:34-35[a] while Matthew omitted the exchange recorded in Mark 14:30-31[a]. (The editorial comment "and they all said the same" comes at the end of the whole episode.)

On three separate occasions Jesus warned Peter that he would deny Him [at least] three times before a rooster crowed during that night. Peter's responses became increasingly belligerent until after the third warning he even contradicted the Lord with an emphatic double negative (Mat. 26:35). Finally the Lord lost His patience, as it were, and said in effect, "Listen, not only will you deny me three times before a rooster crows once, you will deny me another three times before a rooster crows twice!" For answer Peter repeats his prior statement even more vehemently.

The reader will perceive that in answering the second question I have anticipated the answer to the first one. The Lord warned Peter four times, each Gospel recording a separate instance, and there would be [at least] six denials, three before the first crowing of a rooster (John, Luke, Matthew) and another three before the second (Mark). It remains to enquire whether the several accounts of Peter's denials will countenance this proposal. The relevant passages are Matthew 26:57-75, Mark 14:53-72, Luke 22:54-62 and John 18:15-27.

How Many Denials?

A cursory reading of these passages suggests that Peter's denials were provoked by eight different challenges—the maid at the outside entrance (John), a maid in the courtyard (Matthew, Mark, Luke), the same maid a second time (Mark), a different maid in the gateway (Matthew), two different men (Luke, John), and the bystanders on two occasions (John and Matthew, Mark). Although it may be possible to combine one pair or another, there is no reasonable way to get the number down to three. But what if there were at least six denials?

To really get the complete picture we need to plot the relevant information on a chart. We need to know who issued the challenge, where, when, just how was it done, what was Peter's reaction, and if a rooster crowed. Because of constraints of space and paper size, I will do a Gospel at a time, beginning with John.[1]

John 18:15-27:

	1st denial	2nd denial	3rd denial
Who?	the gatekeeper (f)	servants and operatives	a relative of Malchus
Where?	outside gate	by the fire	by the fire (?)
When?	at the beginning of the proceedings	a little while after the first one	a little while after the second one (?)
How was it done?	she asks: "You aren't one of this man's disciples too, are you?"	they ask: "You aren't one of his disciples too, are you?"	he asks: "Didn't I see you with him in the garden?"
What was the reaction?	he says: "I am not!"	he said: "I am not!"	(Peter denied again)
Rooster?	(no)	(no)	immediately a rooster crowed

Luke 22:54-62:

	1st denial	2nd denial	3rd denial
Who?	a servant girl	a man	another man
Where?	by the fire	by the fire (?)	by the fire (?)
When?	fairly early on (?)	a little later	about an hour later
How was it done?	she looked intently and said: "This man was also with him."	he said: "You also are of them."	he confidently affirmed: "Surely this fellow also was with him, for he is a Galilean."
What was the reaction?	he said: "Woman, I do not know him!"	he said: "Man, I am not!"	he said: "Man, I do not know what you are saying!"
Rooster?	(no)	(no)	immediately, while he was yet speaking, a rooster crowed.

---

[1] A comparison of the contents of the four Gospels reveals that in the main John supplies information not recorded in the other three; he wrote last, with the purpose of supplementing their accounts. Here again, the three denials he describes are all new information, not to be found in the other three.

Matthew 26:57-75:

	1st denial	2nd denial	3rd denial
Who?	a servant girl	another girl	bystanders
Where?	by the fire	in the gateway	by the fire (?)
When?	fairly early on (?)	a little later	a little later
How was it done?	approached him saying: "You too were with Jesus the Galilean."	says to the others: "This fellow also was with Jesus the Natsorean."	come up to Peter and say: "Really, you too are one of them, because your very accent gives you away!"
What was the reaction?	denied before them all: "I don't know what you are saying."	denied with an oath: "I do not know the man!"	began to curse and to swear: "I do not know the man!"
Rooster?	(no)	(no)	immediately a roster crowed

Mark 14:53-72:

	1st denial	2nd denial	3rd denial
Who?	a servant girl	the same girl	bystanders
Where?	by the fire	in the fore-court (?)	by the fire (?)
When?	fairly early on (?)	a little later	a little later
How was it done?	looked at him and said: "You also were with Jesus the Nazarene."	says to the bystanders: "This is one of them."	say to Peter again: "Surely you are one of them; for you are a Galilean and your speech shows it!"
What was the reaction?	denied, saying: "I neither know nor understand what you are saying!"	(he denied again)	he began to curse and to swear: "I do not know this man of whom you speak!"
Rooster?	he went out to the fore-court and a rooster crowed	(no)	a rooster crowed a second time.

If you compare all the parameters—who, where, when, how, what—there really is no way to come out with only three denials; even to come out with only six requires some gymnastics (something I attempted to do in an early draft). Let us try to arrange the events in chronological sequence and see what happens.

John 18:17 gives us what is clearly the first challenge—as the maid who kept the outside door let Peter in, at John's request, she asked, "You aren't one of this man's disciples too, are you?"[1] Even though John was evidently standing right there, Peter denied, "I am not". He then went in to stand near the fire in the courtyard. The other Gospels have Peter sitting, while John has him standing. Evidently there were quite a few people about—they could not all sit close to the fire. Presumably they would take turns standing near the fire to warm up and then move away a bit to sit down. Thus they, including Peter, would be alternately sitting and standing.

All four Gospels have Peter in the courtyard near the fire (Mat. 26:58 and 69, Mark 14:54 and 66, Luke 22:55, and John 18:18 and 25) and three of them (Matthew, Mark, John) give some account of the council's dealings with Jesus before going on with Peter's denials.[2] We know from Luke 22:61 that Jesus was at a window that looked out on the courtyard, only with His back to it. John is the only one who records that the high priest asked Jesus about His disciples (v. 19)—he is facing Jesus and therefore the open window, and would be speaking loudly enough for everyone in the room to hear clearly, so the people in the courtyard also heard everything he said—then in verse 25 we read, "<u>Therefore</u> they said to him, 'You aren't one of his disciples too, are you?'" I suggest that verse 25 gives us the second challenge and denial. The guards around the fire, presumably prompted by the high priest's questioning Jesus about His disciples, put their question to Peter. He answers them as he did the girl at the gate, "I am not". So far the chal-

---

[1] Everyone there, including the girl, knows that John belongs to Jesus, so her question is perfectly natural, without malice—since John is vouching for Peter, she assumes that Peter must also belong to Jesus. John had heard all the warnings, so when Peter denied at the gate, in his presence, John doubtless kept a close eye on him the whole rest of the night. So we have an eyewitness account. Of course Peter himself would also be an eyewitness, but since he was undergoing satanic interference in his mind, his powers of recollection might be impaired.

[2] It is after midnight and chilly in the courtyard, hence the fire; but there must have been over fifty people in the room where the questioning was going on, and all windows would be open.

lengers have only questioned, rather than affirm, but now the tempo quickens.

I take it that the first denials recorded in Matthew (26:69-70), Mark (14:66-68) and Luke (22:56-57) form a single episode. Collating them we may understand the following. A certain serving girl of the high priest came by and saw Peter sitting near the fire. She looked closely at him and said to the others, "This man also was with him" (Luke). She then addressed Peter directly, "You also were with Jesus the Nazarene, of Galilee" (Matthew, Mark). But he denied before them all, saying, "Girl, I don't know him; I neither know nor understand what you're talking about!" He then went out to the forecourt, and a rooster crowed (Mark 14:68). Thus, there were [at least] three denials before the first cockcrow.

I say 'at least' because the third denial in John probably belongs here as well. In 18:26 the verb "to say" is in the present tense, which seems to suggest a brief interval rather than nearly an hour (Luke 22:59); also the challenge is still framed as a question, "Didn't I see you with him in the garden?", rather than a direct accusation, which would fit better toward the beginning than at the end. I see no problem with suggesting that all three of the denials in John were part of the first set and thus he records the first rooster crow. In that event I would understand that there were actually four denials before the first crowing, the three in John plus the first one in the others. Because the rooster crowed "immediately" I imagine that the order would be as follows: the first two in John, in that order, then the first one in the others, and then, as Peter was moving toward the fore-court, the relative of Peter's victim comes alongside and puts his question, so that Peter is at the fore-court when the first rooster crows (Mark 14:68). Actually, I am inclined to suspect that indeed there were four denials before the first cockcrow, which is recorded by both

Mark and John (recall that Jesus neither said nor implied that there would be 'only' three).[1]

Now for the next round. In Mark (14:69) the same girl sees Peter again and starts telling the bystanders, "This fellow is one of them". In Matthew (26:71) a different girl sees him and tells the bystanders, "This fellow was with Jesus the Natsorean". In Luke (22:58) a man saw him and said, "You also are one of them". In order to come out with only three denials in the second set, two of these would have to be combined, but as already stated, I am not aware of anything in the Text that rules out the possibility that there could be more than three. It seems to me that there is a progression in Peter's desperation which culminates in his cursing and swearing. On that basis I would consider the instances in Mark and Luke as forming a single episode (if I had to)—the girl speaks, Peter denies, a man backs the girl up and Peter answers, "Man, I am not!" Then the instance in Matthew would be the sixth denial—notice that now Peter adds an oath! Because of the oath I consider that this denial comes after the other two just mentioned; also, Peter has moved out to the gateway. Actually, I am inclined to suspect that there were also four denials before the second cockcrow, so I will start again on that basis.

The girl that provoked the third denial is not about to let Peter get away with that denial. Whether she followed him out to the forecourt, or he moved back toward the fire, I imagine that Mark 14:69 records the fifth denial. If so, Luke 22:58 records the sixth denial, perhaps near the fire. Peter is definitely uncomfortable; he is getting altogether too much unwelcome attention. He moves out to the gateway (perhaps thinking of abandoning the premises)[2] where he is challenged by a different girl (Matthew 26:71); Peter denies with an oath (number

---

[1] The satanic interference in Peter's mind was so effective that not even the rooster's crowing woke him up.

[2] So why didn't Peter just bolt out the gate at that point? I would say that there was supernatural intervention—he simply was not allowed to leave.

seven). Luke (22:59) puts 'about an hour' between denials six and eight, so perhaps Peter was left alone for a bit. However, the 'trial' is over but the bosses are waiting for dawn so they can take Jesus to Pilate. Since the bosses are not going home, the guards and employees cannot either—they are obliged to wait out in the cold, bored stiff—so Peter is now the only show in town.

For the eighth denial three Gospels offer a candidate (Mat. 26:73-74, Mark 14:70-72, Luke 22:59-60). The accounts in Matthew and Mark are very similar and evidently parallel. Since Matthew has the rooster crowing "immediately" and Mark "the second time" this has to be last denial—since by now Peter is cursing and swearing it is fitting that it should be. By that time most of the people on the premises would be aware of Peter and his denials. After listening for a while they closed in, citing his accent. The account in Luke has just one man speaking, but his words are in the same vein. This also has to be the last denial because we are told that the rooster crowed while Peter was still speaking. Evidently a number of people were speaking at once (but not in unison), or in rapid succession, and different writers preserve some of the variety of statement. It would appear that they were ganging up on Peter, because he is driven to curse and to swear. And so we have a second set of four denials, before the second cockcrow. Even then it took a direct look from the Lord (Luke 22:61) to break Satan's spell and bring Peter to a realization of what he had done.

But the question may well be asked, why did each Gospel writer report and speak of only three denials (albeit giving different selections) if there were really six or eight?[1] I suggest

---

[1] Some 50% of the Greek manuscripts that contain the Gospels have colophons; these colophons state that Matthew was 'published' 8 years after Christ's ascension, Mark 10 years after, Luke 15 years after and John 32 years after Christ's ascension. (So the four Gospels are arranged in chronological order, not only in our Bibles but in the vast majority of the Greek manuscripts.) "To the Jew first, . ."—since Matthew wrote for a Jewish audience, God's priorities dictated that Mat-

that we are looking at a prime example of the grace and sensitivity of God. It would be quite humiliating enough to have denied the Lord three/four times, but to go on to do so another three/four times, even after hearing a rooster crow, would be almost too much to bear. Rather than put the full extent of Peter's ignominy on display the Holy Spirit had each writer give only a partial account, enough for the purposes of the record but without flaying Peter unnecessarily. I find it interesting to note that it is Mark who furnishes the necessary clue that there was to be a second set of denials. The opinion is widely held that Peter influenced the composition of this Gospel—this is overtly stated in the introduction to the Gospel found in many manuscripts—and if so he may have insisted on including the hint as to the extent of his humiliation, whereas the others delicately avoided it.

The Text-critical Problem

Although there are around a hundred textual differences reflected in the printed editions of the Greek Text (in the passages considered), I will confine my remarks here to the set

---

thew's should be the first inspired account of our Savior's life on earth to circulate. Then Mark, with Matthew's Gospel open in front of him, and Peter at his elbow, wrote for the Roman mind (since Romans would care nothing for Hebrew Scriptures, Mark removed virtually all reference to fulfilled prophecy). Then Luke, with both Mark and Matthew to hand, wrote the third, for the Greek mind. Then John, with the first three open, wrote to fill in the gaps, preserving important information not provided by the others, for all minds. Now let's consider Peter's denials within that framework. Matthew wrote first, with one cockcrow. Mark says there were really two cockcrows and changes the second denial (1 and 3 are the same in Mark and Matthew). Luke speaks of just one cockcrow, changes the second denial yet again and provides added information (specific) about the third. So just with these three accounts we are up to five denials. John speaks of just one cockcrow but records three new denials, not mentioned by the other three. If these are inspired accounts, then God did it on purpose, and it is up to us to try to figure out why (see my concluding paragraph).

that is especially bothersome in terms of the subject matter of this article.

There are four places in Mark's account that relate to the two cockcrows: "twice" in 14:30, "and a rooster crowed" in 14:68, "the second time" and "twice" in 14:72. Instances 1, 3 and 4 go together and appear to contradict the account in Matthew, Luke and John. Instance 2 is apparently even worse because according to Mark's account Peter had only denied once when the rooster 'jumped the gun' and crowed before he was supposed to (Jesus had said there would certainly be three denials, as recorded in the other three Gospels). Accordingly, ever since the second century there have been those who tried to 'help' Mark out of his difficulties, tampering with the text.

According to the present state of our knowledge it appears that seven Greek MSS omit "twice" in 14:30 (but they do so in two different ways), nine MSS omit "and a rooster crowed" in 14:68 (but in two ways), five omit "the second time" in 14:72[a], and seven omit "twice" in 14:72[b] (two others omit the whole clause). The roster of MSS shifts in each case, as does the versional evidence that sides with the omissions. Only three witnesses are thoroughgoing and omit all four: Codex Aleph, cursive 579 and the Old Latin 'c' (it[c]). This is a curious state of affairs. If the purpose of the omissions was to make Mark conform to the other Gospels, only Aleph, 579 and it[c] have succeeded. Of the seventeen MSS involved, twelve omit only one of the four; one MS omits two of them; and two MSS omit three (there is some doubt here). Unless someone is prepared to show why Aleph and 579 are to be preferred above every other MS (some 1700 for Mark), and it[c] above all the rest of the versional evidence, Latin and otherwise, there is really no reason to take the omissions seriously. However, the eclectic school does take them seriously, even without the requisite demonstration.

It appears that the 'harder reading' canon has come to the aid of the vast majority of the MSS, at least as far as the editors of the 'critical' or eclectic texts presently in vogue are concerned. Instances 1, 3, and 4 are retained in all Nestle and UBS editions (although UBS ascribes "a considerable degree of doubt" to 1 and 3, and "some degree of doubt" to 4—the change in grade here is strange). However, when it comes to instance 2 ("and a rooster crowed") we get some variety: Nestle editions 1 to 25 omit the words; Nestle[26] and all three UBS editions retain them, but in single brackets (the UBS editors ascribe "a very high degree of doubt" to these words, along with the brackets which themselves signify "dubious textual validity"). Presumably the crucial datum here is that Codex B joins the evidence for omission with instance 2 (but not the others). From W-H through N[25] that was enough to banish the words from the Text. One supposes that it was the "harder reading" canon that restored them to UBS and N[26], if only in brackets. It seems to me that this case affords a clear example of the superficiality that characterizes the work of the eclectic school— to challenge the authenticity of a reading supported by over 99% of the MSS is unreasonable at any time, but to do so in the face of a perfectly obvious motivation for the omission is irresponsible.

The English versions that I have consulted all retain instances 1, 3 and 4, but deal variously with instance 2. AV, LB, NKJV, Phillips and TEV all retain "and a rooster crowed", but LB favors us with a footnote: "This statement is found in only some of the MSS". What might the purpose of such a footnote be? From the use of the word "only" it would appear that the purpose is to raise a doubt in the reader's mind about the reliability of the Text. Why would they want to do that? The use of the word "some" also invites comment: it is their way of referring to some 1700 MSS, against nine! Will the reader not be deceived?

Jerusalem, NASB, NEB, NIV and RSV all omit the clause, but only Jerusalem does so without comment. The footnote in NEB reads, "Some witnesses insert 'and a cock crew'." As in LB, by "some" they mean some 1700 MSS, not to mention massive versional support and almost unanimous lectionary support. Will the reader not be deceived? The footnote in RSV reads, "Other ancient authorities add 'and the cock crowed'." The footnote in NIV reads, "Some early MSS add 'and the rooster crowd'." The footnote in NASB reads, "Later mss. add: 'and a cock crowed'." In order to evaluate such footnotes we would need to know the precise definitions for "ancient", "early" and "later". However, I submit that the uninitiated reader of such footnotes will certainly be misled as to the massive evidence against omission.

The case of the NIV invites special comment. It is the only version that offers a footnote at all four instances. At 14:30 we read, "Some early MSS omit 'twice'." At 14:68 we read, "Some early MSS add 'and the rooster crowed'." At 14:72[a] we read, "Some early MSS omit 'the second time'." At 14:72[b] we read, "Some early MSS omit 'twice'." (The meaning of "some" in the second instance is quite different from that in the other three.) What possible reason could the editors have had for including these footnotes? The immediate effect is to call in question the reliability of the Text at those points. Since the NIV editors held to a high view of Scripture, why would they want to do that? I suppose that it was precisely their concern for the inerrancy of the Text that was at work here. It appears that they did not see any other solution to the seeming discrepancy between Mark and the other Gospels than to imply that Aleph and Old Latin 'c' might be right after all. Alas!

The NIV editors are barking up the wrong tree. The worst thing to be done here would be to follow Aleph in deleting all four instances. As already pointed out, the four Gospels record eight different challenges resulting in denials, but no two Gospels have the same selection. So to follow Aleph would force us to try to accommodate eight denials before the first rooster crow, which seems to me to be hopeless. The best thing to be done here is to follow the true Text, which God has graciously caused to be preserved, in this case, in over 99% of the evidence. Peter denied three/four times before the first rooster crow and another set of three/four before the second. The Lord had warned him: "Simon, Simon, indeed Satan has asked for you, that he may sift you as wheat" (Luke 22:31). Peter should have paid attention.

Implications

One question that arises is this: What about the internal integrity of each account? For instance, in John's account, even if we were to claim that two of the denials occurred before the first rooster crow, while the third denial came after the first and before the second, would this claim do violence to the integrity of John's Gospel? Why would it? Let us review the record. In John 13:38 Jesus said to Peter, "Most assuredly I say to you, a rooster shall not crow till you have denied me three times!" The Lord did not say "only" three times—the emphasis is on the obligatory absence of any rooster crow until Peter has denied three times, at least three times (there is nothing in the Lord's turn of phrase to preclude the possibility that there could be more than three). In the Greek text there is no definite article with "rooster" and there is an emphatic double negative with the verb "to crow"—"a rooster shall not crow!" (These observations also apply in Luke 22:34; in fact, in all four Gospels, in both the predictions and the fulfilments, it is always "a" rooster.)

Turning to John's account of the denials themselves, the first one, at the outside door (18:17), poses no difficulty. The second denial (18:25) likewise poses no difficulty—these two occurred before any rooster crow. But what if the third denial (in John's account, 18:26-27) came after the first crowing?[1] I see no problem, in principle. The Lord made a statement of fact, correctly recorded by John—there had to be three denials before the first rooster crow. This was precisely fulfilled,

---

[1] As the reader knows, I believe the third denial in John comes before the first cock crow, but I am covering this possibility for the sake of those who may prefer to have it in the second set.

the others supplying the third denial. Nothing in John's account precludes the possibility that there should be subsequent crowings. (Anyone who has lived near roosters knows that they start crowing off and on anytime after midnight and at daybreak put on a concert—it seems obvious to me that the first two crowings were overtly controlled by God so as to match Christ's predictions.) In 18:27, after the third denial recorded by John, we read, "and immediately a rooster crowed". John does not say that it was the first crowing. Someone without access to the other Gospels would naturally assume that John records the first rooster crow, and that the three denials he gives are the whole story—but <u>nothing in John's statement demands that interpretation</u>; it simply arises from incomplete information. The other three present several added denials that are clearly distinct. The several Evangelists provide distinct sets of details, much like the pieces of a puzzle, that must be fitted together to get the whole picture. The several accounts are complementary, not contradictory.

But how about the internal integrity of Mark's account? He is the only one who mentions the second rooster crow, as such, and in fact his account is tied to it. Jesus said, "before a rooster crows twice you will deny me three times," and Mark records three denials before the second rooster crow. Again, Jesus did not say "only" three times, the emphasis is on "you" and "twice". The other Gospels are needed to get the full picture, but Mark's account is entirely self-consistent.

And how about Luke? In the warning the emphasis is on the obligatory absence of a rooster crow until Peter has denied three times—at least three times (Jesus did not say "only" three times). After describing three of the denials Luke writes, "and immediately, while he was still speaking, a rooster crowed". "A" rooster—he does not say it was the first. Then Luke has Peter remembering that Jesus said, "Before a rooster crows you will deny me three times". Presumably Peter remembered every detail of all the warnings, but Luke (and each of the other Evangelists) gives only a partial description—in fact, Luke has him recalling the warning recorded by Matthew, not the one he himself gave. A reader having only Luke's account may assume that he told the whole story, but it is an unwarranted assumption. Luke's account is internally consistent yet the precise turn of phrase is such that it does not preclude my proposal.

So what about Matthew? Virtually everything said about Luke above can be repeated here. He has Peter remembering the warning he himself recorded. Again it is "a" rooster. Matthew's account is internally consistent yet the turn of phrase will accommodate my proposal without being violated. All of which brings us back to the question: Why does each Gospel speak of three denials, rather than six, eight or whatever? I do not know; we are not told. My best guess is that God chose to draw a veil over the full extent of Peter's ignominy (and perhaps to test our disposition when faced with the unexplained). But it remains a plain fact that each Gospel offers a different assortment of challenges and denials, giving a total of at least eight denials.

Another question that I have heard concerns the validity of attempting an exercise such as this at all. I believe that God deliberately brings difficulties into our lives (Job in the ash heap, Abraham on Moriah, Moses herding sheep, Joseph in prison, Daniel with the lions, and on, and on), and puts puzzles in the world, to test our disposition and fiber, and to cause us to grow. "It is the glory of God to conceal a matter, but the glory of kings is to search out a matter" (Proverbs 25:2). [Even if you are not a king, you get the point.] The case of John the baptizer in prison comes closer to home. He is frustrated, maybe disillusioned; he did his job but his expectations are not being realized. So he sends two disciples to ask Jesus for an explanation. In effect Jesus answers, "Check the evidence; do your homework", and closes with, "And blessed is he who is not offended because of me" (Matthew 11:6). When faced with the difficult or unexplained we must be careful not to rebel. It is much better to obey the command recorded in 1

Peter 3:15. "Sanctify the Lord God in your hearts, and always be ready to give a defense to everyone who asks you a reason for the hope that is in you, . . ." Since opponents of a Text with objective authority have used the accounts of Peter's denials as an argument against any idea of inerrancy, I consider that a defense of that inerrancy is in order.

Harmonizing the accounts of the Resurrection

A rough sequence within the parallel accounts

Matthew 27:62-28:1;
Mark 16:1-3 // Luke 24:1;
Matthew 28:2-4;
John 20:1-10;
Matthew 28:5-8 // Mark 16:4-8 // Luke 24:2-8;
Mark 16:9 // John 20:11-18;
Matthew 28:9-15;
Luke 24:13-35;
Luke 24:36-43 // John 20:19-31.

The presumed sequence of events

0. [Saturday—guards seal the stone and set up a watch (Matthew 27:62-66).]

1. Jesus rises from the dead.[1]

2. Early Sunday morning the women set out for the tomb—Magdalene (John 20:1); Magdalene and Mary (Matthew 28:1); Magdalene, Mary and Salome (Mark 16:1-2); Magdalene, Mary, Joanna and others (Luke 23:55-24:1, 10).[2]

---

[1] None of the Evangelists mentions the moment of the resurrection; probably because that information was never revealed. The fact is taken for granted (the "firstborn from the dead"—Col. 1:18, Rev. 1:5; the "firstfruits"—1 Cor. 15:20, 23).

[2] The several accounts say it was very early, as the day began to dawn, while it was still dark, but by the time they got to the tomb the sun had risen. There is no discrepancy: recall that the garden is on the west side of a mountain, so even after the sun had risen the tomb would be in shadow, besides the shade of the trees. It

3. On the way they worry about the stone (Mark 16:3).

4. Before they arrive an angel rolls back the stone, complete with earthquake, etc. (Matthew 28:2-4).[1]

5. They arrive and see that the stone has been rolled back, but the angel was no longer visible outside (Mark 16:4, Luke 24:2, John 20:1).[2]

6. Magdalene takes off immediately to tell Peter—Peter and John run to the tomb to see (John 20:2-3).[3]

7. Before Peter and John get there the other women enter the tomb, and see and hear the angels (Luke 24:3-8, Mark 16:5-7, Matthew 28:5-7).[4]

---

was still darkish when they started out, but away from the mountain it was already day by the time they arrived—the tomb area would still be gloomy.

[1] The removal of the stone was not to let Jesus out; it was to let witnesses in! If we only had Matthew's record, we could assume that the women saw the shining angel outside the sepulcher, but a comparison of the other accounts leads to a different understanding. So how do we know those details? Matthew 28:11 says that "some" of the guard reported to the priests and accepted big money to spread a false report, but what happened to the other guards? I have no doubt that some of those guards were soundly converted and gave an eyewitness account to the Christian community.

[2] If the angel had been visible, Magdalene would not have taken off, because she would not have thought that the body had been stolen. The hypothesis that she came once alone, before the others, is highly improbable (see the next note).

[3] Her use of the plural "we", verse 2, indicates that she was not alone at the tomb.

[4] I take Matthew and Mark to be parallel, describing the same event: the angel who rolled away the stone is now inside the sepulcher, sitting on the right side; he has turned off his neon and appears to be a young man clothed in white; each account furnishes a few distinct details in the angel's speech—Mark includes "and Peter" [was Peter looking over his shoulder?]. The women were not sure they were happy with the situation, and the 'young man' may well have said more than Matthew and Mark record. I take it that Luke records a second inning: the women are having trouble assimilating the missing body (they were loaded with spices to put on that body—was their effort to be wasted?); so the angel calls in a colleague and they both turn on their neon—a little shock treatment; then they appeal to Jesus' own words, which the women remember, and with that they are convinced and go their way.

8. They leave the tomb in fear, saying nothing to the guards or anyone they chance to meet (Mark 16:8, Matthew 28:8[a]).

9. Probably right after the women leave, and before Peter and John arrive, the guards take off (Matthew 28:11-15).

10. Peter and John come and go [to their own homes] (John 20:4-10; cf. Luke 24:12 that is an historical aside).[1] No mention is made of either angels or guards, so presumably Peter and John saw no one—the place appeared to be abandoned.

11. Magdalene returns to the sepulcher but does not get there until everyone is gone (that is why she thought Jesus was the gardener); Jesus appears to her first (Mark 16:9, John 20:11-17).[2]

12. Then Jesus appears to the other women and they go on their way to tell the disciples (Matthew 28:9-10, Luke 24:9-11).[3]

---

[1] Verse 8 says that John (the author) "saw and believed". What did John 'see' that made him 'believe'? He saw the linen strips 'lying', that is, in the form of the body, only there was no body inside them! If someone had stolen the body, as Magdalene supposed, they would have taken the wrapped package (much easier to carry) and there would have been no linen strips. If someone had unwrapped the body, for whatever reason, there would have been a sizable mound of linen strips and spices piled up (how much cloth would it take to wrap up a hundred pounds of spices?). No, Jesus simply passed through the cloth, as He would later pass through the wall of the upper room, leaving the package like a mummy case or empty cocoon. When John saw that, he understood that the only possible explanation was resurrection.

[2] When the disciples took off running, of course Magdalene followed them back to the tomb. But she was winded, and could not keep up with them (actually, in that culture women probably seldom ran, so she would really be out of breath, but she was not about to be left out of the action, either). She may have arrived as they were leaving; if not they would pass her on the road. In verse 12 John says that she saw two 'angels'. How did John know they were angels? He had just been there and knew there were no human beings around (the guards were presumably gone before the two got there). The angels were in white, but probably not shining, or Magdalene would have been shaken out of her despair. She was so locked in to her sorrow that not even seeing the wrappings collapsed without the body sank in.

[3] The question may reasonably be asked: How could Magdalene have time to go and come and Jesus appear to her first and still have time to appear to the wom-

13. Magdalene goes and tells the disciples (Mark 16:10-11, John 20:18).

14. Later in the day Jesus appears to Peter (cf. Luke 24:34).[1]

15. The Emmaus road episode (Luke 24:13-35, Mark 16:12-13).[2]

---

en before they got to the disciples, the more so since Matthew 28:8 says the women "hurried and ran"? I offer the following considerations in relief of the perceived difficulty: 1) The Jerusalem of that day was small and distances were short ("nearby", John 19:42)—it was probably less than a mile, or even half a mile, between the tomb and Peter's house, as well as where the other disciples were staying; 2) the women were probably slow in entering the tomb—the guards making like dead men, dark, spooky (it's a cemetery), all very strange, Magdalene the impulsive one wasn't there; they would be leery—Magdalene may have been almost to Peter's house before they worked up the courage to enter the tomb; 3) Magdalene, Peter and John were excited and had extra adrenalin—it didn't take that long; 4) the women ran out of the tomb and the garden, but not necessarily all the way to the disciples—once they got away from the garden and on 'safe' ground they may well have slowed down, or even stopped, to get a grip on themselves and discuss what had happened (Mary, the mother of James, was no longer young, and none of the women was used to running, not to mention the type of clothing they wore). Putting it all together, I see no reason to doubt that it all happened just like the Text says.

[1] I see no way of determining the correct sequence of items 14 and 15, it could have been the other way around. Also, during resurrection Sunday (we don't know just when) many resurrected saints "went into the holy city and appeared to many" (Matthew 27:53), which would have been **dramatic** confirmatory evidence to those who were visited.

[2] Some have alleged a discrepancy between the two accounts—their mistake is to tie both accounts to the Eleven, which was not the case. There were other people in the upper room, besides the Eleven. The Eleven were reclining at a table, the 'others' would be nearer the door. The two from Emmaus come bursting in, all excited and probably feeling just a little important; it is the 'others', probably to 'prick their balloon', who say, "Oh, we already know that; He has appeared to Simon". (Human nature hasn't changed, and they didn't have the Holy Spirit yet.) While the two from Emmaus are talking with the 'others', not the Eleven, Jesus Himself appears and interacts with the Eleven (and they think He's a ghost!). Mark, writing for a Roman audience, is emphasizing that the disciples were not gullible, did not 'believe' because they wanted to—in verse 11 they didn't believe Magdalene, in verse 13 nor the two, in verse 14 Jesus rebukes their unbelief. There is nothing here to impugn the genuineness of these verses—they were certainly written by Mark at the same time that he wrote the rest. According to Matthew 28:17 many days later some were still doubting. It is scarcely credible that any of the Eleven would still be in doubt, but there were certainly others present,

16. Jesus appears to the eleven, Thomas being absent (Luke 24:36-48, Mark 16:14-18, John 20:19-23).

17. After Jesus leaves, Thomas comes in and they tell him (John 20:24-25).

Post resurrection day events

1. The next Sunday Jesus appears to them again and deals with Thomas (John 20:26-29).

2. Jesus appears to the seven beside the Sea of Galilee (John 21:1-22).

3. On a mountain in Galilee (Matthew 28:16-20).

4. Jesus appears to over 500, also to James (1 Corinthians 15:6-7).[1]

5. The ascension from Olivet (Mark 16:19-20, Luke 24:49-51, Acts 1:3-12).

Conclusion

In sum, I see no reason for doubt: it all happened just as the Text describes it. There are no discrepancies, in spite of the variety of details supplied by various eyewitnesses (including converted guards) and written down by four different Evangelists. It is just what we should expect from an inspired Text—inspired and preserved, to this day.

Some related anomalies in Matthew's genealogy of the Christ

Matthew's purpose is to demonstrate that Jesus, the Messiah, has a <u>legal</u> right to sit on David's throne (perhaps answering

---

including Jesus' half-brothers. In any group of people there are always differing levels of belief and unbelief. People's heads work differently, and at different speeds.

[1] I see no way of determining the correct sequence of the events in items 3 and 4.

the Lord's own question in Matthew 22:42). Although there are many kings in the genealogy, David is the only one who is described as 'the king', twice. Since David's throne has to do with the covenant people, and that covenant began with Abraham, the genealogy does as well. It ends with Joseph, Jesus' 'father' by adoption, since Jesus had none of Joseph's genes.[1] It was sufficient to Matthew's purpose to show that Joseph was a linear, and legal, descendant of David, the number of intervening generations was beside the point. Matthew's Gospel was directed primarily to a Jewish audience, to whom legal rights were important.

Matthew divides his genealogy of the Christ into three groups of fourteen 'generations'. A comparison of his genealogy with the OT record indicates that it is not a 'normal', straightforward genealogy—there are some anomalies.[2] In an effort to understand the purpose behind the anomalies, I will begin with the second group, which may be said to be made up of (mostly) sovereign kings of Judah. Going back to the OT we discover that there were seventeen such kings, not fourteen. But, Matthew says 'generations', not reigns, and since Ahaziah reigned only one year, Amon only two, and Abijah only three, they can be assimilated into the fourteen generations. That said, however, we next observe that Abijah and Amon are duly included in the list, while Ahaziah is not, followed by Joash and Amaziah. The three excluded names form a group between Jehoram and Uzziah.

Verse eight says that "Joram begot Uzziah", the verb 'begot' being the same one used throughout, but in fact Uzziah was

---

[1] Indeed He could not, because of the prophesies in Jeremiah 22:30 and 36:30, wherein Jeconiah and Jehoiakim are cursed. However, Jesus received some of David's genes through Mary (please see the note that accompanies Luke 3:23 in my translation).

[2] I believe that Matthew composed his Gospel under divine guidance, which leads me to the conclusion that the anomalies were deliberate, on God's part. Therefore, my attempt to unravel the anomalies tries to understand the Holy Spirit's purpose in introducing them into the record.

Joram's (Jehoram's) great-great-grandson. So we see that 'begot' refers to a linear descendant, not necessarily a son. We also see that the number 'fourteen' is not being used in a strictly literal sense (whatever the author's purpose may have been). It also appears that 'generation' is not being used in a strictly literal sense. It follows that we are looking at an edited genealogy, edited in accord with the author's purpose.

In an effort to understand why the group of three was excluded, I ask: What might they have in common? They had in common genes from Ahab and Jezebel, as also a direct spiritual and moral influence from them. Ahaziah's mother was Athaliah, daughter of Ahab and Jezebel, so 50% of his genes were from Ahab. 2 Kings 8:27 says that Ahaziah was a son-in-law of the house of Ahab, referring to the mother of Joash, so 75% of his genes were from Ahab. Since Joash married Jehoaddan of Jerusalem, the contamination in Amaziah was down to 37%, and then in Uzziah it was below 20%.[1] This is my best guess as to why that group was excluded; a rebuke after the fact. (Matthew is giving an edited genealogy of the Christ, and Ahab's genes were definitely undesirable.)

We come now to another anomaly: 14 x 3 = 42, but only 41 names are given; what to do? We begin by noticing that both David and Jeconiah are mentioned on both sides of a 'boundary'. I will consider the second boundary first. Verse eleven says that "Josiah begot Jeconiah and his brothers", passing over Jehoiakim, Jeconiah's father. But according to the Record, it was Jehoiakim who had "brothers", not Jeconiah. Since we need the real Jeconiah in the third group to make fourteen names, I place Jeconiah in the third group—counting both Jeconiah and Christ we get fourteen names.[2] But why was Je-

---

[1] It was Dr. Floyd N. Jones who started me thinking along this line (*Chronology of the Old Testament: A Return to the Basics*, Kings Word Press, 1999, pp. 38-42).

[2] Of course, if four people were omitted from the second group, some may also have been omitted from the third, but we have no way of knowing, and it would make no difference to the purpose of this genealogy.

hoiakim not named? So far as I know, he was the only king who had the perversity to actually cut up a scroll with God's Word and then throw it in the fire, Jeremiah 36:23, and the curse that follows in verse 30 is stated to be a consequence of that act. If we count David in the second group, Jehoiakim would make fifteen. Without Jehoiakim we would need David in the second group to make fourteen. But that raises another difficulty: we also need David in the first group, to make fourteen. Because of the "brothers", I consider that the 'Jeconiah' before the captivity actually stands for Jehoiakim, whose name is omitted because of his heinous crime in destroying the scroll. In that event, we have fourteen without David, so he can be assigned to the first group.

If the second group is made up of kings, the first group is made up of patriarchs. Acts 2:29 calls David a 'patriarch', so we may not disqualify him on that basis, but of course he is better known as a king—indeed he is expressly called that in the genealogy (the only one who is). Although David may be both patriarch and king, he may not be two people, nor two generations. In consequence, I am decidedly uncomfortable with the proposal that David must be placed in both groups—we should neither split him in two, not double him. To my mind, he belongs in the first group, but what if we placed him in the second? That would leave only thirteen for the first one. However, I tentatively assign David to the first group, making fourteen. Since David is used as the first boundary, and the purpose of the genealogy is to establish Jesus' right to David's throne, his name is repeated, but I do not count him in the second group.

But consider Rahab and Ruth (and if four people were omitted from the second group, why could not some also be omitted from the first?). There were 340 years between the death of Joshua and the birth of David, and Salmon married Rahab while Joshua was still alive, presumably. That sort of obliges Boaz, Obed and Jesse to do their begetting at age 100, or thereabouts (perhaps not impossible, but certainly improbable). But what if 'begot' is being used for a grandson, as we have already seen? (Josiah begot Jeconiah, with no mention of Jehoiakim.) If Athaliah's genes were enough to disqualify Ahaziah, what about Rahab's genes? She was not even an Israelite, and worse, she was a prostitute. Now the Law says some rather severe things about prostitutes.[1] "You shall not bring the wages of a harlot or the price of a dog [catamite] to the house of the LORD your God, . . . for both of these are an abomination to the LORD your God" (Deuteronomy 23:18). For a priest to marry a harlot would profane his posterity (Leviticus 21:13-15), so how about an ancestor of the Messiah? Of course it is possible for a prostitute to be saved, but why was she even mentioned? And why were Tamar, Ruth, and Uriah's wife mentioned? Women were not normally included in genealogies.[2]

Now consider Ruth. She was a Moabitess, and according to Deuteronomy 23:3 a Moabite could not enter the assembly of the LORD to the tenth generation. [To me it is an astonishing example of the grace of God that she was included in the Messiah's line.] She embraced Naomi's God, but what about her genes? 'Ten generations' has to do with genes, not spiritual conversion. Moab was a son of Lot, and the first 'Moabite' would be his son, probably a contemporary of Jacob. From Jacob to Salmon we have seven generations, certainly fewer than ten, so Ruth could not enter. Could it be possible that Rahab and Ruth each represent a missing generation? Could

---

[1] However, "the law was given through Moses, but grace and truth came through Jesus Christ" (John 1:17). This being an edited genealogy of the Messiah, perhaps Rahab, and the other women, were included to emphasize the grace of the Messiah.

[2] None of the decent, honest, honorable, responsible mothers are mentioned, only 'exceptions'!

that be why they are mentioned?[1] If we divide 300 years by five, then the average begetting age would be 60, certainly within the bounds of reason (and if more than two generations were skipped, the number would be further reduced). I repeat that this is not a 'normal' genealogy. Why did Matthew want three 'equal' groups, and why did he choose 'fourteen'? Perhaps for stylistic (symmetry, balance) and mnemonic reasons. However, my concern has been to address any perceived errors of fact, which an inspired Text should not have.

To conclude: Matthew gives us an edited genealogy of the Messiah. If on the one hand it emphasizes the Messiah's grace, on the other it reflects the Messiah's holiness—He cannot overlook sin and its consequences (the four excluded names in the second group are due to that holiness). If the four women were included as a reflection of the Messiah's grace, it is also true that the consequences of sin are not hidden—the fourth is called simply 'Uriah's wife' (not 'widow', even though Solomon was conceived after the murder of Uriah—David did not marry a widow, he stole someone else's wife).

The 'Legion' and the pigs; where was it?

We need to start with the evidence supplied by the Greek manuscripts. We encounter the episode in three of the Gospels.

Matthew 8:28: γεργεσηνων 98% (Gergesenes) AV, NKJV

γαδαρηνων 2% (Gadarenes) NIV, NASB, LB, TEV, etc.

NIV footnote: "Some manuscripts *Gergesenes*; others *Gerasenes*".

---

[1] Tamar had suffered a severe injustice, and David's sin with Bathsheba was unusually perverse (cowardly murder), but Rahab was probably a victim of circumstances, and Ruth was certainly not to blame for having been born a Moabitess.

Mark 5:1: γαδαρηνων 95,5% (Gadarenes) AV, NKJV

γεργεσηνων 4,1% (Gergesenes)

γερασηνων 0,3% (Gerasenes) NIV, NASB, LB, TEV, etc.

NIV footnote: "Some manuscripts *Gadarenes*; other manuscripts *Gergesenes*".

Luke 8:26: γαδαρηνων 97% (Gadarenes) AV, NKJV

γεργεσηνων 2% (Gergesenes) TEV

γερασηνων 0,3% (Gerasenes) NIV, NASB, LB, etc.

NIV footnote: "Some manuscripts *Gadarenes;* other manuscripts *Gergesenes;* also in verse 37".

Luke 8:37: γαδαρηνων 96% (Gadarenes) AV, NKJV

γεργεσηνων 3,5% (Gergesenes) TEV

γερασηνων 0,3% (Gerasenes) NIV, NASB, LB, etc.

I will begin with Mark. Jesus arrived at "the region [not 'province'] of the Gadarenes". Gadara was the capital city of the Roman province of Perara, located some six miles from the Sea of Galilee. Since Mark was writing for a Roman audience,[1] "the region of the Gadarenes" was a perfectly reasonable description of the site. Lamentably, the eclectic Greek text currently in vogue follows about five Greek manuscripts of objectively inferior quality (against at least 1,700 better ones) in reading 'Gerasenes' (to be followed by NIV, NASB, LB, TEV, etc.). The NIV footnote is dishonest: to use 'some' to describe over 1,700 manuscripts against five is a dishonest use of the

---

[1] Although, as explained elsewhere, I understand that Matthew was published first, and Mark probably had a copy open before him as he wrote, yet he deliberately changed Matthew's 'Gergesenes' to 'Gadarenes'—to his intended Roman audience 'Gergesa' would be unknown, while some would indeed know about 'Gadara'.

Queen's English (to use 'others' to refer to some 60 is acceptable).

Luke also has Jesus arriving at "the region of the Gadarenes". Since he was writing for a Greek audience, he follows Mark's example. Again NIV has a dishonest footnote. It is most likely that 'Gerasa' is a fiction, a 'place' that never existed. On the other hand, 'Gergesa' certainly did exist, although we no longer know the exact location. As I will explain while discussing Matthew, below, I have no doubt that it was a village near the spot where Jesus landed.

Matthew clearly wrote 'Gergesenes' rather than 'Gadarenes'. Since he was writing for a Jewish audience, and many Galileans would be quite familiar with the Sea of Galilee, he provided a more localized description. Further, try to picture the events in your mind. Do you suppose that the swineherds ran six miles to Gadara? The populace would certainly not run the six miles back. All of that would have taken entirely too long. To me it is obvious that there was a village close by, probably within half a mile, called 'Gergesa'. It was to that village that the swineherds ran, told their story, and brought the residents back. Galileans familiar with the Sea of Galilee would certainly recognize 'Gergesa'.

Not only does Matthew name a different place, he affirms that there were really two demonized men, whereas Mark and Luke mention only one. As a former tax collector, numerical precision was important to Matthew. Neither Mark nor Luke use the number 'one'; they merely commented on the more prominent of the two, the one who wanted to go with Jesus. I understand that indeed there were two of them.

Abiathar is not Ahimelech—Mark 2:26 X 1 Samuel 21:1

Some of my readers may be aware that this verse has destroyed the faith of at least one scholar in our day, although he was reared in an evangelical home. He understood Jesus to be saying that Abiathar was the priest with whom David dealt, when in fact it was his father, Ahimelech. If Jesus stated an historical error as fact, then he could not be God. So he turned his back on Jesus. I consider that his decision was lamentable and unnecessary, and in the interest of helping others who may be troubled by this verse, I offer the following explanation:

> "How he entered the house of God (making Abiathar high priest) and ate the consecrated bread, which only priests are permitted to eat, and shared it with those who were with him."

My rendering is rather different than the 'in the days of Abiathar the high priest' of the AV, NKJV and NIV. We are translating three Greek words that very literally would be 'upon Abiathar high-priest' (but the preposition here, επι, is the most versatile of the Greek prepositions, and one of its many meanings/uses is 'toward'—the standard lexicon, BDAG, lists fully eighteen <u>areas</u> of meaning, quite apart from subdivisions). When we go back to the Old Testament account, we discover that David actually conversed with Ahimelech, Abiathar's father, who was the high priest at that moment (1 Samuel 21:1-9). Within a few days Saul massacred Ahimelech and 84 other priests (1 Samuel 22:16-18), but his son Abiathar escaped and went to David, <u>taking the ephod with him</u> (1 Samuel 22:20-23; 23:6). That David could use it to inquire of the LORD rather suggests that it had to be the ephod that only the high priest wore, since only that ephod had the Urim and Thummim (1 Samuel 23:9-12; cf. Numbers 27:21, Ezra 2:63).

That ephod was to a high priest like the crown was to a king; so how could Abiathar have it? The Text states that David's visit filled Ahimelech with fear, presumably because he too saw Doeg the Edomite and figured what would happen. Now why was Abiathar not taken with the others? I suggest that Ahime-lech foresaw what would happen (Doeg probably took off immediately, and Ahimelech figured he would not have much time), so he deliberately consecrated Abiathar, gave him the ephod, and told him to hide—he probably did it that very day (once the soldiers arrived to arrest Ahimelech and the other 84, it would be too late). Abiathar escaped, but carried the news of the massacre with him; only now he was the high priest.

Putting it all together, it was David's visit that resulted in Abiathar's becoming high priest prematurely, as David himself recognized, and to which Jesus alluded in passing (which is why I used parentheses). But why would Jesus allude to that? I suppose because the Bible is straightforward about the consequences of sin, and David lied to Ahimelech. Although Jesus was using David's eating that bread as an example, He did not wish to gloss over the sin, and its consequences.

Recall that Jesus was addressing Pharisees, who were steeped in the OT Scriptures. A notorious case like Saul's massacre of 85 priests would be very well known. And of course, none of the NT had yet been written, so any understanding of what Jesus said had to be based on 1 Samuel ("Have you never read . . . ?"). If we today wish to understand this passage, we need to place ourselves in the context recorded in Mark 2:23-28. The Pharisees would understand that if Abiathar was in possession of the ephod with the Urim and Thummim, then he was the high priest. And how did he get that way? He got that way because of David's visit. It was an immediate consequence of that visit.

Some may object that 'making' is a verb, not a preposition. Well, the 'in the days of' of the AV, etc., though not a verb, is a phrase. Both a pronoun and an adverb may stand for a phrase, and a preposition may as well. TEV and Phillips actually use a verb: 'when . . . was'; NLT has 'during the days when . . . was'. Where the others used from two to five words, I used only one.

Entering, or leaving Jericho?—Luke 18:35, 19:1 X Mark 10:46 X Matthew 20:29-30

In the NKJV, Luke 18:35 and 19:1 read like this: "Then it happened, as He was coming near Jericho, that a certain blind man sat by the road begging. . . . Then Jesus entered and passed through Jericho." Luke plainly states that Jesus healed a blind man before entering Jericho (he mentions only one, but does not say that there was only one). And Mark 10:46 reads like this: "Now they came to Jericho. As He went out of Jericho with his disciples and a great multitude, blind Bartimaeus, the son of Timaeus, sat by the road begging." Mark plainly states that Jesus healed a blind man upon <u>leaving</u> Jericho (he names the blind man, referring only to him, but does not say that there was only one). And Matthew 20:29-30 reads like this: "Now as they went out of Jericho, a great multitude followed Him. And behold, two blind men sitting by the road, . . ." Matthew plainly states that Jesus healed <u>two</u> blind men upon leaving Jericho.

Well now, entering is one thing, and leaving is another, so which was it? Strange to relate, it was both! The Jericho that Joshua destroyed had been rebuilt (at least partially), and was inhabited. But in Jesus' day Herod had built a new Jericho, perhaps a kilometer away from the old one, also inhabited. So where would an intelligent beggar place himself? Presumably between the two towns. I take it that all three of the accounts before us transpired between the two Jerichos, so Jesus was leaving one and entering the other. There is no discrepancy. Luke and Mark probably give us the same incident, but what about Mathew? Besides stating that the men were two, he says that Jesus "touched their eyes", whereas according to Luke and Mark He only spoke. It is entirely probable that there was more than one beggar along that stretch of road, and any shouting could be heard for quite a ways. I take it that Matthew records a different incident. I suppose that Bartimaeus was healed first, and he shouted so loud that the two heard it all and knew what to do when their turn came.

Who bought what from whom, and where?— Stephen X Genesis

Acts 7:15-16—"So Jacob went down to Egypt; and he died, he and our fathers; and they were transferred to Shechem and placed in the tomb that Abraham bought for a sum of money from the sons of Hamor of Shechem."

When we compare this text with the relevant passages in Genesis, we appear to be confronted with some discrepancies. Who bought what from whom, and where? Genesis 33:19 informs us that <u>Jacob</u> bought a plot from Hamor, in Shechem. On the other hand, Genesis 23:16-20 explains that Abraham bought an area that included the cave of Machpelah from Ephron, in Hebron. That cave became the sepulcher of Abraham and Sarah, of Isaac and Rebecca, and of Jacob and Lea, because Jacob insisted upon being buried there, as indeed he was (Genesis 49:29-30, 50:13). Looking again at Acts 7, it was 'our fathers' that were buried in Shechem, not Jacob. Indeed, Joshua 24:32 states explicitly that Joseph's bones were buried in Shechem.

Yes but, whenever did Abraham buy anything in Shechem? I believe Genesis 12:6-7 gives us the clue. Abraham stopped in Shechem and built an altar. Now then, to build on someone else's property, with that someone looking on, probably won't work very well. I believe we may reasonably deduce that Abraham bought a plot "from the sons of Hamor of Shechem". The 'Hamor' of Jacob's day would be a descendant of the 'Hamor' in Abraham's (sons were often named after their fathers). In Genesis 14:14 we read that Abraham "armed his three hundred and eighteen trained servants who were born in his own house". If we add women and children, the total number of people under Abraham's command was probably over a thousand. Well now, with such a crowd it is not at all unlikely that someone died while they were stopped at Shechem. (People older than Abraham would not have been 'born in his own house', but there were doubtless older persons in that crowd.) In that event Abraham would need space for a cemetery, if the plot he had already bought for the altar was not big enough, or appropriate. That sort of information may have been available to Stephen from an extra-biblical document, or he may have figured it out as I have done (in his case guided by the Holy Spirit—Acts 7:55).

Going back to Genesis 33:19, it is possible that Jacob increased the area that Abraham had bought, by purchase. But why were all of Jacob's sons buried in Shechem? I believe the answer lies in Genesis 34:27-29. We read that Jacob's sons killed all the men of Shechem, looted everything, but <u>kept the women and children</u>. And what do you suppose they did with the women? So where did you think they found wives for so many men? They got them from Shechem. Since Shechem was the source of their wives and material possessions, it would be a natural place for them to be buried.

To conclude: there is no discrepancy. Both Abraham and Jacob bought land in Shechem. It was Jacob's sons who were buried there, not Jacob himself.

How many animals?—Matthew 21:1-7 X Mark 11:1-10, Luke 19:29-36, John 12:12-15

Mark, Luke and John are agreed in mentioning a single animal, a donkey colt. It was loosed, brought to Jesus, garments placed upon it, and then Jesus rode on it. Matthew insists on telling us that there were really two animals, the colt and its mother. The AV (KJV) has a most unfortunate translation of both Matthew 21:5 and Zechariah 9:9 (that has been corrected in the NKJV, fortunately). In Zechariah the AV has, "riding upon an ass, and upon a colt the foal of an ass." In Matthew the AV has, "sitting upon an ass, and a colt the foal of an ass." The obvious difficulty is that the AV makes Jesus ride two animals, when in fact He only rode one. For the correct rendering of both Zechariah and Matthew, at this point, please see the NKJV. That said, however, the fact remains that Matthew clearly has the disciples fetching two animals and placing garments on both.

Why do you suppose the Holy Spirit had Matthew supply the added information? I was not there, of course, but I offer my understanding of the event. Mark and Luke specify that no one had ever sat on the colt; they say that the colt was tied, but Matthew says it was really the mother that was tied. Evidently the colt was so young that it was still staying close to 'mother', so if she was tied, he was too, in effect (they were out in the street, and that may have been a new experience for the colt). Jesus was going to subject the colt to a strange and even frightening situation. From the peace and quiet of his little village, he would be surrounded by a shouting crowd. Strange things would be put on his back, and then someone who was probably bigger and heavier than he was would sit on him! I believe that Jesus had the mother brought along as moral support for her son. Clothes were put on her too (and of course she was surrounded by the shouting crowd as well), and seeing that she was calm would encourage the colt. Just by the way, Jesus probably had to lift His feet to keep them from dragging; it must have been a comical sight. It gives me a warm feeling to see that the Lord Jesus was concerned for the well-being of the colt.

'Gall', or 'myrrh'?—Matthew 27:34 X Mark 15:23

In the NKJV, Matthew 27:34ª reads like this: "they gave Him sour wine mingled with gall to drink." And Mark 15:23ª reads like this: "Then they gave Him wine mingled with myrrh to drink." That Mark used a generic term, 'wine', for the more precise 'sour wine' (or 'wine vinegar'), need not detain us. But what was the mixture? 'Gall' is one thing, an animal substance, and 'myrrh' is another, a vegetable substance; it was either one or the other, but which? Was Matthew influenced by Psalm 69:21? "They also gave me gall for my food, and for my thirst they gave me vinegar to drink." (Matthew wrote for a Jewish audience, and seems to have mentioned fulfilled prophecy whenever he could.) More to the point, perhaps, is Acts 8:23, where Peter says to Simon (the ex-sorcerer), "for I see that you are in a gall of bitterness" (so the Greek Text). Evidently 'gall' was used as a generic term for any bitter substance. I take it that Matthew, perhaps influenced by Psalm 69:21, used the generic term. I conclude that the precise substance used was myrrh, as Mark indicates.

How many people?—Acts 7:14 X Genesis 46:26 X Genesis 46:27

Again, we need only pay close attention to each context, and the precise wording of the text. The three verses give us three different numbers: 75, 66 and 70, respectively. I will begin with the smallest number, which is in Genesis 46:26: "All the persons who went with Jacob to Egypt, who came from his body, besides Jacob's sons' wives, were sixty-six persons in all." The crucial datum is 'from his body', so who were they? Reuben + four sons = 5, Simeon + six sons = 7, Levi + three sons = 4, Judah + five sons = 6, Issachar + four sons = 5, Zebulun + three sons = 4, that add up to 31, but we must include Dinah to get the total of 32 from Leah. Gad + seven sons = 8, Asher + six sons = 7, but we must add a daughter (mentioned in the record) to get the total of 16 from Zilpah. Joseph + two sons = 3, Benjamin + ten sons = 11, that add up to 14 from Rachel. Dan + one son = 2, Naphtali + four sons = 5, that add up to 7 from Bilhah. The grand total 'from his body' is 69. But of course Joseph and his two sons were already in Egypt, so that leaves 66 who 'went with Jacob to Egypt'.

Genesis 46:27 says, "All the persons of the house of Jacob who went to Egypt were seventy." This includes Joseph and Jacob himself, so there is no discrepancy. But what about Acts 7:14? "Then Joseph sent and called his father Jacob and all his relatives to him, seventy-five people." The 75 presumably refers to 'all his relatives', which excludes Jacob and of course Joseph. I take it that nine wives came to Egypt (the wives are mentioned in Genesis 46:26), the other two having died before the migration. (If we include Jacob, there would be eight wives.)

Mary's genealogy—Luke 3:23

Και αυτος ην ο Ιησους , ωσει ετων τριακοντα αρχομενοφ, ων (ως ενομιζετο) υιος Ιωσηφ, του Ηλει, του Ματθαν, του Λευι, του Μελχι( )))

There are four words here that invite special attention: *και, αυτος(ην* and *ως)* Since verse 22 ends with a statement from the Father at Jesus' baptism, it is clear that verse 23 begins another section. But the conjunction that signals the transition is *και* and not *δε*, as one would expect—this means that 'Jesus' continues as the topic. But in that event, how does one explain the personal pronoun *αυτος*, the more so in such an emphatic position? If the author's purpose was simply to register Jesus as a son of Joseph, as many suppose, why did he not just write *και ο Ιησους ην υιος Ιωσης*, etc.?

But then, why write *ως ενομιζετο*? It seems to me that the normal meaning of "as was supposed" is to affirm that Jesus was in fact Joseph's son; but that is precisely what Jesus **was not**. Luke has already made clear that Jesus' real Father was the Holy Spirit—1:34-35, 43, 45; 2:49. So what Luke is really saying is that although the people supposed Jesus to be Joseph's son, He actually had a different lineage—we should translate "so it was supposed". (Recall that a faithful and loyal translation seeks to transmit correctly the meaning intended by the <u>author</u>.)

The verb $\eta\nu$ is the only independent one in the whole paragraph, verses 23-38. Is it working with the participle $\alpha\rho\chi o\mu\varepsilon\nu o\varsigma$ in a periphrastic construction? That appears to be the tendency of the eclectic text that places the participle right after Jesus (following less than 2% of the Greek MSS), which makes Jesus out to be in fact Joseph's son. It seems to me to be far more natural to take the participial clauses as being circumstantial: "beginning at about thirty years of age" and "being (so it was supposed) a son of Joseph". Setting those two clauses aside, the independent clause that remains is $\eta\nu\ o\ I\eta\sigma o\upsilon\varsigma\ \tau o\upsilon\ H\lambda\varepsilon\iota$, "Jesus was of Eli".

The participle 'beginning' requires an object, that the Text leaves implicit; from the context it seems clear that we may supply 'His ministry', or some such thing, which is why most versions do so. I suggest the following rendering: "Beginning *His ministry* at about thirty years of age, being (so it was supposed) a son of Joseph, Jesus was actually of Eli, of Mathan, of Levi, . . ." I take it that the emphatic pronoun $\alpha\upsilon\tau o\varsigma$ heightens the contrast between what the people imagined and the reality. Jesus was a grandson of Eli, Mary's father—Luke gives the genealogy of Jesus through His mother, while Matthew gives it through His stepfather. Jesus received some of David's genes through Mary and Nathan; the glorified body now at the Father's right hand, and that will one day occupy David's throne, has some of his genes.

The eclectic text gives our verse a different wording: $\kappa\alpha\iota\ \alpha\upsilon\tau o\varsigma\ \eta\nu\ I\eta\sigma o\upsilon\varsigma\ \alpha\rho\chi o\mu\varepsilon\nu o\varsigma\ \omega\sigma\varepsilon\iota\ \varepsilon\tau\omega\nu\ \tau\rho\iota\alpha\kappa o\nu\tau\alpha,\ \omega\nu\ \upsilon\iota o\varsigma,$ $\omega\varsigma\ \varepsilon\nu o\mu\iota\zeta\varepsilon\tau o,\ I\omega\sigma\eta\varsigma\ \tau o\upsilon\ H\lambda\iota\ \tau o\upsilon\ M\alpha\theta\theta\alpha\tau\ \tau o\upsilon\ \Lambda\varepsilon\upsilon\iota\ \tau o\upsilon\ M\varepsilon\lambda\chi\iota(\ )$ $)\ )$ The RSV translates it like this: "Jesus, when he began his ministry, was about thirty years of age, being the son (as was supposed) of Joseph, the son of Heli, the son of Matthat, . . ." Is not the normal meaning of this rendering that Jesus was in fact the son of Joseph? However, every version that I recall seeing has

"Joseph, the son of Heli", which directly contradicts Matthew, "Jacob begot Joseph". The word 'son' (without the article) occurs only with Joseph, although most versions supply it on down the genealogy. But Luke is precisely correct in not using it, because it would not hold for the first and last names in the list—Eli did not beget Jesus (nor Joseph) and God did not beget Adam.

So then, properly understood Luke does not contradict Matthew (with reference to Joseph's father), nor does he affirm an error of fact (with reference to Jesus' father).

Chapter IV: POISON

It has been commonly argued, for at least 200 years,[1] that no matter what Greek text one may use no doctrine will be affected. In my own experience, for over fifty years, when I have raised the question of what is the correct Greek text of the New Testament, regardless of the audience, the usual response has been: "What difference does it make?" The purpose of this article is to answer that question, at least in part.

The eclectic Greek text presently in vogue, N-A[26]/UBS[3] [hereafter NU] represents the type of text upon which most modern versions are based.[2] The KJV and NKJV follow a rather different type of text, a close cousin of the Majority Text.[3] The discrepancy between NU and the Majority Text is around 8% (involving 8% of the words). In a Greek text with 600 pages that represents 48 solid pages' worth of discrepancies! About a fifth of that reflects omissions in the eclectic text, so it is some ten pages shorter than the Majority Text. Even if we grant, for the sake of the argument, that up to half of the differences between the Majority and eclectic texts could be

---

[1] John Bengel, a textual critic who died in 1752, has been credited with being the first one to advance this argument.

[2] *Novum Testamentum Graece*, Stuttgart: Deutsche Bibelstiftung, 26th ed., 1979. *The Greek New Testament*, New York: United Bible Societies, 3rd ed., 1975. The text of both these editions is virtually identical, having been elaborated by the same five editors: Kurt Aland, Matthew Black, Carlo Martini, Bruce Metzger and Allen Wikgren. Most modern versions were actually based on the 'old' Nestle text, which differs from the 26th edition in over 700 places. UBS[4] and N-A[27] do not offer changes in the text, just in the apparatus—it follows that the text was determined by the earlier set of five editors, not the present five (Matthew Black and Allen Wikgren were replaced by Barbara Aland [Kurt's wife, now widow] and Johannes Karavidopoulos).

[3] *The Greek New Testament According to the Majority Text*, Nashville: Thomas Nelson Publishers, 2nd ed., 1985. This text was edited by Zane C. Hodges and Arthur L. Farstad. Very similar to this is *The New Testament in the Original Greek: Byzantine Textform 2005*, Southborough, MA: Chilton Book Publishing, 2005. This text was edited by Maurice A Robinson and William G. Pierpont. These differ somewhat from the *Textus Receptus* upon which the KJV and NKJV are based.

termed 'inconsequential', that leaves some 25 pages' worth of differences that are significant (in varying degrees). In spite of these differences it is usually assumed that no cardinal Christian doctrine is at risk (though some, such as eternal judgment, the ascension and the deity of Jesus, are weakened). **However**, the most basic one of all, the divine inspiration of the text, is indeed under attack.

The eclectic text incorporates errors of fact and contradictions, such that any claim that the New Testament is divinely inspired becomes relative, and the doctrine of inerrancy becomes virtually untenable. If the authority of the New Testament is undermined, all its teachings are likewise affected. For well over a century the credibility of the New Testament text has been eroded, and this credibility crisis has been forced upon the attention of the laity by the modern versions that enclose parts of the text in brackets and have numerous footnotes of a sort that raise doubts about the integrity of the Text.

The consequences of all this are serious and far-reaching for the future of the Church. It seems unreasonable that individuals and organizations that profess to champion a high view of Scripture, that defend verbal plenary inspiration and the inerrancy of the Autographs, should embrace a Greek text that effectively undermines their belief.[1] Since their sincerity is

---

[1] For years it has been commonly stated that no two known Greek manuscripts of the NT are in perfect agreement (however, for Galatians, Ephesians, Philippians, Colossians, 1 & 2 Thessalonians, 1 & 2 Timothy, Titus, Philemon, James, 1 & 2 Peter, 1 & 2 & 3 John and Jude I have in my possession copies of at least two identical manuscripts—not the same two for each book). In consequence, claims of Biblical inerrancy are usually limited to the Autographs (the very original documents actually penned by the human authors), or to the precise wording contained in them. Since no Autograph of the NT exists today (they were probably worn out within a few years through heavy use) we must appeal to the existing copies in any effort to identify the original wording.

The text-critical theory underlying NU presupposes that the original wording was 'lost' during the early centuries and that objective certainty as to the original wording is now an impossibility. A central part of the current debate is the argument that the text in use **today** is not inerrant—this is a recurring theme in *The*

evident, one must conclude that they are uninformed, or have not really looked at the evidence and thought through the implications. So I will now set out some of that evidence and discuss the implications. I wish to emphasize that I am not impugning the personal sincerity or orthodoxy of those who use the eclectic text; I am challenging the presuppositions that lie behind it and calling attention to the 'proof of the pudding'.

In the examples that follow, the reading of the Majority Text is always given first and that of NU second, followed by any others. (Where NU uses brackets, or some modern version follows Nestle[25], that will be clearly explained.) Immediately under each variant is a literal equivalent in English. To each variant is attached a statement of manuscript support taken from my edition of the Greek Text of the New Testament.[1] The set of variants with their respective supporting evidence is followed by a discussion of the implications. First I will present errors of fact and contradictions, then serious anomalies and aberrations.

Errors of Fact and Contradictions

Luke 4:44 της Γαλιλαιας—f[35] A,D (94.7%) CP,HF,RP,TR,OC
[in the synagogues] of Galilee

της Ιουδαιας—P[75] ℵB,C,Q (4.1%) NU
[in the synagogues] of Judea

των Ιουδαιων—W (0.2%)

Proceedings of the Conference on Biblical Inerrancy 1987 (Nashville: Broadman Press, 1987), for example.

This book offers objective evidence in support of the contention that the original wording was **not** 'lost' during the early centuries. I further argue that it is indeed possible to identify with reasonable certainty the original wording, based on objective criteria—today.

[1] The Greek New Testament According to Family 35, Second Edition, may be purchased from Amazon.com. It may also be downloaded free from www.prunch.org and/or www.walkinhiscommandments.com; the last footnote in Matthew, for example, explains the apparatus and the symbols used.

αυτων—(0.5%)
further variants—(0.4%)

Problem: Jesus was in Galilee (and continued there), not in Judea, as the context makes clear.

Discussion: In the parallel passage, Mark 1:35-39, all texts agree that Jesus was in Galilee. Thus NU contradicts itself by reading Judea in Luke 4:44. Bruce Metzger makes clear that the NU editors did this on purpose when he explains that their reading "is obviously the more difficult, and copyists have corrected it . . . in accord with the parallels in Mt 4.23 and Mk 1.39."[1] Thus the NU editors introduce a contradiction into their text which is also an error of fact. This error in the eclectic text is reproduced by LB, NIV, NASB, NEB, RSV, etc. NRSV adds insult to injury: "So he continued proclaiming the message in the synagogues of Judea."

Luke 23:45 εσκοτισθη—f^{35} A,D,Q,W (96.8%) CP,HF,RP,TR
[the sun] was darkened

εκλιποντος—P^{75}אC (0.4%) NU
[the sun] being eclipsed

εκλειποντος—B (0.4%) OC
εσκοτισθεντος—(0.7%)
conflations—(1.2%)
three further variants—(0.6%)

Problem: An eclipse of the sun is impossible during a full moon. Jesus was crucified during the Passover, and the Passover is always at full moon (which is why the date for Easter moves around). NU introduces a scientific error.

---

[1] *A Textual Commentary on the Greek New Testament*, New York: United Bible Societies, 1971, pp. 137-38.

Discussion: The Greek verb εκλειπω is quite common and has the basic meaning 'to fail' or 'to end', but when used of the sun or the moon it refers to an eclipse ('eclipse' comes from that Greek root). Indeed, such versions as Moffatt, Twentieth Century, Authentic, Phillips, NEB, New Berkeley, NAB and Jerusalem overtly state that the sun was eclipsed. While versions such as NASB, TEV and NIV avoid the word 'eclipse', the normal meaning of the eclectic text that they follow is precisely "the sun being eclipsed."[1]

Mark 6:22 αυτης της Ηρωδιαδος—f[35] A,C,N (96.5%) HF,RP,CP,TR,OC
[the daughter] herself of Herodias

αυτου &&& Ηρωδιαδος—אB,D (0.4%) NU
his [daughter] Herodias

--- της Ηρωδιαδος—(1.3%)
αυτης &&& Ηρωδιαδος—W (0.7%)
αυτου της Ηρωδιαδος—(0.9%)
two further variants—(0.2%)

Problem: NU in Mark 6:22 contradicts NU in Matthew 14:6.

Discussion: Matthew 14:6 states that the girl was the daughter of Herodias (Herodias had been the wife of Philip, King Herod's brother, but was now living with Herod). Here NU makes the girl out to be Herod's own daughter, and calls **her** "Herodias". Metzger defends the choice of the NU Committee with these words: "It is very difficult to decide which reading is the least unsatisfactory" (p. 89)! (Do the NU editors consider that the original reading is lost? If not it must be 'unsatisfacto-

---

[1] Arndt and Gingrich (*A Greek-English Lexicon of the New Testament and Other Early Christian Literature*. Chicago: University of Chicago Press, 1957, p. 242), referring to this passage, state: "Of the sun **grow dark**, perh. **be eclipsed**". One suspects that this statement was designed specifically to defend the reading of the eclectic text. We are not surprised to find Metzger dismissing the reading of 97% of the MSS as "the easier reading" (p. 182).

ry', but are those editors really competent to make such a judgment? And just what might be so 'unsatisfactory' about the reading of over 97% of the MSS? I suppose because it creates no problem.) The modern versions that usually identify with NU part company with them here, except for NRSV that reads, "his daughter Herodias".

1 Corinthians 5:1 ονομαζεται—**f**^{35} (96.8%) HF,RP,OC,TR,CP
is named

--- —P^{46}ℵA,B,C (3.2%) NU

Problem: It was reported that a man had his father's wife, a type of fornication such that not even the Gentiles talked about it. However, the NU text affirms that this type of incest does not even exist among the Gentiles, a plain falsehood. Every conceivable type of sexual perversion has existed throughout human history.

Discussion: Strangely, such evangelical versions as NIV, NASB, Berkeley and LB propagate this error. I find it interesting that versions such as TEV, NEB and Jerusalem, while following the same text, avoid a categorical statement.[1]

Luke 3:33 του Αμιναδαβ(του Αραμ—**f**^{35} A(D) [95%] CP,HF,
                                                                                RP,TR,OC
          of Aminadab   of Aram

          του Αμιναδαβ, του Αδμιν, του Αρνι—none!! NU
          of Aminadab of Admin of Arni

       του Αδμειν, του Αρνει—B
          του Αδαμ(του Αρνι?—syr^s
          του Αδαμ,   του Αδμιν, του Αρνει—ℵ

---

[1] The UBS apparatus gives no inkling to the user that there is serious variation at this point (but N-A does); in consequence Metzger doesn't mention it either. He would probably have told us that the reading of 96.5% of the MSS is "unsatisfactory".

του Αδαμ ,   του Αδμειν, του Αρνει—cop^{sa}
  του Αδμειν,   του Αδμιν, του Αρνι—cop^{bo}
  του Αμιναδαβ, του Αδμιν,   του Αρνει—ℵ^c
  του Αμιναδαβ, του αδμιν,   του Αρηι—f¹³
  του Αμιναδαβ, του Αδμη,   του Αρνι—X
  του Αμιναδαβ, του Αδμειν, του Αρνι—L
  του Αμιναδαβ, του Αραμ ,   του Αρνι—N

Problem: The fictitious Admin and Arni are intruded into Christ's genealogy.

Discussion: UBS has misrepresented the evidence in their apparatus so as to hide the fact that no Greek MS has the precise text they have printed, a veritable 'patchwork quilt'. In Metzger's presentation of the UBS Committee's reasoning in this case he writes, "the Committee adopted what seems to be the least unsatisfactory form of text" (p. 136). Is this not a good candidate for 'chutzpah' of the year? The UBS editors concoct their own reading and proclaim it "the least unsatisfactory"! And just what might be "unsatisfactory" about the reading of over 95% of the MSS except that it doesn't introduce any difficulties?

There is complete confusion in the Egyptian camp. That confusion must have commenced in the second century, resulting from several easy transcriptional errors, simple copying mistakes. *APAM* to *APNI* is very easy (in the early centuries only upper case letters were used); with a scratchy quill the cross strokes in the *A* and *M* could be light, and a subsequent copyist could mistake the left leg of the *M* as going with the *Λ* to make *N*, and the right leg of the *M* would become *I*. Very early "Aminadab" was misspelled as "Aminadam", which survives in some 25% of the extant MSS (in the minuscule MSS the *beta* was frequently written like a *mu*, only without the 'tail'). The "Adam" of Aleph, syr^s and cop^{sa} arose through an easy instance of homoioarcton (the eye of a copyist went from the first *A* in "Aminadam" to the second, dropping "Amin-" and leaving "Adam"). *A* and *Λ* are easily confused, especially when written by hand—"Admin" presumably came from "AMINadab/m", though the process was more complicated. The *'i'* of "Admin" and "Arni" is corrupted to *'ei'* in Codex B (a frequent occurrence in that MS—perhaps due to Coptic influence). Codex Aleph conflated the ancestor that produced "Adam" with the one that produced "Admin", etc. The total confusion in Egypt does not surprise us, but how shall we account for the text and apparatus of NU in this instance? And whatever possessed the editors of NASB, NRSV, TEV, LB, Berkeley, etc. to embrace such an egregious error?

Matthew 19:17 Τι με λεγεις αγαθον ουδεις αγαθος ει μη εις ο Θεος—

f³⁵ C,W (99%) RP,HF,OC,CP,TR

Why do you call me good? No one is good but one, God.

Τι με ερωτας περι του αγαθου εις εστιν ο αγαθος—

א(B,D) (0.9%) NU

Why do you ask me about the good? One is good.

Problem: NU in Matthew 19:17 contradicts NU in Mark 10:18 and Luke 18:19 (wherein all texts agree with the Majority here).

Discussion: Presumably Jesus spoke in Hebrew, but there is no way that whatever He said could legitimately yield the two translations into Greek given above.[1] That the Latin versions offer a conflation suggests that both the other variants must have existed in the second century—indeed, the *Diatessaron* overtly places the Majority reading in the first half of that century. The Church in Egypt during the second century was dominated by Gnosticism. That such a 'nice' Gnostic variant came into being is no surprise, but why do modern editors embrace it? Because it is the "more obscure one" (Metzger, p. 49). This

---

[1] In His teaching on general themes the Lord presumably repeated Himself many times, using a variety of expressions and variations on those themes, and the Gospel writers preserve some of that variety. In this case we are dealing with a specific conversation, which presumably was not repeated.

'obscurity' was so attractive to the NU Committee that they printed another 'patchwork quilt'—taking the young man's question and this first part of the Lord's answer together, the precise text of NU is found only in the **corrector** of Codex B; further, with reference to the main Greek MSS given as supporting the eclectic text here (ℵ,B,D,L,Θ,f¹), the fact is that no two of them precisely agree! (Should they be regarded as reliable witnesses? On what basis?) Most modern versions join NU in this error also.

Acts 19:16 αυτων—**f³⁵** [90%] HF,RP,OC,TR,CP
them

αμφορερων—ℵA,B,D [5%] NU
both of them

two other variants—[5%]

Problem: The sons of Sceva were seven, not two.

Discussion: To argue that 'both' can mean 'all' on the basis of this passage is to beg the question. An appeal to Acts 23:8 is likewise unconvincing. "For Sadducees say that there is no resurrection—and no angel or spirit; but the Pharisees confess both." 'Angel' and 'spirit' if not intended as synonyms at least belong to a single class, spirit beings. The Pharisees believed in "both"—resurrection and spirit beings. There is no basis here for claiming that "both" can legitimately refer to seven (Acts 19:16).[1] Still, most modern versions do render "both" as "all".

---

[1] Arndt and Gingrich's note (p. 47) seems designed to protect the reading of the eclectic text here. Metzger's discussion is interesting: "The difficulty of reconciling [seven] with [both], however, is not so great as to render the text which includes both an impossible text. On the other hand, however, the difficulty is so troublesome that it is hard to explain how [seven] came into the text, and was perpetuated, if it were not original, . . ." (pp. 471-72). Notice that Metzger assumes the genuineness of "both" and discusses the difficulty that it creates as if it were fact. I would say that his assumption is gratuitous and that the difficulty it creates is an artifact of his presuppositions.

NASB actually renders "both of them", making the contradiction overt!

Matthew 1:7-8 Ασα—**f³⁵** W [98%] RP,HF,OC,CP,TR
Asa

Ασαφ—P¹ᵛℵ,B,C [2%] NU (twice)
Asaph

Problem: Asaph does not belong in Jesus' genealogy.

Discussion: Asaph was a Levite, not of the tribe of Judah; he was a psalmist, not a king. It is clear from Metzger's comments that the NU editors understand that their reading refers to the Levite and should not be construed as an alternate spelling of Asa; he overtly calls Asaph an "error" (p. 1). In fact, "Asaph" is probably not a misspelling of "Asa". Not counting Asa and Amon (see v. 10) Codex B misspells 13 names in this chapter, while Codex Aleph misspells 10, which undermines their credibility. However, their misspellings involve dittography, gender change, or a similar sound (z̲ for s̲, d̲ for t̲, m̲ for n̲)—not adding an extraneous consonant, like f̲, nor trading dissimilar sounds, like s̲   for n̲.

In response to Lagrange, who considered "Asaph" to be an ancient scribal error, Metzger writes: "Since, however, the evangelist may have derived material for the genealogy, not from the Old Testament directly, but from subsequent genealogical lists, in which the erroneous spelling occurred, the Committee saw no reason to adopt what appears to be a scribal emendation" (p. 1). Metzger frankly declares that the spelling they have adopted is "erroneous". The NU editors have deliberately imported an error into their text, which is faithfully reproduced by NAB (New American Bible) and NRSV. RSV and NASB offer a footnote to the effect that the Greek reads "Asaph"—it would be less misleading if they said that a tiny fraction of the Greek MSS so read. The case of Amon vs.

Amos in verse 10 is analogous to this one. Metzger says that "Amos" is "an error for 'Amon'" (p. 2), and the NU editors have duly placed the error in their text.

Matthew 10:10 μηδε ραβδους—**f³⁵** C,N,W [95%] RP,HF,CP
neither staves

μηδε ραβδον—ℵ,B,D [5%] OC,TR,NU
neither a staff

Problem: In both Matthew 10:10 and Luke 9:3 NU has "neither a staff," thus contradicting Mark 6:8 where all texts have "only a staff".

Discussion: In Luke and Matthew the Majority text reads "neither staves", which does not contradict Mark—the case of the staves is analogous to that of the tunics; they were to take only one, not several. A superficial reader would probably expect the singular; that some scribe in Egypt should have trouble with "staves" and simplify it to "a staff" comes as no surprise, but why do the NU editors import this error into their text? Almost all modern versions follow NU both here and in Luke 9:3.

Mark 1:2 εν τοις προφηταις—**f³⁵** A,W (96.7%) HF,RP,CP,TR,OC
[as it is written] in the prophets

εν τω Ησαια τω προφητη—ℵB (1.3%) NU
[as it is written] in Isaiah the prophet

Ησαια τω προφητη—D (1.8%)

Problem: The NU text ascribes extraneous material to Isaiah.

Discussion: The rest of verse 2 is a quote from Malachi 3:1 while verse 3 is from Isaiah 40:3. Once again Metzger uses the 'harder reading' argument, in effect (p. 73), but the eclectic choice is most probably the result of early harmonizing activity. The only other places that Isaiah 40:3 is quoted in the New Testament are Matthew 3:3, Luke 3:4 and John 1:23. The first two are in passages parallel to Mark 1:2. The quote in John is also used in connection with John the Baptist. The crucial consideration, for our present purpose, is that Matthew, Luke and John all identify the quote as being from Isaiah (without MS variation). It seems clear that the "Alexandrian-Western" reading in Mark 1:2 is simply an assimilation to the other three Gospels. It should also be noted that the material from Malachi looks more like an allusion than a direct quote. Further, although Malachi is quoted (or alluded to) a number of times in the New Testament, he is never named. Mark's own habits may also be germane to this discussion. Mark quotes Isaiah in 4:12, 11:17 and 12:32 and alludes to him in about ten other places, all without naming his source. The one time he does use Isaiah's name is when quoting Jesus in 7:6. In the face of such clear evidence the 'harder reading' canon cannot justify the forcing of an error into the text of Mark 1:2. Almost all modern versions agree with NU here.

Luke 9:10 εις τοπον ερημον πολεως καλουμενης Βηθσαιδα(ν)—f[35] (A)C (N)W [98%] CP,HF,RP,TR,OC
into a deserted place belonging to a town called Bethsaida

εις πολιν καλουμενην Βηθσαιδα—(P[75])B [0.5%] NU
into a town called Bethsaida

εις κωμην λεγομενην βηδσαιδα—D
εις τοπον ερημον—א [0.5%]
four further variants—(0.4%)

Problem: NU has Jesus and company going into Bethsaida, but in verse 12 the disciples say they are in a deserted area; thus a contradiction is introduced. NU here is also at variance with NU in the parallel passages.

Discussion: In Matthew 14:13 all texts have Jesus going to a deserted place, and in verse 15 the disciples say, "the place is deserted . . . send the crowd away to the towns". In Mark 6:31-32 all texts have Him going to a deserted place, and in verse 35 the disciples say it is a deserted place, etc. So NU not only makes Luke contradict himself, but sets him against Matthew and Mark. The modern versions do not surprise us.

John 18:24 απεστειλεν—**f³⁵** A [90%] CP,HF,RP,OC,TR
[Annas] had sent [Him bound to Caiaphas]

απεστειλεν ουν—B,C,W [9%] NU, some TRs
then [Annas] sent [Him bound to Caiaphas]

απεστειλεν δε—ℵ [1%]

Problem: The NU variant sets up a contradiction within the immediate context. Verse 13 says Jesus was taken first to Annas, but all four Gospels are agreed that Peter's denials and the judging took place in the house of Caiaphas—here in John, verses 15-23 happened there. The NU variant puts verses 15-23 in the house of Annas, making John contradict the other three Gospels.

Discussion: Only John records that Jesus was taken first to Annas; the other three go directly to Caiaphas, so for them the difficulty of changing houses does not arise. After penning verses 15-23, John saw that his readers could get the idea that Jesus was still with Annas, so he wrote verse 24 to avert that misunderstanding. Verse 24 should be translated in parentheses: (Annas had sent Him bound to Caiaphas the high priest).

John 6:11 τοις μαθηταις οι δε μαθηται—**f³⁵** D [97%] CP,HF,
RP,OC,TR
to the disciples, and the disciples

---   ---   --- ---   ---   —P⁶⁶,⁷⁵ᵛ ℵ A,B,W [3%] NU

Problem: The NU text contradicts itself. In Matthew 14:19, Mark 6:41 and Luke 9:16, parallel passages, NU agrees with the Majority that Jesus handed the bread to the disciples, who in turn distributed it to the people. Here in John NU omits the disciples and has Jesus Himself distributing the bread to the people.

Discussion: This variant may be explained as an easy transcriptional mistake, a case of homoioarcton, a similar beginning—in this case jumping from one τοις to the next. There is no need to appeal to the 'harder reading' canon. If this were the only instance, it could be explained away, but when added to the others it has a cumulative effect.

I am well aware that the foregoing examples may not strike the reader as being uniformly convincing. However, I submit that there is a cumulative effect. By dint of ingenuity and mental gymnastics it may be possible to appear to circumvent one or another of these examples (including those that follow), but with each added instance the strain on our credulity increases. One or two circumventions may be accepted as possible, but five or six become highly improbable; ten or twelve are scarcely tolerable.

Serious Anomalies/Aberrations

John 7:8 ουπω—f³⁵ P⁶⁶,⁷⁵B,N,T,W [96.5%] CP,HF,RP,OC,TR
      not yet

      ουκ—ℵD [3%] NU
      not

      --- —[0.5%]

Problem: Since Jesus did in fact go to the feast (and doubtless knew what He was going to do), the NU text has the effect of ascribing a falsehood to Him.

Discussion: Since the NU editors usually attach the highest value to P^{75} and B, is it not strange that they reject them in this case? Here is Metzger's explanation: "The reading ["not yet"] was introduced at an early date (it is attested by P^{66,75}) in order to alleviate the inconsistency between ver. 8 and ver. 10" (p. 216). So, they rejected P^{66,75} and B (as well as 96.5% of the MSS) because they preferred the "inconsistency". NASB, RSV, NEB and TEV stay with the eclectic text here.

John 6:47 εις εμε—**f**^{35} A,C,D,N (99.5%) CP,HF,RP,OC,TR
[believes] into me

--- --- —P^{66}אB,T,W (0.5%) NU
[believes]

Problem: Jesus is making a formal declaration about how one can have eternal life: "Most assuredly I say to you, he who believes into me has everlasting life." By omitting "into me" the NU text opens the door to universalism.

Discussion: Since it is impossible to live without believing in something, everyone believes—the object of the belief is of the essence. The verb 'believe' does occur elsewhere without a stated object (it is supplied by the context), but not in a formal declaration like this. The shorter reading is probably the result of a fairly easy instance of homoioarcton—three short words in a row begin with E. And yet Metzger says of the words "in me", "no good reason can be suggested to account for their omission" (p. 214). The editors grade the omission as {A}, against 99.5% of the MSS plus 2nd century attestation! TEV, NASB, NIV, NRSV and Jerusalem reproduce the UBS text precisely.

Acts 28:13 περιελθοντεϕ—**f³⁵** A,048 [95%] HF,RP,OC,TR,CP
tacking back and forth [we reached Rhegium]

περιελοντεϕ—ℵB [5%] NU
taking away (something) [we reached Rhegium]

Problem: The verb chosen by NU, περιαιρεω, is transitive, and is meaningless here.

Discussion: Metzger's lame explanation is that a majority of the NU Committee took the word to be "a technical nautical term of uncertain meaning" (p. 501)! Why do they choose to disfigure the text on such poor evidence when there is an easy transcriptional explanation? The Greek letters O and Q are very similar, and being side by side in a word it would be easy to drop one of them out, in this case the *theta*. Most modern versions are actually based on the 'old' Nestle text, which here agrees with the Majority reading. NRSV, however, follows NU, rendering it as "then we weighed anchor".

Mark 16:9-20 (have)—every extant Greek MS (a. 1,700) except three; HF,RP,CP,TR,OC[[NU]]

(omit)—ℵᶜ,B,304

Problem: A serious aberration is introduced—it is affirmed that Mark's Gospel ends with 16:8.

Discussion: UBS³ encloses these verses in double brackets, which means they are "regarded as later additions to the text", and they give their decision an {A} grade, "virtually certain". So, the UBS editors assure us that the genuine text of Mark ends with 16:8. But why do critics insist on rejecting this passage? It is contained in every extant Greek MS (about 1,700) except three (really only two, B and 304—Aleph is not properly 'extant' because it is a forgery at this point).[1] Every extant Greek Lectionary (about 2,000?) contains them (one of them, 185, doing so only in the Menologion). Every extant Syriac MS except one (Sinaitic) contains them. Every extant Latin MS (8,000?) except one (k) contains them. Every extant Coptic MS except one contains them. We have hard evidence for the 'inclusion' from the II century (Irenaeus and the *Diatessaron*), and presumably the first half of that century. We have no such hard evidence for the 'exclusion'.

In the face of such massive evidence, why do the critics insist on rejecting this passage? Lamentably, most modern versions also cast doubt upon the authenticity of these verses in one way or another (NRSV is especially objectionable here). As one who believes that the Bible **is** God's Word, I find it to be inconceivable that an official biography of Jesus Christ, commissioned by God and written subject to His quality control, should omit proofs of the resurrection, should exclude all post-resurrection appearances, should end with the clause

---

[1] Tischendorf, who discovered Codex Aleph, warned that the folded sheet containing the end of Mark and the beginning of Luke appeared to be written by a different hand and with different ink than the rest of the manuscript. However that may be, a careful scrutiny reveals the following: the end of Mark and beginning of Luke occur on page 3 (of the four); pages 1 and 4 contain an average of 17 lines of printed Greek text per column (there are four columns per page), just like the rest of the codex; page 2 contains an average of 15.5 lines of printed text per column (four columns); the first column of page 3 contains only **twelve** lines of printed text and in this way verse 8 occupies the top of the second column, the rest of which is blank (except for some designs); Luke begins at the top of column 3, which contains 16 lines of printed text while column 4 is back up to 17 lines. On page 2 the forger began to spread out the letters, displacing six lines of printed text; in the first column of page 3 he got desperate and displaced **five** lines of printed text, just in one column!

In this way he managed to get two lines of verse 8 over onto the second column, avoiding the telltale vacant column (as in Codex B). That second column would accommodate 15 more lines of printed text, which with the other eleven make 26. Verses 9-20 occupy 23.5 such lines, so there is plenty of room for them. It really does seem that there has been foul play, and there would have been no need for it unless the first hand did in fact display the disputed verses. In any event, Aleph as it stands is a forgery (in this place) and therefore may not legitimately be alleged as evidence against them.

"because they were afraid"! If the critics' assessment is correct we seem to be between a rock and a hard place. Mark's Gospel as it stands is mutilated (if it ends at v. 8), the original ending having disappeared without a trace. But in that event what about God's purpose in commissioning this biography?

John 1:18 ο μονογενης υιος—**f**^{35} A,C,W (99.6%) (CP)HF,RP,OC,TR
the only begotten Son

&& μονογενης θεος—P^{66}אB,C (0.3%) NU
an only begotten god

ο μονογενης θεος—P^{75} (0.1%)
the only begotten god

Problem: A serious anomaly is introduced—God, as God, is not begotten.

Discussion: The human body and nature of Jesus Christ was indeed literally begotten in the virgin Mary by the Holy Spirit; God the Son has existed eternally. "An only begotten god" is so deliciously Gnostic that the apparent Egyptian provenance of this reading makes it doubly suspicious. It would also be possible to render the second reading as "only begotten god!", emphasizing the quality, and this has appealed to some who see in it a strong affirmation of Christ's deity. However, if Christ received His 'Godhood' through the begetting process then He cannot be the eternally pre-existing Second Person of the Godhead. Nor is 'only begotten' analogous to 'firstborn', referring to priority of position—that would place the Son above the Father. No matter how one looks at it, the NU reading introduces a serious anomaly, and on the slimmest of evidence.

Presumably μονογενης is intended to mean something more than just μονος, 'only'. In Luke 7:12, even though for reasons of style a translator may put "the **only** son of his mother", we must understand that he is her own offspring—he could not be an adopted son. The same holds for Luke 8:42 and 9:38. In Hebrews 11:17, with reference to the promise and to Sarah, Isaac was indeed Abraham's "only begotten", even though he in fact had other sons with other women. Note that in Genesis 22:12 and 16 God Himself calls Isaac Abraham's "only" son. John uses μονογενης five times, always referring to the Son of God (John 1:14, 18; 3:16, 18; 1 John 4:9). I see nothing in New Testament usage to justify the rendering 'unique'.

That P[75] should have a conflation of the first two readings is curious, but demonstrates that the discrepancy arose in the second century. (Articles modify nouns not adjectives, when in a noun phrase such as we have here, so the article is part of the same variation unit.) Most modern versions avoid a straightforward rendering of the NU reading. NIV offers us "but God the only [Son]"—a bad translation of a bad text. (A subsequent revision has "God the One and Only"—a pious fraud since none of the variants has this meaning.) TEV has "The only One, who is the same as God"—only slightly better. NASB actually renders "the only begotten God"! (the reading of P[75]). Not to be outdone Amplified serves up a conflation, "the only unique Son, the only begotten God". Ho hum!

John 7:53-8:11 (retain)—f[35] D [85%] CP,HF,RP,OC,TR[[NU]]

(omit)—P[66,75]אB,N,T,W [15%]

Problem: UBS[3] encloses these verses in double brackets, which means they are "regarded as later additions to the text", and they give their decision an {A} grade, "virtually certain". The omission introduces an aberration.

Discussion: The evidence against the Majority Text is stronger than in any of the previous examples, but assuming that the passage is spurious (for the sake of the argument), how could it ever have intruded here, and to such effect that it is attested by some 85% of the MSS? Let us try to read the larger passage without these verses—we must go from 7:52 to 8:12 directly. Reviewing the context, the chief priests and Pharisees had sent officers to arrest Jesus, to no avail; a 'discussion' ensues; Nicodemus makes a point, to which the Pharisees answer:

> (7:52) "Are you also from Galilee? Search and look, for no prophet has arisen out of Galilee."
> (8:12) Then Jesus spoke to them again, saying, "I am the light of the world . . . ."

What is the antecedent of "them", and what is the meaning of "again"? By the normal rules of grammar, if 7:53-8:11 is missing then "them" must refer to the "Pharisees" and "again" means that there has already been at least one prior exchange. But, 7:45 makes clear that Jesus **was not there** with the Pharisees. Thus, NU introduces an aberration. And yet, Metzger claims that the passage "interrupts the sequence of 7.52 and 8.12 ff." (p. 220)! To look for the antecedents of 8:12 in 7:37-39 not only does despite to the syntax but also runs afoul of 8:13—"the Pharisees" respond to Jesus' claim in verse 12, but "the Pharisees" are somewhere else, 7:45-52 (if the pericope is absent).

Metzger also claims that "the style and vocabulary of the pericope differ noticeably from the rest of the Fourth Gospel"—but, would not the native speakers of Greek at that time have been in a better position than modern critics to notice something like that? So how could they allow such an 'extraneous' passage to be forced into the text? I submit that the evident answer is that they did not; it was there all the time. I also protest their use of brackets here. Since the editors clearly regard the passage to be spurious they should be consistent and delete it, as do NEB and Williams. That way the full extent of their error would be open for all to see. NIV, NASB, NRSV,

Berkeley and TEV also use brackets to question the legitimacy of this passage.

1 Timothy 3:16 θεος—f^{35} A,C^v [98.5%] RP,HF,OC,TR,CP
God [was manifested in flesh]

ος—א [1%] NU
who [was manifested in flesh]

ο—D
that [was manifested in flesh]^1

Problem: A grammatical anomaly is introduced. "Great is the mystery of godliness, who was manifested in flesh" is worse in Greek than it is in English. "Mystery" is neuter in gender while "godliness" is feminine, but "who" is masculine!

Discussion: In an effort to explain the "who" it is commonly argued that the second half of verse 16 was a direct quote from a hymn, but where is the evidence for this claim? Without evidence the claim begs the question.[2] That the passage has some poetic qualities says no more than that it has some poetic qualities. "Who" is nonsensical, so most modern ver-

---

[1] For a more thorough and complete discussion of the evidence, the interested reader may go to pages 115-117 in my book, *The Identity of the New Testament Text IV*.

[2] A pronoun normally requires an antecedent, but quoted material might provide an exception. Thus, 1 Corinthians 2:9 is sometimes offered as an instance: the quote from Isaiah 64:4 begins with a pronoun, without a grammatical antecedent (although "mystery" in verse 7 is presumably the referential antecedent). However, the words from Isaiah are formally introduced as a quotation, "as it is written", whereas the material in 1 Timothy 3:16 is not, so there is no valid analogy. Colossians 1:13 or 1:15 have been suggested as analogies for "who" in 1 Timothy 3:16, even claimed as "hymns", but there is no objective support for the claim. The antecedent of the relative pronoun in Colossians 1:15 is "the son" in verse 13, and the antecedent of the relative pronoun in verse 13 is "the father" in verse 12. Again, there is no valid analogy.

sions that follow NU here take evasive action: NEB and NASB have "he who"; Phillips has "the one"; NRSV, Jerusalem, TEV and NIV render "he". Berkeley actually has "who"! The Latin reading, "the mystery . . . that," at least makes sense. The true reading, as attested by 98.5% of the Greek MSS, is "God". In the early MSS "God" was written ΘC (with a cross stroke above the two letters to indicate an abbreviation), "who" was written OC, and "that" was written O. The difference between "God" and "who" is just two cross strokes, and with a scratchy quill those could easily be light (or a copyist could be momentarily distracted and forget to add the cross strokes). The reading "who" can be explained by an easy transcriptional error. The reading "that" would be an obvious solution to a copyist faced with the nonsensical "who". Whatever the intention of the NU editors, their text emasculates this strong statement of the deity of Jesus Christ, besides being a stupidity—what is a 'mystery' about any human male being manifested in flesh? All human beings have bodies.

2 Peter 3:10 κατακαησεται—**f^{35}** A,048 (93.6%) RP,HF,OC,TR,CP
[the earth . . .] will be burned up

ευρεθησεται—(P^{72})אB (3.2%) NU
[the earth . . .] will be found

---   —(2.8%)
one further variant—C

Problem: The NU reading is nonsensical; the context is clearly one of judgment.

Discussion: Metzger actually states that their text "seems to be devoid of meaning in the context" (p. 706)! So why did they choose it? Metzger explains that there is "a wide variety of readings, none of which seems to be original"—presumably if "shall be burned up" were the only reading, with unanimous attestation, he would still reject it, but he can scarcely argue that it is meaningless. The NU editors deliberately chose a variant that they believed to be "devoid of meaning in the context". NASB abandons UBS here, giving the Majority reading; NEB and NIV render "will be laid bare"; TEV has "will vanish".

Jude 15 παντας τους ασεβεις—**f³⁵** A,B,C (97.8%) RP,HF,OC,TR,CP
[to convict] all the ungodly [among them of all their ungodly deeds]

πασαν ψυχην—P⁷²ℵ(only one other MS) NU
[to convict] every soul [of all their ungodly deeds]

---   ---   —(1.6%)

Problem: NU introduces a serious anomaly.

Discussion: Certain very evil persons have been rather graphically described in verses 4, 8 and 10-13. In verse 14 Jude introduces a prophecy "about these men", the same ones he has been describing, and the quotation continues to the end of verse 15. Verse 16 continues the description of their perversity, but verse 17 draws a clear distinction between them and the believers that Jude is addressing. So, Enoch cannot be referring to "every soul"—the NU reading is clearly wrong, introducing an aberration on the flimsiest of evidence. In fact, Nestle²⁵ and UBS² stayed with the Majority, reading "all the ungodly". UBS³ changes to "every soul", without comment! Is this not a curious proceeding? The UBS editors reverse an earlier position, following just three MSS and the Sahidic version, and do not even mention it in their apparatus. This is especially unfortunate, given the serious nature of the change. Most modern versions are with the Majority here, but NRSV has "convict everyone".

Matthew 5:22 εικη—**f³⁵** D,W (96.2%) RP,HF,OC,CP,TR
without a cause

--- —P⁶⁴ℵB (1.9%) NU
a long omission (1.9%)

Problem: The NU omission has the effect of setting up a conflict with passages like Ephesians 4:26 and Psalm 4:4, where we are commanded to be angry, and even with the Lord's own example, Mark 3:5.

Discussion: God hates injustice and will judge it; but He also hates evil and commands us to do likewise, Psalm 97:10. The NU variant has the effect of forbidding anger, which cannot be right. Again, if this were the only instance, it could be explained away, but when added to the others it has a cumulative effect.

Mark 10:24 τουφ πεποιθοταφ επι χρημασιν—**f³⁵** A,C(D)N
(99.5%)
HF,RP,CP(TR)OC

for those who trust in riches

---   ---   ---   ---   —ℵB (0.4%) NU

πλουσιον—W

Problem: The NU variant has Jesus saying: "How difficult it is to enter the Kingdom of God!" Within the context this is a stupidity, besides having the effect of making Him contradict Himself, since in other places He gives an open invitation: "Come unto me, all you who labor and are heavy laden, and I will give you rest" (Matthew 11:28).

Discussion: Within the context the Majority reading is clearly correct. Taking into account all that Scripture offers on the subject, being rich in itself is not the problem; the problem is precisely one of trust—are you really trusting God, or is it your wealth? Or to put it differently, where is your treasure? Most modern versions follow NU here, and some offer a footnote that says, "some (later) manuscripts add, 'for those who trust in riches'." It is their way of referring to 99.5% of the manuscripts; and the Latin and Syriac versions take the Majority reading back to the 2nd century. Such footnotes are clearly perverse.

Matthew 1:25 ετεκεν τον υιον αυτης τον πρωτοτοκον—f³⁵ C, D,N,W (99.5%) RP,HF,OC,CP,TR
she had given birth to her son, the firstborn

ετεκεν υιον—‭א‬B (0.5%) NU
she had given birth to a son

Problem: NU turns a strong, clear statement into an empty one, with serious theological consequences, and they do so on the flimsiest of evidence.

Discussion: We need to remember the context, beginning with verse 18.

> 18 Now the birth of Jesus Christ was like this: After His mother Mary was betrothed to Joseph, before they joined together, she was found to be pregnant by the Holy Spirit. 19 Then Joseph her husband,[1] being a just man and not wanting to humiliate her publicly, decided to repudiate her secretly. 20 But while he pondered these things, wow, an angel of the Lord appeared to him in a dream saying: "Joseph, son of David, do not be afraid to receive Mary as your wife, because that which has been conceived in her is of the Holy Spirit. 21 And she will give birth to a Son and you will call His name Jesus, because He will save His people from their sins." 22 Now all this happened so that what was spoken by the Lord through the prophet should be fulfilled, namely: 23 "Behold, the virgin will become pregnant and bear a Son, and they shall call His name Emmanuel", which being translated is, 'God with us'. 24

---

[1] The betrothal was legally binding, so the man was then called 'husband', even before the physical union.

Then Joseph, being aroused from sleep, did as that angel of the Lord commanded him and received his wife,[1] 25 but did not know her until[2] she had given birth to her son, the firstborn. And he called His name JESUS.

Only 0.5% of the Greek manuscripts, of objectively inferior quality, demonstrably so, omit "her" and "the firstborn" (as in NIV, NASB, LB, TEV, etc.). That is eight manuscripts against 1,454 that have been collated, but there are over 200 others yet to be collated that will swell the number against the eight. Why do so-called 'evangelical' scholars insist on damaging the Text based on such ridiculously inferior and inadequate 'evidence'? The point of the 'her' is to reinforce the fact that the son was not Joseph's, nor any other man's—if a man was involved it would be 'his' son.

Matthew is said to have 'published' his Gospel in about 39 AD. By then Mary would be past the age when she could have children, even if she was still alive. So for Matthew to write 'firstborn' means there were others later; if Mary had had only one child Matthew would have written 'only born' (in John 3:16 it is 'only begotten'). This is important because of the Roman doctrine of the 'perpetual virginity' of Mary, denying that she had any children with Joseph.

There are many further examples, some of which, taken singly, may not seem to be all that alarming. But they have a cumulative effect and **dozens** of them should give the responsible reader pause. Is there a pattern? If so, why? But for now enough has been presented to permit us to turn to the implications.

---

[1] Apparently there was some urgency involved; it sounds like he did it that same night (Mary was at least three months pregnant)—at night there would not be any onlookers.

[2] The use of this conjunction indicates that they had normal relations after Jesus' birth, and in fact they had at least six children together. In the Bible the verb 'to know' is used to refer to sexual intercourse.

Implications

How is all of this to be explained? I believe the answer lies in the area of presuppositions. There has been a curious reluctance on the part of conservative scholars to come to grips with this matter. To assume that the editorial choices of a naturalistic scholar will not be influenced by his theological bias is naive in the extreme.

To be sure, both such scholars and the conservative defenders of the eclectic text will doubtless demur. "Not at all", they would say, "our editorial choices derive from a straightforward application of the generally accepted canons of NT textual criticism" ["generally accepted" by whom, and on what basis—that is, what are the presuppositions behind them?]. And what are those canons? The four main ones seem to be: 1) the reading that best accounts for the rise of the other reading(s) is to be preferred; 2) the harder reading is to be preferred; 3) the shorter reading is to be preferred; 4) the reading that best fits the author's style and purpose is to be preferred. It could be said that the first canon sort of distills the essence of them all, and therefore should be the ruling canon, but in practice it is probably the second that is most rigorously applied. From B.M. Metzger's presentation of the NU Committee's reasoning in the examples given above it appears that over half the time they based their decision on the 'harder reading' canon (for four of them he has no comment because the UBS apparatus does not mention that there is any variation; for two of them he says that all the variants are unsatisfactory!). But, how are we to decide which variant is 'harder'? Will not our own theological bias enter in?

Let us consider an example: in Luke 24:52 the Nestle editions 1-25 omit "they worshipped him" (and in consequence NASB, RSV and NEB do too). UBS[3] retains the words, but with a {D} grade, which shows a "very high degree of doubt". Only one solitary Greek manuscript omits the words, Codex D, supported by part of the Latin witness. In spite of the very slim external evidence for the omission it is argued that it is the 'harder' reading—if the clause were original, what orthodox Christian would even think of removing it? On the other hand, the clause would make a nice pious addition that would immediately become popular, if the original lacked it. However, not only did the Gnostics dominate the Christian church in Egypt in the second century, there were also others around who did not believe that Jesus was God—would they be likely to resist the impulse to delete such a statement? How shall we choose between these two hypotheses? Will it not be on the basis of our presuppositions? Indeed, in discussing this variant set, along with Hort's other "Western non-interpolations", Metzger explains (p. 193) that a minority of the UBS committee argued that "there is discernible in these passages a Christological-theological motivation that accounts for their having been added, while there is no clear reason that accounts for their having been omitted". (Had they never heard of the Gnostics?)

Why Use Subjective Canons?

It is clear that the four canons mentioned above depend heavily upon the subjective judgment of the critic. But why use such canons? Why not follow the manuscript evidence? It is commonly argued that the surviving MSS are not representative of the textual situation in the early centuries of the Church. The official destruction of MSS by Diocletian (AD 300), and other vagaries of history, are supposed to have decimated the supply of MSS to the point where the transmission was totally distorted—so we cannot be sure about anything. (Such an argument not only 'justifies' the eclectic proceeding, it is used to claim its 'necessity'.) But, the effectiveness of the Diocletian campaign was uneven in different regions. Even more to the point are the implications of the Donatist movement which developed right after the Diocletian campaign passed. It was predicated in part on the punishment that was deserved by those who betrayed their MSS to destruction. Evidently some did **not** betray their MSS or there would have been no one to judge the others. Also, those whose commitment to Christ and His Word was such that they withstood the torture would be just the sort who would be most careful about the pedigree of their MSS. So it was probably the purest exemplars that survived, in the main, and from them the main stream of transmission derives.

Since the Byzantine (Majority) textform dominates over 90% of the extant MSS, those who wish to reject it cannot grant the possibility that the transmission of the text was in any sense normal. (If it was, then the consensus must reflect the original, especially such a massive consensus.) So it is argued that the 'ballot box' was 'stuffed', that the Byzantine text was imposed by ecclesiastical authority, but only after it was concocted out of other texts in the early IV century. But, there is simply no historical evidence for this idea. Also, numerous studies have demonstrated that the mass of Byzantine MSS are not monolithic; there are many distinct strands or strains of transmission, presumably independent. That at least some of these must go back to the III century (if not earlier) is demonstrated by Codex Aleph in Revelation, in that it conflates some of those strands. Asterius (d. 341) used MSS that were clearly Byzantine—presumably most of his writing was not done on his deathbed, so his MSS would come from the III century. There are further lines of evidence that militate against the eclectic position, not least the very nature of their canons.

"The shorter reading is to be preferred." Why? Because, we are told, scribes had a propensity to add bits and pieces to the text. But that would have to be a deliberate activity. It is demonstrable that accidental loss of place results in omission far more often than addition—about the only way to add accidentally is to copy part of the text twice over, but the copyist would have to be really drowsy not to catch himself at it. So, any time a shorter reading could be the result of *parablepsis* it should be viewed with suspicion. But even when deliberate, omission should still be more frequent than addition. If there is something in the text that you do not like it draws your attention and you are tempted to do something about it. Also, it requires more imagination and effort to create new material than to delete what is already there (material suggested by a parallel passage could be an exception). Further, it is demonstrable that most scribes were careful and conscientious, avoiding even unintentional mistakes. Those who engaged in deliberate editorial activity were really rather few, but some were flagrant offenders (like Aleph in Revelation).

"The harder reading is to be preferred." Why? The assumption is that a perceived difficulty would motivate an officious copyist to attempt a 'remedy'. Note that any such alteration must be deliberate; so if a 'harder' reading could have come about through accidental omission (e.g.) then this canon should not be used. But in the case of a presumed deliberate alteration, how can we really ascribe degrees of 'hardness'? We do not know who did it, nor why. Due allowance must be made for possible ignorance, officiousness, prejudice and malice. In fact, this canon is unreasonable on the face of it—the more stupid a reading is, whether by accident or design, the stronger is its claim to be 'original' since it will certainly be the 'hardest'. It does not take a prophet to see that this canon is wide open to satanic manipulation, both in the ancient creation of variants and in their contemporary evaluation. But in any case, since it is demonstrable that most copyists did not make deliberate changes, where there is massive agreement among the extant MSS this canon should not even be considered. Indeed, where there is massive agreement among the MSS none of the subjective canons should be used—they are unnecessary and out of place. Of the 6,000+ differences between NU and the Majority Text, the heavy majority of the readings preferred by the NU editors have slender MS attestation.

The Myth of Neutrality

We need to lay to rest the myth of neutrality and scholarly objectivity. Anyone who has been inside the academic community knows that it is liberally sprinkled with bias, party lines, personal ambition and spite—quite apart from a hatred of the Truth.[1] Neutrality and objectivity should never be assumed, and most especially when dealing with God's Truth—because in this area neither God nor Satan will permit neutrality. In Matthew 12:30 the Lord Jesus said: "He who is not with me is against me, and he who does not gather with me scatters abroad." God declares that neutrality is impossible; you are either for Him or against Him. Jesus claims to be God. Faced with such a claim we have only two options, to accept or to reject. (Agnosticism is really a passive rejection.) The Bible claims to be God's Word. Again our options are but two. It follows that when dealing with the text of Scripture neutrality is impossible. The Bible is clear about satanic interference in the minds of human beings, and most especially when they are considering God's Truth. 2 Corinthians 4:4 states plainly that the god of this age/world blinds the minds of unbelievers when they are confronted with the Gospel. The Lord Jesus said the same thing when He explained the parable of the sower: "When they hear, Satan comes immediately and takes away the word that was sown in their hearts" (Mark 4:15, Luke 8:12).

Furthermore, there is a pervasive satanic influence upon all human culture. 1 John 5:19 states that "the whole world lies in the evil one". The picture is clearly one of massive influence, if

---

[1] By "the Truth" I mean the fact of an intelligent and moral Creator, Sovereign over all, to whom every created being is accountable. Many scholars will sacrifice the evidence, their own integrity and other people rather than face the Truth.

not control—NASB, RSV, NEB and Jerusalem render "in the power of", TEV has "under the rule of", NIV has "under the control of", NKJV has "under the sway of". All human culture is under pervasive satanic influence, including the culture of the academic community. Ephesians 2:2 is even more precise: "in which you once walked according to the course of this world, according to the prince of the power of the air, the spirit who now works in the sons of the disobedience." Satan actively works in the mind of anyone who rejects God's authority over him. Materialism has infiltrated the Church in Europe and North America to such an extent that what the Bible says on this subject has been largely ignored. But I submit that for someone who claims to believe God's Word to accept an edition of the Bible prepared on the basis of rationalistic assumptions is really to forget the teaching of that Word.

Interpretation is preeminently a matter of wisdom. A naturalistic textual critic may have a reasonable acquaintance with the relevant evidence, he may have knowledge of the facts, but that by no means implies that he knows what to do with it. If "the fear of the LORD is the **beginning** of wisdom" (Proverbs 9:10), then presumably the unbeliever does not have any, at least from God's point of view. Anyone who edits or translates the text of Scripture needs to be in spiritual condition such that he can ask the Holy Spirit to illumine him in his work as well as protect his mind from the enemy.

In Jesus' day there were those who "loved the praise of men more than the praise of God" (John 12:43), and they are with us still. But, the "praise of men" comes at a high price—you must accept their value system, a value system that suffers direct satanic influence. To accept the world's value system is basically an act of treason against King Jesus, a type of idolatry. Those conservative scholars who place a high value on 'academic recognition' on being acknowledged by the 'academic community', etc., need to ask themselves about the presuppositions that lie behind such recognition. Please note that I am not decrying true scholarship—I have three earned graduate degrees myself—but I am challenging conservatives to make sure that their definition of scholarship comes from the Holy Spirit, not from the world, that their search for recognition is godly, not selfish. I rather suspect that were this to happen there would be a dramatic shift in the conservative Christian world with reference to the practice of NT textual criticism and to the identity of the true NT text.

Conclusion

To sum it up, I return to the opening question: "What difference does it make?" Not only do we have the confusion caused by two rather different competing forms of the Greek text, but one of them (the eclectic text) incorporates errors and contradictions that undermine the doctrine of inspiration and virtually vitiate the doctrine of inerrancy; the other (the Majority Text) does not. The first is based on subjective criteria, applied by naturalistic critics; the second is based on the consensus of the manuscript tradition down through the centuries. Because the conservative evangelical schools and churches have generally embraced the theory (and therefore the presuppositions) that underlies the eclectic text (UBS^3/N-A^{26}),[1] there has been an ongoing hemorrhage or defection within the evangelical camp with reference to the doctrines of Biblical inspiration and inerrancy (especially). The authority of Scripture has been undermined—it no longer commands immediate and unquestioned obedience. As a natural consequence there is a generalized softening of our basic commitment to Christ and His Kingdom. Worse yet, through our missionaries we have been exporting all of this to the emerging churches in the 'third world'. Alas!

---

[1] UBS^4 and N-A^{27} have changes in the apparatus, but not the text, so the text is still that of the prior editions.

So what shall we do, throw up our hands in despair and give up? Indeed no! 'It is better to light one candle than to sit and curse the darkness.' With God's help let us work together to bring about a reversal of this situation. Let us work to undo the damage. We must start by consciously trying to make sure that all our presuppositions, our working assumptions, are consistent with God's Word. When we approach the evidence (Greek MSS, patristic citations, ancient versions) with such presuppositions we will have a credible, even demonstrable, basis for declaring and defending the divine preservation, the inspiration and the inerrancy of the New Testament text. We can again have a compelling basis for total commitment to God and His Word.[1] The present printed Majority Text (whether H-F or R-P) is a close approximation to the original, free from the errors of fact and contradictions discussed above. (All modesty aside, I consider that my Greek Text is even closer.)

---

[1] For a more thorough discussion, please see "The root cause of the continuous defection from biblical infallibility" in chapter V.

Chapter V: DOCTRINAL TOPICS

Judgment begins at the house of God

Let me begin by explaining why I am writing such an article as this. I am looking for a way (if it is still possible) to stop, and even turn back, the satanic steamroller that is destroying the culture and taking over all aspects of life in the country where I live, Brazil. (Of course the same is true of other countries as well.) The only possible 'medicine' is the love of the truth (2 Thessalonians 2:10, see below), so the bottom line is this: what can we do to promote the love of the truth? Lamentably, the vast majority of the churches are part of the problem, rather than being part of the solution. I venture to say that less than 1% of the churches want a Bible with objective authority.[1] The culture outside the church is totally dominated by relativistic humanism, and most church members have been heavily influenced by that worldview. On the way to promoting the love of the truth, we must defend the objective authority of the biblical Text,[2] and the place to begin is with the churches.[3] **To promote truth necessarily involves exposing lies**.

Any surgeon knows that for certain pathological conditions the only alternative to a premature physical death is radical surgery. The patient will not like the news, but if the surgery is successful, he will end up thanking the surgeon. Similarly, a brother probably will not appreciate being told that he has embraced a lie, but if he will stop and think, and change, he

---

[1] In consequence, they are lacking in spiritual power and spiritual discernment.

[2] It is the biblical Text that defines and teaches the Truth, and in order to arrive at the Truth we must understand that the Text has objective authority. Relativistic humanism is inimical to objective authority, and any attempt to relativize the authority of Scripture only serves the enemy.

[3] Our only hope of correcting the national culture depends upon first correcting the churches.

will end up thanking us. In desperate times 'business as usual' is not enough; it is necessary to take risks.[1]

Now consider 1 Peter 4:17—"Because the time has come for judgment to begin at God's house; now if it starts with us, what will be the end of those who keep disobeying the Gospel of God?" Although the 'publishing' of this letter is often stated to have been around 60 AD, or even later, I suspect it may have been at least ten years earlier. In any case, although the nation of Israel will yet return to center stage, beginning with the day of Pentecost Sovereign Jesus has been interacting with the world using mainly His body, the Church. Since Peter is writing to Christians, he is referring to them as "God's house". It is possible to translate the verse above as 'from God's house', that house being the point of departure. It seems clear that God's judgment does not stop with us; it goes on to the world.

God has always judged His people

Once the blood of God's Lamb had been shed, thus paying for the sin of the world, the judgment against those "who keep disobeying the Gospel of God" became more direct. But since judgment starts with God's house, the demands upon those claiming to belong to Christ also became more direct. The fate of Ananias and Sapphira is an emphatic case in point.[2] What I wish to emphasize is that God's judging His house began at the beginning, it began on the day of Pentecost, with reference to the Church. When we cry out to God to judge the world, the judging of God's house as a prior condition is not a factor[3]—God has been judging His house right along.[1] Howev-

---

[1] In order to try to save the 'patient', I must take the risk of being rejected and hated. On the other hand, Ezekiel 3:20-21 explains an even more serious risk.

[2] They were not given any warning, nor any chance to repent or explain.

[3] For many years I had the idea that it was a prior condition that had not yet been fulfilled—don't ask me where I got it!

er, I would say that judging is one thing, but correcting is another. The correcting of the culture begins with, and depends on, the correcting of the churches.

Consider what happened to the apostle Paul. The Holy Spirit had told him repeatedly **NOT** to go to Jerusalem, but he went anyway. When he got there he kowtowed to big boss James, who was well on his way back into Judaism. Do you remember his pitch to Paul? "You see, brother, how many tens of thousands are the Jews who have believed, and they are all zealous for the law; but they have been informed about you that you teach all the Jews who are among the Gentiles to forsake Moses, telling them not to circumcise their children nor to walk according to our customs" (Acts 21:20-21).[2] If his "many tens of thousands" was not a blatant exaggeration, as I suspect, then the whole church in that area was in a bad way (which it probably was anyway). Was Paul judged? He spent the next five years, at least, in chains.[3]

Was James judged? He was killed, not long after. Was the church in Jerusalem judged? The city was destroyed in 70 AD, and the Jerusalem church ceased to exist. The city was little more than a ruin for centuries.[4] And now consider 1 Corinthians 11:29-30: "He who eats and drinks unworthily eats and drinks judgment to himself, not distinguishing the Lord's body. Because of this many among you are weak and sick, and a good many have died." Paul declares that God had already visited sickness on many, and death on even more. God was judging His people. A variety of further texts could be men-

---

[1] Of course this has always been true. The O. T. is full of God's judgment upon His people, Israel. Adam was judged; Moses was judged. God has always required an accounting based on the benefits and blessings one receives.

[2] "The law", "Moses", "our customs" = Judaism.

[3] Try living in chains for just twenty-four hours, and see how you like it!

[4] References during the early centuries to especially good NT manuscripts in Jerusalem are probably just pious hogwash. The center of gravity of the Church had moved north.

tioned, but Hebrews will do. Please read 2:1-3, 3:12-4:13, 6:3-8, 10:26-31, and 12:28-29. "It is a dreadful thing to fall into the hands of the Living God", "because our God is indeed a consuming fire!"

And then there are the seven letters that the glorified Jesus sent to the seven churches. Each letter ends with a promise to "the one who overcomes"; so what happens to you if you don't? Although He had some good things to say about the church in Ephesus, He said He would remove their 'lampstand' if they did not return to their first love. Indeed, in due time all seven of those churches lost their lampstand. Two of the letters refer to the doctrine and works of the Nicolaitans, that Sovereign Jesus says He hates. The etymology of the term suggests the beginning of the distinction between clergy and laity. It may have begun with James in Jerusalem.[1] Before the end of the first century, a certain Clement was the bishop of Rome. The term 'bishop' came to be used of a presbyter who had authority over the other presbyters in his area, the boss presbyter.[2]

Attempting to control someone else's spiritual life is forbidden

But the concept of special spiritual authority being vested in a 'bishop' soon ran afoul of Sovereign Jesus' words in Matthew 23:8-12 and John 4:23-24. First Matthew:

---

[1] The Jews were accustomed to a high priest, a single individual at the top of the religious pyramid. Evidently that attitude invaded the churches.

[2] In the writings of the 'church fathers' that have come down to us, there appears to be no mention of 'apostles' after the first century. This means that there was no 'apostolic succession'; the more so since apostles are designated by God, not ordained by men. Since the second century there has only been 'discipolic' succession. Any claims in our day based on apostolic succession are spurious (as were any such claims after the first century).

"But you (pl.), do not be called 'Rabbi'; because your Teacher is <u>one</u>, the Christ,[1] and you are all brothers. 9 And do not call anyone on earth your 'father'; because your Father is <u>one</u>, He who is in the heavens. 10 Neither be called leaders/guides; because your Leader is <u>one</u>, the Christ. 11 On the contrary, the greatest among you must be your servant. 12 And whoever exalts himself will be humbled, and whoever humbles himself will be exalted."

In verse 9, since the second person here is plural, the Lord is evidently referring to calling someone your spiritual father; He is not saying not to acknowledge your physical father. "Your (pl.) Father is <u>one</u>"—obviously they did not all have the same physical father. Verse 10 may be why we have no record in Scripture of a Christian calling someone his disciple; even in 1 Corinthians 3:4 Paul evidently avoids using the term. **I take it that our Lord is forbidding any effort by one Christian to control the spiritual life of another**. We may point the way, we may encourage, we may discipline when occasion warrants, but the rest is up to the Holy Spirit.[2] The Lord had already told the Samaritan woman that the Father must be worshipped "in spirit and truth" (John 4:23-24).

"The time is coming, in fact now is, when the genuine worshipers will worship the Father in spirit and truth. Really, because the Father is looking for **such** people to worship Him. 24 God is <u>Spirit</u>,[3] and those who worship Him must worship in spirit and truth."

---

[1] Perhaps 4% of the Greek manuscripts omit "the Christ" (as in NIV, NASB, LB, TEV, etc.).

[2] It is normal, indeed inescapable, that a new Christian will receive his first ideas about spiritual things from the older Christians around him. But as he grows and matures, he should learn to depend directly upon Scripture and the Holy Spirit.

[3] Again the lack of the definite article presents us with an ambiguity; the rendering 'a spirit' is possible. But as I indicate by the underlining, I understand that the quality inherent in the noun is being emphasized, which is another use of an absent article (in Greek).

The Father "is looking" for those who will worship Him in spirit and truth.[1] It may be that we have here a window on the reason why God created a race such as ours—persons in His image with the capacity to **choose**. God "is looking" for something, which means He does not have it, at least not automatically, nor in sufficient quantity. I take it that He wants to be appreciated for who He is, but to have meaning such appreciation cannot come from robots—it has to be voluntary. So He created a type of being with that capacity, but He had to take the risk that such a being would choose not to appreciate Him. Unfortunately, most human beings make the negative choice, and with that negative choice come all sorts of negative consequences. Ever since Adam human beings are born with an inclination toward sin,[2] so for someone to choose to appreciate God is definitely not automatic, nor even easy. No one can reasonably accuse God of having 'stacked the deck' in His own favor, of 'buying votes'—He seems to have done just the opposite. If a human being, against his natural inclination, chooses to appreciate God, then God receives what He is looking for.

"In spirit and truth" presumably means that it cannot be faked, cannot be forced or imposed, cannot be merely physical, cannot be merely emotional (though both body and emotions can, and often will, be utilized). The concept of 'bishop' (and in our day even of lowly pastors) as someone having the authority to control the spiritual life of others is an open rebellion against Sovereign Jesus, who forbids any such attitude or proceeding.[3] But rebellion against God is Satan's 'thing', and

---

[1] See also 2 Chronicles 16:9, that tells you how to have God's help.

[2] Babies have to be self-centered in order to survive, but self-centeredness is the essence of sin, which, however, is not charged to the account until the person can understand what he is doing. At that point, the person needs to receive adequate instruction, to escape from that self-centeredness (Proverbs 22:6).

[3] A typical proceeding is to dictate who may, or may not, participate in the 'Lord's Supper', as though the 'table' belongs to the leaders of the congregation, rather than to the Lord—after all, it is the 'Lord's Table'.

will certainly call down God's judgment (see the discussion of 2 Thessalonians 2:9-12 below).

Someone who wishes to control the spiritual life of others must develop a doctrinal 'package'; he must define what they may and may not believe, and/or do. But of course that gave rise to competing 'packages', and competition between 'bishops', to the point that they were mutually excommunicating each other, and so on. That gave rise to different 'churches', and in our day to different 'denominations'. This mentality guarantees the perpetuation of the falsehoods that have been incorporated into the denominational 'packages'. In some cases they reached the point of declaring that only those who were within their ranks could be saved. Anyone who embraces a 'package' elevates that package above God's inspired Word, and that is idolatry. Such idolatry offends the Holy Spirit, who has a special interest in that Word; such idolaters no longer listen to the Holy Spirit (if they ever did). Such idolaters condemn their 'package' to become an 'old wineskin', devoid of spiritual power.

I would say that the only way to avoid becoming an 'old wineskin' is to be constantly listening to the Holy Spirit and obeying what He says. Unfortunately, few Christians are in the habit of consulting the Holy Spirit, and those who do are marked for persecution. <u>No Establishment can tolerate anyone who listens to the Holy Spirit</u>. Surely, or have you forgotten John 3:8? "The wind blows where it wishes, and you (sg) hear its sound, but you do not know where it comes from or where it goes. So it is with everyone who has been begotten by the Spirit." Notice that the Lord is saying here that it is **we** who are to be unpredictable, like the wind, or the Spirit ("comes" and "goes" are in the present tense). If you are really under the control of the Spirit you will do unexpected things, just like He does, and that definitely will not please the 'bosses'.[1] (Since Satan is for-

---

[1] But what about Hebrews 13:17? "Obey your leaders and submit, for they keep watch over your souls, as those who must give account." In the first place, I

ever muddying the water with excesses and abuses, spiritual discernment is needed, but lamentably such discernment appears to be a rare commodity in the churches.) An Establishment is defined by its 'straightjacket' (or 'package'), and the Holy Spirit does not like straightjackets, and vice versa.

The love of the Truth

During the middle ages the Church all but died out, at least in the West. And why did the Church almost die out? It was because the Church became part of the problem, rather than being part of the solution. And how did it become part of the problem? It became part of the problem by rejecting the love of the truth (see the discussion of 2 Thessalonians 2:9-12 below). When the Church becomes part of the problem, the surrounding culture is condemned. Did you get that? **When the Church becomes part of the problem, the surrounding culture is condemned.** Surely, because salvation begins at the house of God.

Consider 1 Timothy 3:15—"so that you may know how it is necessary to conduct oneself in God's household, which is the Church of the living God, pillar and foundation of the truth." My first impression would be that the truth should be sustaining the Church, not vice versa. But it is the Church that has the responsibility to promote and defend the truth in the society at large—in education, health, commerce, government, everywhere. Salvation can come to an individual just by reading God's Word, all by himself, but to transform a whole culture requires the Church. Remember also what Jesus said to the Samaritan woman in John 4:22, "salvation is from the Jews". Quite so. The Lamb of God is a Jew, and the O.T. canon came

---

would say that the reference is to administrative matters, so that things be done 'decently and in order'. But the minute a leader attempts to impose a falsehood, he should not be obeyed; he is no longer listening to the Holy Spirit. As Peter said to the council, "We must obey God rather than men" (Acts 5:29). I treat 1 Peter 5:5 similarly. Some 4% of the Greek manuscripts, of inferior quality, omit "submitting to one another" (as in NIV, NASB, LB, TEV, etc.).

through the Jewish people (for that matter, most, if not all, of the N.T. was written by Jews as well). As Paul says in Romans 3:2, "they were entrusted with the oracles of God". The Oracles of God are His written revelation to the human race.

Then came the Protestant Reformation, but because of its emphasis on reason it was born deformed. It was not long before 'packages' developed within the Reformation, and in the nineteenth century it was besieged by three satanic sophistries (2 Corinthians 10:5): 1) Darwin's theory of evolution, 2) the so-called 'higher criticism' of the Bible, and then 3) the text-critical theory of Westcott and Hort.[1] These were followed by materialism, humanism, relativism, etc. A biblical Text with objective authority barely limped into the twentieth century, but then came the onslaught of liberal theology.[2]

To understand the full impact of the onslaught of liberal theology, one must take account of the milieu. Reason has always been important to the historic or traditional Protestant denominations. In consequence, academic respectability has always been important to their graduate schools of theology. The difficulty resides in the following circumstance: for at least two centuries academia has been dominated by Satan, and so the terms of 'respectability' are dictated by him. Those terms include 'publish or perish', but of course he controls the technical journals. Since he is the father of lies (John 8:44), anyone who wished to tell the whole truth has always had a hard time getting an article published, no matter how good it was. To

---

[1] The W-H theory did away with any notion of a NT text with objective authority. My demonstration that that theory is a tissue of falsehoods was first published in 1977 (the book having gone through at least six revisions since), and so far as I know, it has never been refuted. *The Identity of the New Testament Text* (Nashville: Thomas Nelson Inc., Publishers, 1977); *The Identity of the New Testament Text IV* (self-published with Amazon.com, 2014).

[2] One response to liberal theology was the so-called Neo-orthodoxy; it holds that the Bible is made up of divine parts and human parts, so that the whole cannot be said to **be** God's Word. Since that view offers no way to know which parts are and which are not, it also does away with any notion of a NT text with objective authority.

get an article published one had to toe the party line. 'Taking account of the existing literature' obliges one to waste a great deal of time reading the nonsense produced by Satan's servants, all of which was designed to keep the reader away from the **truth**—the 'reader' in this case being the students who in their turn would become pastors and church leaders, seminary professors, etc.[1]

The TRUTH—aye, there's the rub. Consider 2 Thessalonians 2:9-12:

> That one's coming is according to the working of Satan with all power[2] and signs and lying wonders, 10 and with all wicked deception among those who are wasting themselves,[3] because they did not receive the love of the truth so that they might be saved. 11 Yes, because of this God will send them an active delusion so that they will believe the lie 12 and so that all may be condemned who have not believed the truth but have taken pleasure in wickedness.[4]

Although verse ten is in the context of the activity of the Antichrist, who will find an easy target in 'those who are wasting themselves' (my translation), it does not follow that no one will be wasting himself before that activity. Obviously, people have been wasting themselves all down through history, and

---

[1] The systematic contamination of successive generations of future pastors inevitably resulted in the contamination of the congregations as well.

[2] When Satan fell he did not lose his power.

[3] The verb here, $\alpha\pi\omega\lambda\lambda\upsilon\mu\iota$, often rendered 'to perish' (John 3:16 in KJV), is used in a variety of contexts, but I take the core meaning to be 'waste'. The participial form here is ambiguous as to voice, either middle or passive, but the basic form of the verb is middle. Ephesians 1:5-14 makes clear that a basic objective of our redemption is that we be "to the praise of His glory", which was part of the original Plan (Isaiah 43:7). Only as we live for the glory of God can we realize or fulfill our potential, our reason for being. If you live for any other reason, you are wasting yourself.

[4] 'Taking pleasure in wickedness' involves rejecting the Truth of a moral Creator who will demand an accounting, or even overt rebellion against that Creator (like Lucifer/Satan).

the underlying cause for that 'wasting' has never changed—"they did not receive the love of the truth". (It began in the Garden.)

Consider Romans 1:18: "Now the wrath of God is revealed from Heaven upon all ungodliness and unrighteousness of the people who suppress the truth by unrighteousness." To 'suppress the truth' is a deliberate act, an evil choice that invites God's wrath. (Romans 1:24-25 and 2:8 give more detail.) To hear a sermon about 'the love of God' is easy enough, but how many have you heard (or preached) about 'the wrath of God'? 'God hates sin but loves the sinner' is standard fare, but consider Psalm 5:4-6.

> "For You are not a God who takes pleasure in wickedness, nor shall evil dwell with You. The boastful shall not stand in your sight; You **hate** all workers of iniquity. You shall destroy those who speak falsehood; the LORD abhors the bloodthirsty and deceitful man."

This is not an isolated text; there are a fair number of others in the same vein. Someone who deliberately chooses to be evil and to promote evil, having rejected the truth, thereby makes God his enemy, makes himself an object of His wrath.[1] God has been judging sin for six thousand years.

Consider also Luke 16:31 "He said to him, 'If they do not listen to Moses and the prophets, they will not be persuaded even if someone should rise from the dead'." Abraham states a disquieting reality: people who reject God's written revelation are self-condemned. As Jesus said in John 8:31-32, "If you abide in my word, you really are my disciples; and you will know the Truth, and the Truth will make you free." So what happens if you don't abide?

---

[1] A person who sells himself to evil will spend eternity in the Lake of fire and brimstone, but usually gets a taste of God's wrath in this life as well.

Consider further 2 Timothy 4:4, "They will turn their ears away from the Truth and be turned aside to fables." Notice the progression: first they choose to turn away from the Truth, but after that someone else takes over and leads them into ever greater stupidities—that someone else is Satan, using his servants.

But to return to Thessalonians, please notice carefully what is said there: it is God Himself who sends the "active delusion"![1] And upon whom does He send it? Upon those who do not receive the love of the truth—it is a direct judgment upon their rejection of the truth.[2] And what is the purpose of the strong delusion?—the condemnation of those who do not believe the truth. Dear me, this is heavy. Notice that the truth is **central** to anyone's salvation. This raises the necessary question: just what is meant by 'the truth'?

In John 14:6 Sovereign Jesus declared Himself to be 'the truth'. Praying to the Father in John 17:17 He said, "Thy Word is truth". Once each in John chapters 14, 15 and 16 He referred to the third person of the Trinity as "the Spirit of the truth". Since the Son is back in Heaven at the Father's right hand, and the Spirit is not very perceptible to most of us, most of the time, and since the Word is the Spirit's sword (Ephesians 6:17), our main access to 'the truth' is through God's Word, the Bible. The Bible offers propositional truth, but we need the Holy Spirit to illumine that truth, and to have the Holy Spirit we must be adequately related to Sovereign Jesus—it is Jesus who baptizes with the Holy Spirit (Matthew 3:11). If that is 'the Truth', then what is 'the lie'? I suggest that 'the lie' is short for Satan's kingdom and all it represents. In

---

[1] I understand 'active' in the sense of 'aggressive'; it is not a passive delusion that lies quietly in your brain, allowing you to go your merry way. It is aggressive, it tries to control how you think, and therefore what you do and who you are.

[2] Please note that it is not enough to merely 'accept' the truth; it is required that we <u>love</u> the truth. Satan tantalizes us with fame and fortune (on his terms, of course), so to love the truth requires determination; since the love in question is αγαπη, it involves an act of the will.

that event, we could also say that 'the Truth' is short for Christ's Kingdom and all it represents.

Now then, for something to be received, it must be offered; one cannot believe in something he has never heard about (Romans 10:14). A baby born to Satanist parents and dedicated to him may well grow to adulthood without ever having been exposed to 'the truth'. The same holds for cultures that have no knowledge at all of Christianity. In such circumstances a person can be serving 'the lie' because that is all he knows. He has not rejected 'the truth', because he has no knowledge of it. For such a person there is hope; if some day 'the truth' is presented to him, he has the option of embracing it, as has happened many times.

The use of the verb 'receive' clearly implies an act of volition on the part of those not receiving the truth; that love was offered or made available to them but they did not want it; they wanted to be able to lie and to entertain lies told by others. But the consequences of such a choice are terrible; they turned their back on salvation. Notice in verse 11 that God sends the active delusion <u>so that they will believe the lie</u>; God pushes them toward the lie! In John 8:44 Sovereign Jesus stated that Satan is the father of lying, there being no truth in him. So if God Himself sends delusion, He is turning the victims over to Satan. So if God turns you over to Satan, what are your chances?

Notice the sequence: first they reject the love of the truth; it is as a consequence of that choice that God sends the delusion. The implication is that there is a **point of no return;**[1] God sends the delusion so that they may be condemned. The only intelligent choice is to embrace the truth! If God offers you

---

[1] However, since God is gracious and longsuffering, He may grant a number of opportunities to repent before a person reaches that point. In my own experience, I threw off a variety of falsehoods that I was taught, one at a time over a period of years. That said, I should not assume that I am now totally free from false ideas; I need to keep listening to the Holy Spirit as I study the Scriptures.

the truth and you reject it, your choice turns Him into your enemy—not a good idea!

A correct solution depends upon a correct diagnosis

Why did I write this article? I am looking for a way (if it is still possible) to stop, and even turn back, the satanic steamroller that is destroying the culture and taking over all aspects of life in the country where I live, Brazil. (Of course the same is true of other countries as well.) The only possible 'medicine' is the love of the truth, so the bottom line is this: what can we do to promote the love of the truth? Lamentably, the vast majority of the churches are part of the problem, rather than being part of the solution. I venture to say that less than 1% of the churches want a Bible with objective authority.[1] The culture outside the church is totally dominated by relativistic humanism, and most church members have been heavily influenced by that worldview. On the way to promoting the love of the truth, we must defend the objective authority of the biblical Text,[2] and the place to begin is with the churches.[3] To promote truth necessarily involves exposing lies.

The world hates the Truth

Satan never quits with his attacks against the objective authority of God's Word; it began back in the Garden: "Yea, hath God said?" Satan hates the Truth, because as Sovereign Jesus said in John 8:44, "there is no truth in him". Satan is the father of lying (same verse), so whenever we tell a lie we are doing Satan's thing. And whenever we embrace a lie (like evolutionism, Marxism, Freudianism, Hortianism, humanism, relativism,

---

[1] In consequence, they are lacking in spiritual power and spiritual discernment.

[2] It is the biblical Text that defines and teaches the Truth, and in order to arrive at the Truth we must understand that the Text has objective authority. Relativistic humanism is inimical to objective authority, and any attempt to relativize the authority of Scripture only serves the enemy.

[3] Our only hope of correcting the national culture depends upon first correcting the churches.

etc.) we give Satan a foothold in our minds, which he usually turns into a stronghold. When Satan gets someone to sell himself to evil, having rejected the truth, that someone becomes what Jesus called a 'dog' in Matthew 7:6.[1] A 'dog' reacts in an aggressive and violent manner against any presentation of the Truth. The media and academia are filled with such dogs; they are sworn enemies of the Truth. Why did the Sovereign say **not** to offer anything 'holy' to such people? The implication is that it would be a waste of time; they are beyond recovery—their ongoing opposition will also get in the way. However, in order to save the people that they are damaging, it will be necessary to challenge and refute what they represent—before attempting to do this, you had better know how to wield God's power (Ephesians 3:20). To confront a 'dog' is not the same as offering him something 'holy'.

Consider our Lord's words recorded in Luke 17:2—"It would be better for him if a millstone were hung around his neck and he were thrown into the sea, than that he should cause one of these little ones to fall." What is worse than a horrible, premature physical death? Spiritual death. Whoever destroys the faith of a 'little one' is self-condemned. What about all the professors and pastors who make it their business to destroy the faith of their students and hearers?

Consider also 2 Peter 3:5—"This because they deliberately ignore that heavens and land (out of water and through water) had been existing from of old by the word of God." It appears to me that the term "deliberately" has a direct bearing on the intended meaning of the Greek term usually rendered as 'forget'. How can one 'forget' deliberately? To 'ignore' is deliberate; to 'pretend' is deliberate. When a professor, a scholar, or a scientist ignores the scientific evidence for a worldwide flood, he is deliberately deceiving his students or readers. To do so is to be perverse, to do so is to serve Satan.

---

[1] 1 Timothy 6:5 and 2 timothy 3:8 may refer to such 'dogs' as well.

Comparing Romans 1:18: the wrath of God is upon those who suppress the truth, with Psalm 5:5: God hates all workers of iniquity, with what Jesus said in John 6:44: "No one is able to come to me unless the Father who sent me draws him", we may reasonably conclude that the Father will not draw someone whom He hates. So anyone who has become a 'dog' is condemned. Just by the way, have you not noticed that those who were brought up in a Christian environment but then turned their back on Jesus are often more virulent in their opposition to God's truth than those who were brought up as pagans? There is no way to save a 'dog', but we should work to save their students and readers—how can we do this apart from demonstrating that what the 'dog' teaches is wrong? To confront a 'dog' is not the same as offering him something 'holy'; we are not trying to save him, we are refuting him for the sake of his students and readers.

False doctrines in the churches

I suspect that not many Christians in the so-called 'first world' really believe what Sovereign Jesus said in Matthew 7:14: those who find the way of Life are **few**![1] We need to consider carefully Revelation 22:15; "whoever loves and practices a lie" is excluded from the heavenly City.[2] The Text has 'a' lie, not 'the' lie. The verb here is φιλεω, that refers to emotional love;

---

[1] Consider also Romans 9:27, "the remnant will be saved". The context is about Israel, but the statement is descriptive of all human history. At any moment during the last 6,000 years, only a very small percentage of the total population was seriously committed to God. The same is true of the Christian population during the last 2,000 years. What percentage of a wheat plant is edible grain (Luke 3:17)? And then there is Matthew 24:37—after 1,650 years of human procreation, how many people would there have been on the earth? Probably well over a million. And how many were saved? Sovereign Jesus said that at His coming it will be like it was in the days of Noah.

[2] Help! "A lie" is rather general, open-ended. What happens if I accepted a lie without realizing that it was one? But the text does not say 'accepts'; it says 'loves' and 'practices'. The implication is that the contrary evidence, to the lie, is available, but has been rejected, or deliberately ignored—the person sold himself to the lie.

someone who sells himself to a lie usually becomes emotionally attached to it, and they react aggressively (often irrationally) if you challenge their lie. In contrast, in 2 Thessalonians 2:10 the love of the truth is αγαπη love, that refers to an act of the will whereby you align yourself with the truth.

Consider 1 Timothy 4:1-2—"Now the Spirit says explicitly that in later times some will fall away from the faith, paying attention to deceiving spirits and to things taught by demons— through hypocritical liars whose own consciences have been cauterized." Notice that one cannot "fall away from the faith" unless he was first with the faith. Be not deceived, the churches (with exceptions, of course) are filled with a variety of 'doctrines' of demonic origin. The enemy uses a certain type of person to 'sell' them. Whatever its origin, any false doctrine gives the enemy an entrance into the life of the church, and then into the persons who attend there.

But let us return to Revelation 22:15. The verb 'practice' indicates a value that orients your conduct. If you are practicing a lie, that lie has become part of what you are, part of your private 'package'. Depending on the nature of the lie, its contaminating influence could end up touching all areas of your life. A lie like 'God does not exist' touches everything. Obviously, the more lies that someone practices, the worse off that he will be. Notice, however, that the verbs "loves" and "practices" are in the present tense, which means that while there is life there is hope; it is still possible to repent and change and escape condemnation. Anyone who is overtaken by death while practicing a lie will be excluded from the City.[1]

Now notice what it says in Ezekiel 18; I encourage you to read the whole chapter with care. Each person is responsible for his own destiny, and it is possible to change destinies. Verses 21-

---

[1] All of us have received false information that we assumed to be true, and in some cases may even have acted upon it, but if it did not become part of our ongoing practice, then it will not necessarily result in keeping us out of the City.

22 teach that someone who starts out wrong can change to right, and live. Verse 23: "Do I have any pleasure at all that the wicked should die?" says the Lord GOD, "and not that he should turn from his ways and live?" But verse 24 teaches that the reverse is true; someone who starts out right can change to wrong, and die. While there is life there is hope, except for certain irreversible conditions.[1]

If you consult the Holy Spirit on a given matter, He will not permit you to believe a lie. "He will guide you into all truth" (John 16:13). He is the Spirit of the Truth (John 15:26) and He cannot lie (Titus 1:2). It follows that He hates lies. "These six things the LORD hates, yes, seven are an <u>abomination</u> to Him: a proud look, **a lying tongue**, . . ." (Proverbs 6:16-17). "Lying lips are an abomination to the LORD" (Proverbs 12:22). And remember that liars cannot enter the New Jerusalem (Revelation 21:27, 22:15). The case of Joshua and the Gibeonites provides a negative example. The Text says explicitly that they did not seek the Lord's guidance (Joshua 9:14), and the negative consequences lasted for centuries.

I will now discuss some of the lies that Satan has succeeded in 'selling' to many Christians, precisely because they did not consult the Holy Spirit before embracing them. It may be that most people simply accept what they are taught because they trust the teacher, as well as not feeling competent to attempt an independent judgement—and many of them may stop short of 'loving' and 'practicing'. It is also lamentably true that very few churches teach how to consult the Holy Spirit, but none of this changes the consequences of a lie. Such lies often become strongholds of Satan in their minds, that they then defend emotionally. Have you never noticed that when you challenge certain doctrines the people simply explode? They are incapable of discussing the question rationally; they do not know all that the Bible says on the subject. <u>For all that, to</u>

---

[1] These will be discussed below in the section, "Sins that lead to death".

<u>promote the truth we must expose lies</u>. If the promoting of the love of the Truth is our top priority, then we must accept the consequences of exposing and denouncing lies. If all Christians were to throw off all of the eight cherished falsehoods discussed below, the world would see an outpouring of God's power unprecedented in human history.

Sovereign grace: The doctrine of 'sovereign grace' is obviously false. God is indeed sovereign, but no single one of His attributes can be, by simple logic, since it is constrained by all the others. God is certainly grace, but He is also love (which necessarily includes the hate of evil, because of the consequences to loved ones), truth, wisdom, power, justice, wrath, eternity, and doubtless others that our finite minds cannot comprehend. Nowhere does the Bible teach that grace is sovereign; the doctrine is an invention. Those who use the idea of sovereign grace to protect sin and comfort the sinner[1] are in for a terrible surprise. Anyone who has embraced the notion of 'sovereign grace' did not consult the Holy Spirit before doing so.

Unconditional love: The doctrine that God's love is 'unconditional' is also false. Since we have no way of deserving His love beforehand, presumably God offers His love without prior condition—it is unconditional only in that sense. But the minute someone receives God's love, then His expectations come into play. From John 4:23-24 it is clear that the Father is looking for a response to His love; He wants to be reciprocated. This is also clear from John 14:21 and 23. If God's love is unconditional, why then does He chasten us? "As many as I love, I rebuke and chasten" (Revelation 3:19). "Whom the LORD loves He chastens, and scourges every son whom He receives" (Hebrews 12:6). And why does He demand an accounting? "We must all appear before the judgment seat of Christ, that each one may receive the things done in the body, ac-

---

[1] By 'comfort the sinner' I mean to tell a sinner not to worry about his sin, rather than confronting it.

cording to what he has done, whether good or bad" (2 Corinthians 5:10; see also 1 Corinthians 3:11-15). Those who use the idea of unconditional love to protect sin and comfort the sinner are in for a terrible surprise. Anyone who has embraced the notion of 'unconditional love' did not consult the Holy Spirit before doing so.

Eternal security: The doctrine of 'eternal security', as usually understood, is also false, and even more dangerous to the souls of men than the two discussed above. A crass statement of the 'doctrine' would go something like this: Once saved, always saved, no matter what you do afterwards. When one mentions passages like Ephesians 5:5-6 and 1 Corinthians 6:9-10, that list practices that exclude from the Kingdom, the standard defense is to say that such people never were saved. But do they not beg the question? Both the passages above were written to <u>believers</u>, not unbelievers. Why would the Holy Spirit write such things to believers if it were simply impossible for them to fall into such practices? And why did the glorified Jesus say, "I will not blot out his name from the Book of Life" (Revelation 3:5)? Please note that <u>it is impossible to blot out a name that is not there</u>! To try to argue that the glorified Jesus was using an impossible 'bogey-man' to scare them would make Him out to be a liar, which He cannot be (Titus 1:2). And then there are all the passages that speak of enduring to the end, so as to be saved. But the definitive text on the subject is Hebrews 6:3-6. The descriptions given in verses 4 and 5 can only refer to someone who has been regenerated, as verse 6 makes clear. The only way to "crucify <u>again</u>" is if you have already done so, at least once. To say that the Holy Spirit is using an impossible 'bogey-man' to scare them would make Him out to be a liar, as well, also impossible.[1] Those who use the idea of eternal security to protect sin

---

[1] An appeal to John 10:28-29 reflects a basic misunderstanding of the Text; the crucial point is the semantic area of the verb "snatch". Being snatched is one thing; jumping out is another. You cannot 'snatch' yourself, it must be done by an outside force, and no such force is greater than God. But, if you don't want to go

and comfort the sinner are in for a terrible surprise. Anyone who has embraced the notion of 'eternal security' did not consult the Holy Spirit before doing so.

Salvation without works: The Protestant Reformation correctly rejected the Roman doctrine of salvation by works, but to replace it with 'faith alone' is open to serious misunderstanding. Ephesians 2:8-10 gives us the truth on this subject in a nutshell:

> "For by grace you have been saved, through the Faith[1]— and this not of yourselves, it is the gift of God—9 not by works, so that no one may boast. 10 You see, we are His 'poem',[2] created in Christ Jesus for good works, which God prepared in advance in order that we should walk in them."[3]

We are not saved <u>by</u> good works, but we are indeed saved <u>for</u> good works; we do not do good works in order to be saved, but we must do good works because we are saved. James is very clear on this point; a faith that does not produce <u>cannot</u> save (James 2:14). Faith without works is dead (James 2:17, 20, 26). If you are alive, you do things. The plan of redemption is not just about getting us to heaven, it is about our contributing to Christ's Kingdom down here. To tell someone that all

---

to Heaven, you won't; God will certainly not take you there against your will. Sovereign Jesus puts it very plainly in John 15:6, "If anyone does not abide in me, he is cast out as a branch . . ." 'Abiding' is up to us; we are not forced to do it. If we choose not to, we are out. Note that you cannot be "cast out" unless you are first in.

[1] The Text has 'the' faith; the reference is to a specific Faith, presumably the body of truth that revolves around the person of Jesus.

[2] The English word 'poem' comes from the Greek word here, *poiema*, and is one of its meanings. Just as each poem is an individual creation of the poet, so we are individual creations, not produced by a production line in a factory.

[3] "Prepared in advance"—I imagine that this refers to God's moral code, the rules of conduct that everyone should follow (if everyone did, we would not need jails, rescue missions, etc.).

he has to do is 'believe in Jesus'[1] and 'bang', he goes to heaven, is a cruel falsehood. Anyone who has embraced the notion that he can be saved without working did not consult the Holy Spirit before doing so.

Substitutionism: The doctrine of 'substitution' holds that the Church totally replaces Israel as God's people and that never again will Israel receive any special attention from God. Adherents of substitution are obliged to ignore or mistreat the considerable percentage of the total biblical text that is prophecy relating to the end times. They must also reject plain biblical statements to the contrary, the equivalent of making the Holy Spirit out to be a liar (don't forget that to blaspheme the Holy Spirit is unforgivable). 1 Corinthians 10:32—"Give no offense, either to the Jews or to the Greeks or to the church of God." This text makes clear that during the Church Age there are three categories of people: Jews, non-Jews and the Church (made up of both Jews and non-Jews who are in Christ). Before Pentecost there were two categories: Jews and non-Jews. Substitutionists hold that after Pentecost there were still just two: Church and non-Church, wherein the Church replaced Israel. But it is not so; Israel still exists as a separate entity in God's plan. Chapters nine, ten and eleven of Romans go into some detail on this point. Romans 11:1-2—"I say then, has God cast away His people? Certainly not! . . . God has not cast away His people whom He foreknew."[2] Substitutionism contradicts this plain statement. At the end of Galatians 6:16 we find "the Israel of God". It is very common to hear this

---

[1] Unfortunately, most versions do not translate the Greek text adequately with this clause; the Text never has 'believe in Jesus', it always has 'believe into Jesus', the point being that one must change location from being outside to being inside. To believe into Jesus involves commitment. It is also wrong to use 'accept Jesus' rather than the biblical 'receive Jesus'—one 'accepts' from someone who is inferior in rank, from someone superior in rank one 'receives'. A 'Jesus' that you merely accept cannot save you, since he would be smaller than you are.

[2] Recall that this was written decades after Pentecost and the beginning of the Church.

phrase used as a synonym for the Church, but it is not. According to Greek grammar, the repetition of the preposition 'upon' in two phrases joined by 'and' makes clear that the objects of the prepositions refer to distinct entities. Hence, "the Israel of God" cannot be a reference to the Church, assuming that "those who conform to this rule" refers to those who are "in Christ Jesus". I take "the Israel of God" to refer to sincere, devout Israelites. Anyone who has embraced the notion of 'substitution' did not consult the Holy Spirit before doing so.

Idolatry: Idolatry is certainly sin, but in what sense is it a lie? Well, does it not replace something true with something false? 2 Timothy 3:16 says that Scripture is like God's breath. Psalm 138:2 says: "You have magnified your word above all your name", and a name represents the person. And John 17:17 says: "Your word is truth". To place church tradition above God's Word is a form of idolatry. To place a denomination's doctrinal 'package' above God's Word is a form of idolatry. To place a church leader's word above God's Word is a form of idolatry. Any of the above hinder spiritual growth, and may lead to ultimate loss, because they all contain falsehood. Anyone who has adopted any of those practices did not consult the Holy Spirit before so doing.

Cessationism: The doctrine of 'cessationism' is also false. Cessationism claims that the 'sign gifts' ceased when the NT Canon was completed, or when the last shovelful of dirt landed on the apostle John's grave.[1] The alleged scriptural basis for this is found in 1 Corinthians 13:8^b-10. These verses have received more than their fair share of mistreatment, partly because

---

[1] To affirm that the miraculous gifts ceased when the last shovelful of dirt fell on the apostle John's grave is an historical falsehood. Christians who lived during the second, third and fourth centuries, whose writings have come down to us, affirm that the gifts were still in use in their day. No 20th or 21st century Christian, who was not there, is competent to contradict them. Any 'cessationist' will have a stronghold of Satan in his mind on that subject, because he has embraced a lie. Any doctrine that derives from reaction against excesses and abuses gives victory to Satan. Any argument designed to justify lack of spiritual power cannot be right.

commentators have not linked verse 12 to them (seeing verse 11 as parenthetical). Consider verse 10: "But whenever the complete should come, <u>then</u> the 'in part' will be done away with." If we can pinpoint the 'then', we will have also pinpointed the 'when';[1] and verse 12 pinpoints the 'then'. When will we see 'face to face', when will we know as we are known? 1 John 3:2 has the answer: "Beloved, now we are children of God; and it has not yet been revealed what we shall be, but we know that when He is revealed, we shall be like Him, for we shall see Him as He is." It is at the return of Christ that we will see 'face to face', so "whenever the complete should come" refers to Christ at His second coming. The problem with 'prophecy', 'tongues' and our present 'knowledge' is that they are 'in part', but after the return of Christ we will have no further need for them. Since Christ has not returned yet, these 'in part' things are certainly still with us. The claim that 'the complete' refers to the completed New Testament canon does violence to the Text. If it had really been the Holy Spirit's purpose to tell us that the *charismata* would disappear in a few decades, He presumably could have done a much better job of it. Cessationists also generally choose to ignore all that the Bible says about warfare with Satan and his angels, and in consequence they spend their lives in spiritual defeat, producing much less for the Kingdom than they could and should. They do not even do the same things that Jesus did, much less the greater things (John 14:12). Those who use the idea of cessationism in an attempt to explain and justify their lack of spiritual power are being foolish, if not worse. Anyone who has embraced the notion of 'cessationism' did not consult the Holy Spirit before doing so.

Prosperity gospel: While there may be variations on the theme, the basic 'pitch' is to the hearer's selfish interests, while any serious commitment to Christ and His Kingdom is severely ignored. The emphasis is upon blessings, not the

---

[1] These two temporal adverbs work together.

Blessor, but the blessings are not free; to get them one must contribute heavily to the purveyors thereof. But Sovereign Jesus gave the definitive answer to this stupidity (or should it be 'perversity') in Matthew 6:24—"No one can serve two masters; for either he will hate the one and love the other, or else he will be loyal to the one and despise the other. You cannot serve God and mammon." 'Mammon' is sometimes translated as 'money', but it probably includes more than that, although money is central to it—a materialistic worldview. As Jesus said, someone serving mammon <u>cannot</u> be serving God at the same time. Anyone who wants to go to heaven must reject mammon. Anyone who has embraced any form of the prosperity 'gospel' did not consult the Holy Spirit before doing so.

The reader may well have tired of the refrain, "did not consult the Holy Spirit", but of course there is more to the story than that. Recall what Sovereign Jesus said to the Sadducees, "You are deceived, not knowing the Scripture nor the power of God" (Matthew 22:29). To be ignorant of both the Scripture and the power of God is to be spiritually bankrupt. Anyone who has embraced any of the falsehoods discussed above did not study the Scriptures sufficiently before doing so.

There are many, many more false things being taught in our churches,[1] but I consider that the short list discussed above is sufficient for my present purpose. **If all Christians were to throw off all of the eight cherished falsehoods discussed above, the world would see an outpouring of God's power unprecedented in human history.**[2] I am well aware that one painful consequence of taking Revelation 22:15 seriously is to consider the fate of people we loved and respected who passed on while embracing one or more of the falsehoods discussed above. That is a question that is in God's capable

---

[1] All false teaching has a certain destiny; as Sovereign Jesus said in Matthew 15:13, "Every plant that my heavenly Father did not plant will be uprooted."

[2] The outpouring in Moses' time was limited to a small area, as was the outpouring in Jesus' time. Today there are Christians all around the world.

hands. For ourselves, 2 Corinthians 10:12 comes to mind: "But they, measuring themselves by themselves, and comparing themselves among themselves, are not wise." We had best base what we are and do on God's Text.

I now move on to a topic that has received very little attention, so far as I know. It underscores the importance of promoting the love of the Truth.

Sins that lead to death

Consider 1 John 5:16-17—"If anyone should see his brother sinning a sin not leading to death, let him ask, and He will give him life, for those who do not sin unto death. There is sin leading to death; I am not saying that he should make request about that.[1] 17 All unrighteousness is sin, and there is sin not leading to death." It should be obvious that John is not contradicting Romans 6:23—"The wages of sin is death, but the gracious gift of God is eternal life in Christ Jesus our Lord." Obvious, because the shed blood of God's Lamb delivers the true believer from that death (the spiritual part). Anyone who dies outside of Christ is condemned by his sin.

But notice that John is talking about Christians; "If anyone should see his **brother** . . ." John is saying that for <u>believers</u> there are sins that lead to death and others that do not. A necessary question presents itself; is he talking about a premature physical death (everyone dies sooner or later), or is it spiritual death? John clearly says that a sin leading to death is irreversible, there is no point in praying about it, God will not grant life. A premature physical death is not all that serious if the person still goes to heaven. I think of two possible candidates:

---

[1] I suppose that a request about a sin leading to death simply will not be granted. In that case it does no harm to take a chance, in the hope that you can still make a difference. We ignore this area of truth to our peril.

1) God sometimes kills those who participate in the 'Lord's Table' in an unworthy manner (1 Corinthians 11:29-30). The use of the verb 'sleep' indicates that they do not lose their salvation; I believe it is reserved for the death of believers.

2) Acting in an irresponsible manner (presumptuously) with the intent of obliging God to work a miracle to save you. Satan tried to get Jesus to do this, but did not succeed (Matthew 4:5-7). People who attempt this generally die prematurely.

That said, however, I rather doubt that John was writing about physical death. Consider what is said in Hebrews 10:26-31.

> "Because, if we deliberately keep on sinning after having received the real knowledge of the Truth, there no longer remains a sacrifice for sins, 27 just a certain fearful anticipation of judgment and fierce fire that is ready to consume the hostiles. 28 Anyone who rejected Moses' law died without mercy on the testimony of two or three witnesses. 29 Of how much worse punishment, do you suppose, will he be deemed worthy who has trampled the Son of God under foot, who has regarded as unholy the blood of the covenant by which he was sanctified, and who has insulted the Spirit of grace? 30 For we know Him who said, '"Vengeance is up to me", says the Lord, "I will repay".' And again, 'The LORD will judge His people.' 31 It is a dreadful thing to fall into the hands of the Living God!"

Notice that verse 28 refers to a premature physical death, so the "how much worse punishment" in the next verse must refer to spiritual death. Notice further that from verses 19-25 (same chapter) it is clear that the author is addressing believers. This is confirmed by verse 26: "there no longer remains a sacrifice for sins" can only apply to someone who has already taken advantage of Christ's sacrifice. Notice also the 'after having received the real knowledge of the Truth' and 'by which he was sanctified' (verses 26 and 29).

I will now discuss some possible candidates for sin that condemns a Christian to spiritual death, that causes irreversible spiritual ruin.

1) Matthew 10:33 falls within the instructions that Jesus gave to the twelve apostles before He sent them out two by two: "Whoever denies me before men, him I will also deny before my Father who is in heaven". One possible reference is to a Christian who caves under persecution. Revelation 21:8 consigns 'the cowardly' to the Lake. A Christian who becomes a Mason (Freemason) is clearly condemned. During the initiation ritual the candidate is asked, "Where are you coming from?" and he must answer, "I am coming from darkness". Then he is asked, "What are you coming for?" and he must answer, "I am coming for light". At that moment the candidate has formally denied Jesus before men. Surely, because in John 8:12 Jesus affirmed: "I am the light of the world. He who follows me shall not walk in darkness, but have the light of life." Further, such people generally do so for material gain, thereby switching from Jesus to mammon (Mathew 6:24).

2) Hebrews 10:29 refers to someone "who has trampled the Son of God under foot", evidently referring to a virulent rejection by someone who was once a Christian (sanctified). I can think of several modern day examples. Some years ago there was a very successful Canadian evangelist named Charles Templeton. His evangelistic campaigns filled football stadiums; many thousands of people responded to his invitations; at least one hundred Canadian foreign missionaries received their call under his ministry. But then someone convinced him that he needed more 'culture', more 'sophistication', and he went to a liberal theological seminary in the USA to get it. When he returned he was blaspheming God and cursing Jesus Christ; as a television host his favorite sport was to ridicule the Christian faith. Years later he told someone that he "missed

Jesus", which indicates that he knew that he could not return (Hebrews 6:6).

3) And how about blasphemy against the Holy Spirit? Mark 3:30 defines it as ascribing to Satan something done by the Holy Spirit. Is it impossible for a Christian to do this? Have you never heard someone roundly condemn all things charismatic as being from Satan? I would suggest that to be careless on this point is not to be recommended—better safe than sorry.

Sins for which we may pray

Now then, having said all of that, what might be some sins about which we may, and should, pray? Well, how about the embracing of any one of the lies that I discussed above? If we can get a brother to abandon such a lie, we will be doing him a tremendous favor. I may not enjoy hearing a doctor tell me I have a life-threatening condition, but if I allow him to save me from a premature death, I will end up thanking him. Similarly, a brother probably will not appreciate being told that he has embraced a lie, but if he will stop and think, and change, he will end up thanking us. If we wish to save a brother from Revelation 22:15, it is a risk that we must take.

And then there is Hebrews 3:12-13. "Take care, brothers, that there not be a malignant heart of unbelief in any of you, so as to go away from[1] the living God; 13 rather, exhort yourselves every day, while it is called 'today', so that none of you be hardened through sin's deceitfulness." I rendered "exhort yourselves" because the pronoun here is reflexive, not recip-rocal, but being plural it probably includes both ideas—each one should exhort himself, but we should also exhort each other. If we are attentive and vigilant, there will be no end of

---

[1] Notice the direction. The term 'malignant' implies satanic influence.

things to pray about, things where we can still make a difference.

All of this relates to the purpose of this article in the following way. To promote truth it is necessary to expose and combat falsehood. The obvious place to start with our promoting is with individual believers, and the more so if they are leaders and teachers within their communities. Although they may reject us and our 'impertinence', Ezekiel 3:20-21 bears directly on this question.

> "Again, when a righteous man turns from his righteousness and commits iniquity, and I lay a stumbling block before him, he shall die; because you did not give him warning, he shall die in his sin, and his righteousness which he has done shall not be remembered; but his blood I will require at your hand. 21 Nevertheless if you warn the righteous man that the righteous should not sin, and he does not sin, he shall surely live because he took warning; also you will have delivered your soul."

When we see a brother going in the wrong direction, it is incumbent upon us to warn him, even if he rejects us. Notice again, "his righteousness which he has done shall not be remembered"—how terrible! Allow me to insist that the question before us is not merely theoretical or 'pedantic'; it is terribly practical, it is of the essence. In the words of Deuteronomy 32:47, "It is not a vain thing for you, because it is your life." It is certainly life for each one of us individually, but it is also life for the churches, and then it will be life for the world.

Conclusion

In conclusion, I will review the 'building blocks' that make up the article.

1) Why did I use 1 Peter 4:17? There was a time when I thought that I could not ask God to judge the world because He had not yet judged the Church. But I was mistaken. God has always judged both His 'house' and the world. More to the

point, the world is in the mess that it is because of failure in the Church. Further, judging is one thing, but correcting is another, and the correcting of the culture begins with, and depends on, the correcting of the churches. To correct a group of people begins with getting them to see where they are wrong, which involves denouncing error and showing a way out.

2) Why did I use Matthew 23:8-12 and John 4:23-24? I tried to trace a basic cause of failure in the Church—a correct solution depends upon a correct diagnosis. The Church became part of the problem, rather than being part of the solution, and it became part of the problem by rejecting the love of the Truth. The concept of 'bishop' (and in our day even of lowly pastors) as someone having the authority to control the spiritual life of others is an open rebellion against Sovereign Jesus, who forbids any such attitude or proceeding. But rebellion against God is Satan's 'thing', and will certainly call down God's judgment.

3) Why did I use 2 Thessalonians 2:9-12? This text gives the essence of the problem and the essence of the solution. The consequences of rejecting the love of the Truth are devastating, both to the Church and to the world. It is God Himself who sends the "active delusion"![1] And upon whom does He send it? Upon those who do not receive the love of the truth—it is a direct judgment upon their rejection of the truth.[2] And what is the purpose of the strong delusion?—the condemnation of those who do not believe the truth. The only solution that I can see is to promote the love of the Truth, which necessarily involves denouncing error.

---

[1] I understand 'active' in the sense of 'aggressive'; it is not a passive delusion that lies quietly in your brain, allowing you to go your merry way. It is aggressive; it tries to control how you think, and therefore what you do and who you are.

[2] Please note that it is not enough to merely 'accept' the truth; it is required that we love the truth. Satan tantalizes us with fame and fortune (on his terms, of course), so to love the truth requires determination; since the love in question is αγαπη, it involves an act of the will.

4) Why did I use Revelation 22:15? This text states plainly the terrible consequence of embracing a lie. To promote love of the Truth it is necessary to expose lies, and this is a necessary part of correcting the churches so they can be salt and light in the surrounding culture. A correct solution depends upon a correct diagnosis. Although they may reject us and our 'impertinence', Ezekiel 3:20-21 bears directly on this question. When we see a brother going in the wrong direction, it is incumbent upon us to warn him, even if he rejects us. Notice again, "his righteousness which he has done shall not be remembered" — how terrible!

5) Why did I use 1 John 5:16-17? This text emphasizes the possible terrible end result of being flippant about sin and the Truth. Anyone who is flippant about sin does not have the mind of Christ. We ignore to our peril the instruction given in Hebrews 3:12-13. And then there is 1 Corinthians 9:27—the Greek term *adokimos* is stronger than some commentaries would have you believe.

The future of the Church and of the world depends on the love of the Truth.

When is an 'apostle'?

The beginning

The basic meaning of the term is 'sent one'; in John 13:16 it is used in that way. But within the incipient Christian Church it came to have a specialized meaning: an office or function characterized by special spiritual authority. It began with the twelve disciples who were personally chosen by Jesus; after His resurrection they received the designation, 'apostles' (but the Iscariot had lost his place, leaving eleven). With the exception of four verses (Luke 11:49, John 13:16, Acts 14:4 and 14) I would say that all the occurrences of the term in the four Gospels and Acts, about thirty-five, refer to that group, as do Galatians 1:17, 19; 2 Peter 3:2; Jude 17 and Revelation 21:14.

The purpose of this note is to enquire whether the NT signals any further uses of the term.

Acts 1:13-26 records Peter's initiative to replace the Iscariot. The Text does not say that it was God's idea; and when they asked God to choose between the two candidates, they did not give Him the option of saying "neither". The Text affirms that Matthias was numbered with the Eleven apostles, but he receives no further mention.

Paul (erstwhile Saul of Tarsus) repeatedly refers to himself as an apostle: Romans 1:1, 11:13, 1 Corinthians 1:1, 9:1, 2, 15:9, 2 Corinthians 1:1, Galatians 1:1, Ephesians 1:1, Colossians 1:1, 1 Thessalonians 2:6, 1 Timothy 1:1, 2:7, 2 Timothy 1:1, 11 and Titus 1:1. Luke refers to Paul as an apostle in Acts 14:4 and 14. Jesus personally chose Paul, returning from Heaven to do so. Aside from the Eleven, Paul was the only one personally designated by Jesus.

Jesus Himself is called "the Apostle" of our confession in Hebrews 3:1. Peter calls himself an apostle in 1 Peter 1:1 and 2 Peter 1:1, but of course he is one of the Twelve. James, the half-brother of Jesus, became the 'big boss' in Jerusalem, and evidently was regarded as an apostle—1 Corinthians 15:7 and Galatians 1:19. Luke refers to Barnabas as an apostle: Acts 14:4 and 14. Paul seems to refer to Silvanus and Timothy as apostles: 1 Thessalonians 2:6. It is possible to interpret Romans 16:7 in the same way with reference to Andronicus and Junias. I believe those are the only ones who are actually named.

The discussion up to this point was necessary to provide the background for the questions that are the occasion for this study: did 'apostle' become an established office or function for the ongoing life of the Church, until the return of Christ, and if so, how is an apostle to be designated or recognized? It is my intention to analyze every verse where the term is used, and I will begin with those that may be purely historical, going on from those already dealt with.

In 2 Corinthians 11:5 and 12:11 Paul compares himself to 'the most eminent apostles', which must be limited to his contemporaries. 1 Corinthians 9:5 also must be limited to his contemporaries. 1 Corinthians 15:5 and 7 refer to physical appearances of the resurrected Jesus before His ascension (of necessity historical). 1 Corinthians 4:9 is a little different: "I think that God has displayed us, the apostles, last, as men condemned to death; for we have been made a spectacle to the world, both to angels and to men " (read also verses 10-13). In the context, Paul is complaining about the way he has been treated by some in Corinth, but in this verse he seems actually to be blaming <u>God</u> for the way he has been treated! I suppose that the use of the word 'last' would be a comparison with God's servants in prior ages. Paul is not talking about the future of the Church in this passage, and if we only had this text on the subject, we would have to conclude that to be an apostle was not a good thing.

And now we come to Luke 11:49-51, a most interesting text. "Therefore the wisdom of God also said, 'I will send them prophets and apostles, and some of them they will kill and persecute,' that the blood of all the prophets which was shed from the foundation of the world may be required of this generation, from the blood of Abel to the blood of Zechariah who perished between the altar and the temple. Yes, I say to you, it shall be required of this generation." Jesus is speaking, deriding the lawyers. His citation of "the wisdom of God" appears to have no match in the OT, so what was His meaning? In 1 Corinthians 1:24 Paul refers to Christ as 'the wisdom of God'. In Matthew 23:34 Jesus said, "I send you prophets", so here Jesus may be referring to Himself as 'the wisdom of God'. However that may be, if the "required of this generation" was fulfilled in 70 AD, as I suppose, then the 'apostles' here are also historical.

I will now consider the other places where the phrase 'prophets and apostles' occurs, albeit with the terms in reverse order: Ephesians 2:20 and 3:5, and Revelation 18:20.

Ephesians 2:19-22—"So then, you are no longer strangers and aliens, but fellow citizens with the saints and members of God's household, 20 built upon the foundation of the apostles and prophets, Jesus Christ Himself being the chief corner-stone; 21 in whom the whole building, being joined together, grows into a holy temple in the Lord; 22 in whom you also are being built together to become a habitation of God in spirit." The truth that Paul is expounding is that in Christ Gentiles join Jews as "fellow citizens" and "members of God's household", part of "the whole building". In what sense can that "building" be built upon "the foundation of the apostles and prophets"? Presumably "prophets" is short for the writings that make up the Old Testament Scriptures, or Canon. **The Faith is based on revealed Truth, not individual people**. Analogously, presumably "apostles" is short for the writings that make up the New Testament Scriptures, or Canon. Again, the Faith is based on revealed Truth, not individual people. Our "growing into a holy temple" (verse 21) depends upon the Holy Spirit and His Sword (not individuals whom God used). Note that Paul mentions the 'apostles' first. In any case, the 'apostles' here are historical.

Ephesians 3:1-7—"For this reason I, Paul, the prisoner of Christ Jesus on behalf of you Gentiles—2 surely you have heard of the dispensation of the grace of God that was given to me for you, 3 how that by revelation He made known to me the 'secret'[1] (as I have written briefly already, 4 with reference to which, when you read, you can understand my insight into Christ's secret), 5 which in different generations was not made known to the sons of men, as it has <u>now</u> been revealed by Spirit[2] to His holy apostles and prophets: 6 that the Gentiles

---

[1] I consider that 'secret' is a better rendering than 'mystery'. The truth about the Church is not all that mysterious; it just had not been explained before.

[2] There being no article with 'spirit', it could be either 'by Spirit' (used as a proper name) or 'in spirit' (referring to the manner). Both are true and legitimate, but I have chosen the first option in the translation.

are joint-heirs, of the same body, and fellow partakers of His promise in the Christ through the Gospel, 7 of which I became a servant according to the gift of God's grace, the gift given to me according to the outworking of His power." The use of "now" in verse 5 indicates that Paul is referring to the NT Canon. An apostle, upon receiving a revelation, would also function as a prophet, but people like Mark and Luke were prophets without being apostles. I take the 'apostles' here to be historical.

Revelation 18:20—"Rejoice over her, O heaven, yes you saints and apostles and prophets, because God has pronounced your judgment against her!"[1] Perhaps this verse should be connected to 18:6-7, and in that event the judgment was pronounced in faith. But just who are these apostles? I take it that "saints and apostles and prophets" is in apposition to "heaven", and in that event, whoever they are, they are already in heaven. It follows that this text is irrelevant to the occasion for this study.

The hinge

As a hinge to link the past to the present, I will now consider the two texts that refer to 'false apostles'; they are 2 Corinthians 11:13 and Revelation 2:2.

2 Corinthians 11:12-15—"Further, I will keep on doing what I do in order to cut off the opportunity from those who desire an opportunity to be considered equal with us in the things of which they boast. 13 Such men are really false apostles, deceitful workers, transforming themselves into 'apostles' of Christ.[2] 14 And no wonder, because Satan himself masquer-

---

[1] Instead of "saints and apostles", a small minority of the Greek manuscripts has 'holy apostles', as in AV and NKJV.

[2] There have always been those who want to 'get on the band-wagon', to get a free ride; who traffic in spiritual things for personal, temporal advantage. Since such people only do damage, Paul's desire to expose them stems from his concern for the Corinthians' welfare.

ades as an angel of light. 15 So it is no great thing if his servants also masquerade as ministers of righteousness, whose end will be according to their works." It is well to remember that neither Satan nor his servants are in the habit of appearing with horns and tails. Just because someone 'looks good' does not mean that he is. We need spiritual discernment at all times. Note that Paul affirms that such people are Satan's servants, and they evidently declared themselves to be 'apostles'. In our day we have a veritable plague of self-proclaimed 'apostles' (that I call 'apustles'); now whom do you suppose they are serving?

Going back to the title of this study, when is an apostle? In Galatians 1:1 Paul affirms that his apostleship was "not from men nor through a man", but through both the Father and the Son. Paul's apostleship did not depend upon human ordination or recognition. So what about apostleship today? In Romans 1:1 Paul says he is a "called apostle". I take the point to be that true apostles are not ordained by man; they are designated by God, who has a specific reason for doing so.[1] In the case of Paul, it was "to promote obedience of faith among all ethnic nations" (verse 5). Any genuine apostle will have a specific task to fulfil. Although God does not take back His gifts (Romans 11:29), a gift may be ignored (because the church's doctrine does not allow it), or neglected (1 Timothy 4:14), and hence aborted. Far worse, even an apostle that Jesus chose personally can be 'rejected' (1 Corinthians 9:27). If Paul recognized the possibility for himself, how about all the 'apustles' in our day?

In Revelation 2:2 the glorified Christ is writing to the church in Ephesus: "I know your works, yes the labor, and your endurance, and that you cannot stand those who are evil. And you have tested those who claim to be apostles and are not, and found them *to be* liars." The glorified Christ Himself declares

---

[1] It follows that there is no 'apostolic succession', since an apostle is not 'ordained' by men. There is only 'discipolic' succession.

that there are false apostles (and this at the close of the first century), and that the church in Ephesus knew how to test them.[1] Unfortunately, at least from my point of view, we are not told how they did it, the criteria that they used. There is one text that speaks of the 'signs of an apostle', 2 Corinthians 12:12. "Truly the apostolic signs were produced among you with all perseverance, by signs and wonders and miracles."

Both Stephen and Phillip, 'mere' deacons, performed miracles, but evidently that did not transform them into apostles. And then there are the words of Sovereign Jesus Himself in John 14:12. "Most assuredly I say to you,[2] the one believing into me, he too will do the works that I do; in fact he will do greater works than these,[3] because I am going to my Father."

This is a tremendous statement, and not a little disconcerting. Notice that the Lord said, "will do"; not 'maybe', 'perhaps', 'if you feel like it'; and certainly not 'if the doctrine of your church permits it'! If you believe you **will do!** The verb 'believe' is in the present tense, 2nd person singular; if you (sg)

---

[1] Is there not an implication here that there were also genuine apostles? If there were no such thing as an apostle, there could be no candidates, and hence no need for criteria. When John wrote this he was the last survivor of the Twelve (also Paul), and he himself would soon die.

[2] "Most assuredly" is actually "amen, amen"—rendered "verily, verily" in the AV. Only John registers the word as repeated, in the other Gospels it is just "amen". In the contemporary literature we have no example of anyone else using the word in this way. It seems that Jesus coined His own use, and the point seems to be to call attention to an important pronouncement: "Stop and listen!" Often it precedes a formal statement of doctrine or policy, as here.

[3] Well now, if we cast out demons, heal and perform miracles, is that not enough? Jesus wants more, He wants "greater things" than those just mentioned. Notice again that He said "will do", not maybe, perhaps, or if your church permits. But what could be 'greater' than miracles? This cannot refer to modern technology because in that event such 'greater things' would not have been available to the believers during the first 1900 years. Note that the key is in the Lord's final statement (in verse 12), "because I am going to my Father". Only if He won could He return to the Father, so He is here declaring His victory before the fact. It is on the basis of that victory that the 'greater things' can be performed. Just what are those 'greater' things? For my answer, see my outline, "Biblical Spiritual Warfare", available from www.prunch.org.

are believing you will do; it follows that if you are not doing, it is because you are not believing. 2 + 2 = 4. Doing what? "The works that I do." Well, Jesus preached the Gospel, He taught, He cast out demons, He healed all sorts and sizes of sickness and disease, He raised an occasional dead person, and He performed a variety of miracles (water to wine, walk on water, stop a storm instantaneously, transport a boat several miles instantaneously, multiply food, shrivel a tree—and He implied that the disciples should have stopped the storm and multiplied the food, and He stated that they could shrivel a tree [Peter actually took a few steps on water]). So how about us? The preaching and teaching we can handle, but what about the rest? I once heard the president of a certain Christian college affirm that this verse obviously could not mean what it says because it isn't happening! Well, in his own experience, and in that of his associates (cessationists all), I guess it isn't. But many people today cast out demons and heal, and I personally know someone who has raised a dead person. Miracles are also happening. So how about me? And you? But to get back to the 'signs of an apostle', if all of us are supposed to be producing miracles, that does not make us all apostles, so there must be further criteria. (Please notice the 'further', I am not denying the 'signs'.)

I suggest that we must consider the matter of spiritual authority, and I begin with 2 Corinthians 10:8 and 13:10. 10:8 reads like this: "Now even if I boast a little to excess about our authority (which the Lord gave us for building up, not to tear you down), . . ." 13:10 reads like this: "This is why I write these things while absent, so that when present I may not have to deal harshly, according to the authority that the Lord gave me, for building up and not tearing down." In both verses Paul states that the authority is for building up, not tearing down, although his mention of harsh dealing indicates that such may be included in the process, as circumstance may require. (In fact, on at least two occasions, Paul actually turned someone over to Satan!—1 Corinthians 5:5 and 1 Timothy 1:20.)

Is this not what we are to understand from 1 Timothy 1:3? "You recall that I urged you to remain in Ephesus, when I went into Macedonia, in order that you should command certain persons to stop teaching a different doctrine . . ." Now the church was well established in Ephesus, yet Timothy had authority to command; I suppose that Paul designated him as his deputy. And what about 1 Timothy 5:19-20? "Do not entertain an accusation against an elder except on the basis of two or three witnesses. 20 Those who are sinning rebuke publicly, so that the rest also may be in fear." Evidently Timothy had authority over the elders, being competent to rebuke them publicly.

Now consider Jeremiah 1:10—"See, I have this day set you over the nations and over the kingdoms, to root out and to pull down, to destroy and to throw down, to build and to plant." Of course this was before the Church, but there is a principle here that remains valid. If you plan to build on a site that is covered with ruins and rubble, where must you start? You must remove the wreckage. If God sent you to the church in Laodicea (Revelation 3:14-19), to try to straighten it out, where would you have to start? You might have to depose the leaders, as well as denounce the error. Presumably, also, you would have to be able to establish your authority over them. In Timothy's case, Paul presumably took care of that.

Something similar happened with Titus; consider: "I left you in Crete for this reason, that you should set in order the things that were lacking and appoint elders in every town, as I directed you" (1:5). "Because there really are lots of rebels, loudmouths and deceivers, especially those of the circumcision group, who must be silenced" (1:10-11). "Speak these things, whether you exhort or reprove, with all authority" (2:15). If Titus was to appoint elders, he evidently had authority over them. And to silence 'rebels' evidently requires authority. Now then, does anyone imagine that such situations, requiring apostolic authority, ceased to exist in 100 AD? History records no lack of such situations, and far worse, down through the centuries and millennia. In our day the degree of perversity in the churches is such that I don't know how God can stand the stench! We desperately need people with apostolic authority who are prepared to function.

But to get back to the Text, consider Ephesians 4:11-13. "Yes, He Himself gave some to be apostles, some to be prophets, some to be evangelists, and some to be pastors and teachers,[1]

---

[1] One might imagine that this list follows the chronological sequence of the several ministries. An apostle introduces the Gospel into an area or context; a prophet gets the people's attention and an evangelist urges them to believe; but once people are regenerated then pastors and teachers come to the fore—they are the ones who equip the saints. However, in practice, especially in a pioneer missionary situation, there are seldom that many people around. The missionary preaches the Gospel and it is up to him to teach the first converts; he is alone. A pioneer missionary, the first one to introduce the Gospel to an ethnic group or area, has an apostolic function (whether or not he himself is an apostle). But he must also function as an evangelist and as a teacher (whether or not he has those gifts).

However, most of us live and work where there are established, functioning congregations. So what would be the function of an apostle within an established, functioning congregation? If he lives and worships in that community, probably none at all, in that specific capacity—he might function as a teacher or a prophet. In a country, or area, where there is no more pioneer missionary work to be done, the exercise of the apostolic function would be itinerant, acting as God's special emissary, an official intervener, for disciplinary and correctional purposes.

I will take up evangelist next; what would his function be within an established congregation? Well, can you evangelize someone who is already regenerated? Evidently the function of an evangelist is directed to unbelievers, who should not be members of the congregation (although some often are). Of course an evangelist might also function as a pastor or teacher. A truly gifted evangelist will function beyond the limits of a local congregation.

As for the prophetic function, I will address the question of supernatural revelation of information not available through existing channels. (1 Corinthians 14:3 speaks of 'edification', 'exhortation' and 'comfort' as coming from a prophet, but I will not take up such activity here.) We understand that the Canon of Scripture is closed; God is no longer giving written revelation that is of general or universal application. But that does not mean that God no longer speaks into specific situations. Divine guidance is a type of prophecy; He is giving information not otherwise available. I myself have been contemplated with a prophecy delivered by someone who had no idea who I was, and not in the context of a local congrega-

12 for the equipping of the saints into the work of the ministry, so as to build up the body of Christ, 13 until we all attain into the unity of the faith and of the real knowledge of the Son of God, into a complete man, into the resulting full stature of Christ." If verses 12 and 13 are still being worked on, then the apostles, etc. are still necessary. Verse 13 emphasizes the truth in verse 12—every believer is supposed to grow into full stature. Just because we do not reach a goal does not invalidate that goal. I would say that one of the principal causes for the lamentable spiritual condition of most churches is the total lack of the apostolic function among us—itinerant, acting as God's special emissary, an official intervener, for disciplinary and correctional purposes. The idea of Christian or ministerial 'ethics', where one must not criticize a neighbor, is clearly designed to silence any prophetic or apostolic voice. It is designed to protect error.

Now consider 1 Corinthians 12:27-31. "Now you are the body of Christ, and members individually. 28 And those whom God has appointed in the Church are: first apostles, second prophets, third teachers; after that miracles, then presents of healings, helps, administrations, kinds of languages. 29 All are not apostles, are they? All are not prophets, are they? All are not teachers, are they? All are not miracle workers, are they? 30 All do not have presents of healings, do they? All do not speak

---

tion. The function of a true prophet cannot be limited to one congregation. Indeed, God may use a prophet at city, state or country level. Our world desperately needs prophetic voices.

A teacher will normally reside in a specific community, but his ministry may range beyond it. A pastor's function is local, just as he is chosen and ordained locally. It is simply a fact of life that someone with a shepherd's heart is not necessarily a good teacher, and an honest to goodness teacher often lacks a shepherd's heart. The functions are supposed to be complementary, and the object is to get all true believers involved in the work of the ministry. Life in Christ is not a spectator sport!

languages, do they? All do not interpret, do they?[1] 31 But earnestly desire the best gifts."

It should be observed that the terminology here is clearly hierarchical: '1st, 2nd, 3rd, then, then, . . .' (similar lists in other places lack this terminology) [the Kingdom of God is not a democracy]. Next, if God has appointed these functions, there must be a good reason for them, and to deliberately exclude any of them is to go against God. Here in Brazil, with a few exceptions, the churches have no place for a true teacher; they simply are not allowed. The consequences are not pretty.

Presumably even the most ardent 'cessationist' will grant that "teachers", "helps" and "administrations" are still around. But this letter was written around 55 AD, well into the Church Age, therefore. Why would God "appoint in the Church" things that would be extinguished in a few decades. If miracles come "after" teachers, how can miracles be gone if teachers are still here? We have the command to "earnestly desire the best gifts", so which ones are the best? Presumably those at the top of the hierarchical list. Why would God command us to earnestly desire a gift like apostleship, if He was going to ex-

---

[1] The Greek grammar of verses 29 and 30 is plain: no gift is given to everybody—not everyone is an apostle and not everyone speaks languages. Those churches that teach that speaking in tongues is the <u>necessary</u> sign of being 'baptized in the Spirit' (and until you are 'baptized' you are a 2nd class citizen, if a citizen at all), have done untold damage to their people. Since the Holy Spirit simply does not give 'tongues' to everybody, those who do not get it are out in the cold. But the social pressure is intolerable, so many end up faking it. Since many of the leaders are also faking it, the social problem is solved; the person is 'in'. But since Satan is the source of all lies, someone who fakes it is living a lie and invites Satan into his life. I have been in many Pentecostal, neo-pentecostal, charismatic, whatever churches and have heard thousands of people 'speaking in tongues'—a large majority were faking it, while a few were speaking a real language, but under demonic control. (I am a linguist, PhD, and can tell when I am listening to a real language, even though I don't understand it, because real language has structure. To know whether or not a language is demonic requires spiritual discernment.) A church that teaches a lie invites Satan into the church, and he does not hesitate. Of course some had the genuine gift.

tinguish it before the end of the first century? In such an event the command would be meaningless for the last 1900 years!

The present

Somewhere along the line, I heard this: 'the status quo' is Latin for 'the mess we're in'. Whether Latin or English, I imagine that most of us would agree that the world is in a bad way, and that is at least partly because the Church is in a bad way. By and large, 'Christians' have ceased to be salt and light in the surrounding culture (Matthew 5:13-16); they are part of the problem, rather than part of the solution. As I have already opined, the lamentable spiritual condition of most churches is a direct result of the total lack of the apostolic function among us. It would appear that that 'lack' began early on.

In the writings of the 'church fathers' that have come down to us, there appears to be no mention of 'apostles' after the first century. Already in the second century, the concept of a 'bishop' came into being, an elder having authority over other elders in a given area—so a 'bishop' could exercise the apostolic function within his area (but all too often the bishop became part of the problem, since bishops were not chosen by God). It did not take long before the 'bishop of Rome' started to claim authority over other 'bishops', and then there were archbishops, and so on. If I am correct in defining the apostolic function as someone 'acting as God's special emissary, an official intervener, for disciplinary and correctional purposes', and if there has been a general lack of this function for 1900 years, then we should not be surprised at the 'status quo'.

In our day we have denominations, defined by different doctrinal and procedural 'packages', and there is no end of splitting within such denominations. Here in Brazil we have at least five 'Baptist' denominations, four 'Presbyterian' ones, and no end of 'Assemblies of God', plus any number of 'independent' ones. We have literally thousands of self-proclaimed 'apustles'; everywhere you turn there is an 'apostolic ministry'. It is a generalized ego trip; no one wants to be left behind, or to appear inferior to his neighbor. They are building private empires, and fleecing the sheep in the process. I am not aware of any theological seminary in this country that teaches the students how to study the Bible, and much less how to expound it; expository preaching is almost nonexistent. In consequence, the variety of abject stupidities promulgated from the pulpits appears to be without end, doing ever increasing damage to the hearers. I am not aware of any denomination here where the biblical Text has objective authority.

But it gets worse. We actually have self-proclaimed 'apostles' who pontificate like this: "I am an apostle on a level with Peter or Paul, so I can disagree with them; I can change what the Bible says." And they do; they reject plain biblical teaching and impose their own ideas on their flocks. It should be evident to any true subject of Sovereign Jesus that all such 'apustles' are in the service of Satan. We have already noted Ephesians 2:20, God's household is "built upon the foundation of the apostles and prophets, Jesus Christ Himself being the chief cornerstone." 1 Corinthians 3:11 says that "no one can lay any foundation other than what is laid, which is Jesus Christ." And Revelation 21:14 informs us that the foundations of the New Jerusalem are "the twelve apostles of the Lamb". No pipsqueak 'apustle' of our day is competent to alter the Sacred Text—they obviously do not believe what the glorified Christ said in Revelation 22:18-19.

To someone who intends to be totally committed to Christ and His Kingdom, the following question is obvious and necessary: What can be done to remedy, to correct the calamitous reality I have described? We must cry out to God to raise up true apostles; but this raises another question: How is an apostle to be recognized, and how can he establish his authority so as to be able to bring about necessary changes in actual situations? I see only one way, the use of supernatural power; and that power must be used to clear out wreckage before it can be used to build. I see a difference between a prophet and an apostle in this connection: a prophet warns; an apostle inflicts. In Acts 5 Peter simply executed Ananias and Sapphira, without warning and without chance for repentance. In Acts 13 Paul inflicted blindness on the sorcerer Elymas, again without ado.

It should be obvious that anyone who starts functioning in this way will promptly be declared to be 'public enemy number one'. Any and all leaders who are serving Satan will do all in their power to eliminate a true apostle, because of the threat to them personally and to the perverse structures they have created and maintained. It will be all out war. I am reminded of 1 Corinthians 4:11-13—"To this very hour we go hungry and thirsty; we are poorly dressed, brutally treated, and wander homeless; 12 yes, we labor, working with our own hands. Upon being reviled, we bless; upon being persecuted, we endure it; 13 upon being slandered, we exhort. We have been made as the refuse of the world, the off-scouring of whatever, to this moment." Well now, how many of the plague of self-styled 'apostles' in our day would maintain their pretentions if they had to experience the conditions described above? They would run and hide.

We need to understand what Paul is saying here. To be looked down on and criticized by believers among whom one has labored is one thing. Local people with personal ambition know how to do that. For <u>God</u> to make us "as the refuse of the world" is something very different. How should we understand this? If we insist on proclaiming a 'gospel' that the world considers to be stupid, abject foolishness, we will certainly be ridiculed. But if we insist on biblical values that the world has declared to be 'hate crimes', we will certainly be hated and persecuted, treated as refuse. The choice of Hebrews 13:13 is upon us: "So then, let us go out to Him, outside the camp, bearing His disgrace." The above applies to any true subject of Sovereign Jesus, but any true apostle will be the target of the total fury of the religious leaders as well. In short, to be an apostle is not for the fainthearted.

And now please consider 2 Thessalonians 2:8-12, noting especially verses 10 and 11. "And then the lawless one will be revealed, whom the Lord will consume with the breath of His mouth and abolish by the splendor of His coming; 9 that one's coming is according to the working of Satan with all power and signs and lying wonders, 10 and with all wicked deception among those who are wasting themselves, because they did not receive the love of the truth[1] so that they might be saved.[2] 11 Yes, because of this God will send them an active delusion so that they will believe the lie[3] 12 and so that all may be condemned who have not believed the truth but have taken pleasure in wickedness."[4] Notice the sequence: first they reject the love of the truth; it is as a consequence of that choice that God sends the delusion. The implication is that there is a point of no return; God sends the delusion so that they may be condemned. The only intelligent choice is to embrace the truth!

Consider with me the consequences of the facts enunciated in verses 10-12 for a whole nation, like Brazil, where I now live. We have many thousands of local churches that call them-

---

[1] The use of the verb 'receive' clearly implies an act of volition on their part; that love was offered or made available to them but they did not want it; they wanted to be able to lie and to entertain lies told by others. But the consequences of such a choice are terrible; they turned their back on salvation.

[2] Since there are only two spiritual kingdoms in this world, that of Sovereign Jesus and that of Satan, "those who are wasting themselves", in this text, are still in Satan's kingdom and therefore wide open to his "wicked deception". The Text states plainly that they are wasting themselves "because they did not receive the love of the truth so that they might be saved". They are not saved.

[3] Perhaps "the lie" is best illustrated in our day by the theory of evolution: 'There is no Creator'—so there will not be any accounting; so you can do what you feel like. How terrible will be the awakening!

[4] "Taking pleasure in wickedness" involves rejecting the Truth of a moral Creator who will demand an accounting, or even overt rebellion against that Creator (like Lucifer/Satan).

selves Christian. But I know of almost none that could be characterized as 'loving the truth'. No one wants a Bible with objective authority. Humanistic, relativistic, materialistic values have taken over the churches. Biblical values are no longer acceptable. In consequence, Satan has control of the government, of education, of health services, of commerce, of the entertainment industry, in short, of the whole culture. The churches that have rejected biblical values are part of the problem—since they have rejected "the love of the truth", they have been taken over by "active delusion".

Note that God Himself sends that delusion with the declared objective of condemning all those who believed the lie. If God Himself visits "active delusion" upon a whole country, what possible escape is there? The only possible 'medicine' is "the love of the truth". Those of us who consider ourselves to be true subjects of Sovereign Jesus need to appeal to Him to show us how to promote the love of the truth to the churches and to the society at large. Here in Brazil it may be too late, but if God's grace still offers us a window of opportunity, we must devote ourselves to promoting the love of the truth by all possible means. I imagine that the most effective means would be the exercise of the apostolic function, and that at more than one level. I am thinking of the following: local congregations, whole denominations, and the various levels of civil government.

Dear God, please send us apostles!

The Root Cause of the Continuous Defection from Biblical Infallibility and Consequent Objective Authority

That part of the academic world that deals with the biblical Text, including those who call themselves 'evangelical', is dominated by the notion that the original wording is lost, in the sense that no one knows for sure what it is, or was (if indeed it ever existed as an Autograph).[1] That notion is basic to all that is taught in the area of New Testament (NT) textual criticism in most schools. In an attempt to understand where that notion came from, I will sketch a bit of relevant history.

A Bit of Relevant History

The discipline of NT textual criticism, as we know it, is basically a 'child' of Western Europe and its colonies; the Eastern Orthodox Churches have generally not been involved. (They have always known that the true NT Text lies within the Byzantine tradition.) In the year 1500 the Christianity of Western Europe was dominated by the Roman Catholic Church, whose pope claimed the exclusive right to interpret Scripture. That Scripture was the Latin Vulgate, which the laity was not allowed to read. Martin Luther's ninety-five theses were posted in 1517. Was it mere chance that the first printed Greek Text of the NT was published the year before? As the Protestant Reformation advanced, it was declared that the authority of Scripture exceeded that of the pope, and that every believer had the right to read and interpret the Scriptures for himself. The authority of the Latin Vulgate was also challenged, since the NT was written in Greek. Of course the Vatican library held many Greek MSS, no two of which were identical (at least in the Gospels), so the Roman Church challenged the authenticity of the Greek Text.[2] In short, the Roman Church forced the Reformation to come to grips with textual variation among the Greek MSS. But they did not know how to go about it, because

---

[1] There are those who like to argue that none of the books was written by its stated author, that they are forgeries, the result of editorial activity spread over decades (if not centuries) of time. Of course they were not there, and do not know what actually happened, but that does not deter them from pontificating.

[2] Probably no two MSS of the Latin Vulgate are identical either, but that was not the issue. Indeed, so far as I know, there is no way to establish what may have been the original wording of the Latin Vulgate, in every detail.

this was a new field of study and <u>they simply were not in pos-</u><u>session of a sufficient proportion of the relevant evidence.</u>[1] (They probably didn't even know that the Mt. Athos peninsula, with its twenty monasteries, existed.)

In 1500 the Roman Catholic Establishment was corrupt, moral-ly bankrupt, and discredited among thinking people. The Age of Reason and humanism were coming to the fore. More and more people were deciding that they could do better without the god of the Roman Establishment. The new imagined free-dom from supernatural supervision was intoxicating, and many had no interest in accepting the authority of Scripture (*sola Scriptura*). Further, it would be naive in the extreme to exclude the supernatural from consideration, and not allow for satanic activity behind the scenes. Consider Ephesians 2:2—"in which you once walked, according to the Aeon of this world, the ruler of the domain of the air, the spirit who is now at work in the sons of the disobedience." Strictly speaking, the Text has "according to the Aeon of this world, according to the ruler of the domain of the air"—the phrases are parallel, so 'Aeon' and 'ruler' have the same referent, a specific person or being. This spirit is presently at work (present tense) in 'the sons of the disobedience'. 'Sons' of something are those char-acterized by that something, and the something in this case is 'the' disobedience (the Text has the definite article)—a con-tinuation of the original rebellion against the Sovereign of the universe.[2] 'Sons of the disobedience' joined the attack against

---

[1] Family 35 (for an introduction to this family please see chapter seven of my book, *The Identity of the New Testament Text IV*), being by far the largest and most co-hesive group of MSS with a demonstrable archetype, was poorly represented in the libraries of Western Europe. For that matter, very few MSS of whatever text-type had been sufficiently collated to allow for any tracing of the transmissional history. Worse, the lack of complete collations made it impossible to refute an erroneous hypothesis within a reasonable timeframe.

[2] Anyone in rebellion against the Creator is under satanic influence, direct or indi-rect (in most cases a demon acts as Satan's agent, when something more than the influence of the surrounding culture is required—almost all human cultures have ingredients of satanic provenance; this includes the academic culture). Any-

Scripture. The so-called 'higher criticism' denied divine inspiration altogether.[1] Others used the textual variation to argue that in any case the original wording was 'lost', there being no objective way to determine what it may have been (unfortunately, no one was able to perceive such a way at that time).

The uncritical assumption that 'oldest equals best' was an important factor, and became increasingly so as earlier uncials came to light.[2] Both Codex Vaticanus and Codex Bezae were available early on, and they have thousands of disagreements between themselves, just in the Gospels (in Acts, Bezae is wild almost beyond belief). **If** 'oldest equals best', and the oldest MSS are in constant and massive disagreement between/ among themselves, then the recovery of a lost text becomes hopeless. Did you get that? **Hopeless, totally hopeless**! However, I have argued (and continue to do so) that 'oldest equals worst', and that changes the picture radically. The benchmark work on this subject is Herman C. Hoskier's *Codex B and its Allies: A Study and an Indictment* (2 vols.; London: Bernard Quaritch, 1914). The first volume (some 500 pages) contains a detailed and careful discussion of hundreds of obvious errors in Codex B; the second (some 400 pages) contains the same for Codex Aleph. He affirms that in the Gospels alone these two MSS differ well over 3,000 times, which number does not include minor errors such as spelling (II, 1). [Had he tabulated

---

one in rebellion against the Creator will also have strongholds of Satan in his mind. Since Satan is the 'father' of lies (John 8:44), anytime you embrace a lie you invite him into your mind—this applies to any of his sophistries (2 Corinthians 10:5) currently in vogue, such as materialism, humanism, relativism, Marxism, Freudianism, Hortianism, etc.

[1] The Darwinian theory appeared to be made to order for those who wished to get rid of a Creator, or any superior Authority, who might require an accounting. The 'higher criticism' served the purpose of getting rid of an authoritative Revelation, that might be used to require an accounting. Rebels don't like to be held accountable.

[2] Appeal was made to the analogy of a stream, where the purest water would presumably be that closest to the source. But with reference to NT manuscripts the analogy is fallacious, and becomes a sophistry.

all differences, the total would doubtless increase by several hundreds.] Well now, simple logic demands that one or the other has to be wrong those 3,000+ times; they cannot both be right, quite apart from the times when they are <u>both</u> wrong. **No amount of subjective preference can obscure the fact that they are poor copies, objectively so.**[1] They were so bad that no one could stand to use them, and so they survived physically (but had no 'children', since no one wanted to copy them).

Since everyone is influenced (not necessarily controlled) by his milieu, this was also true of the Reformers. In part (at least) the Reformation was a 'child' of the Renaissance, with its emphasis on reason. Recall that on trial Luther said he could only recant if convinced by Scripture <u>and reason</u>. So far so good, but many did not want Scripture, and that left only reason. Further, since reason cannot explain or deal with the supernatural, those who emphasize reason are generally unfriendly toward the supernatural. [To this day the so-called historic or traditional Protestant denominations have trouble dealing with the supernatural.]

Before Adolf Deissmann published his *Light from the Ancient East* (1910), (being a translation of *Licht vom Osten*, 1908),

---

[1] John William Burgon personally collated what in his day were 'the five old uncials' (ℵ,A,B,C,D). Throughout his works he repeatedly calls attention to the *concordia discors*, the prevailing confusion and disagreement, that the early uncials display among themselves. Luke 11:2-4 offers one example.

> "The five Old Uncials" (ℵABCD) falsify the Lord's Prayer as given by St. Luke in no less than forty-five words. But so little do they agree among themselves, that they throw themselves into six different combinations in their departures from the Traditional Text; and yet they are never able to agree among themselves as to one single various reading: while only once are more than two of them observed to stand together, and their grand point of union is no less than an omission of the article. Such is their eccentric tendency, that in respect of thirty-two out of the whole forty-five words they bear in turn solitary evidence. (*The Traditional Text of the Holy Gospels Vindicated and Established*. Arranged, completed, and edited by Edward Miller. London: George Bell and Sons, 1896, p. 84.)

Yes indeed, <u>oldest equals worst</u>. For more on this subject, please see pages 130-36 in *The Identity of the New Testament Text IV*.

wherein he demonstrated that Koine Greek was the *lingua franca* in Jesus' day, there even being a published grammar explaining its rules, only classical Greek was taught in the universities. But the NT was written in Koine. Before Deissmann's benchmark work, there were two positions on the NT Greek: 1) it was a debased form of classical Greek, or 2) it was a 'Holy Ghost' Greek, invented for the NT. The second option was held mainly by pietists; the academic world preferred the first, which raised the natural question: if God were going to inspire a NT, why would He not do it in 'decent' Greek? The prevailing idea that Koine was bad Greek predisposed many against the NT.

All of this placed the defenders of an inspired Greek Bible on the defensive, with the very real problem of deciding where best to set up a perimeter they could defend. Given the prevailing ignorance concerning the relevant evidence, their best choice appeared to be an appeal to Divine Providence. God providentially chose the TR, so that was the text to be used (the 'traditional' text).[1] I would say that Divine Providence was indeed at work, because the TR is a good Text, far better than the eclectic one currently in vogue.

To all appearances Satan was winning the day, but he still had a problem: the main Protestant versions (in German, English, Spanish, etc.) were all based on the *Textus Receptus*, as were doctrinal statements and 'prayer books'. Enter F.J.A. Hort, a quintessential 'son of the disobedience'. Hort did not believe in the divine inspiration of the Bible, nor in the divinity of Jesus Christ. Since he embraced the Darwinian theory as soon as it appeared, he presumably did not believe in God.[2] His theory

---

[1] Please note that I am not criticizing Burgon and others; they did what they could, given the information available to them. They knew that the Hortian theory and resultant Greek text could not be right.

[2] For documentation of all this, and a good deal more besides, in Hort's own words, please see the biography written by his son. A.F. Hort, *Life and Letters of Fenton John Anthony Hort* (2 vols.; London: Macmillan and Co. Ltd., 1896). The son made heavy use of the father's plentiful correspondence, whom he admired. (In those

of NT textual criticism, published in 1881,[1] was based squarely on the presuppositions that the NT was not inspired, that no special care was afforded it in the early decades, and that in consequence the original wording was lost—lost beyond recovery, at least by objective means. His theory swept the academic world and continues to dominate the discipline to this day.[2]

But just how was it that the Hortian theory was able to take over the Greek departments of the conservative schools in North America? The answer begins with the onslaught of liberal theology upon the Protestant churches of that continent at the beginning of the twentieth century. The great champion of the divine inspiration of Scripture was Benjamin B. Warfield, a Presbyterian. His defense of inspiration is so good that it is difficult to improve it. Somewhere along the line,

---

days a two-volume 'Life', as opposed to a one-volume 'Biography', was a posthumous status symbol, albeit of little consequence to the departed.) Many of my readers were taught, as was I, that one must not question/judge someone else's motives. But wait just a minute; where did such an idea come from? It certainly did not come from God, who expects the spiritual person to evaluate everything (1 Corinthians 2:15). Since there are only two spiritual kingdoms in this world (Matthew 6:24, 12:30; Luke 11:23, 16:13), then the idea comes from the other side. By eliminating motive, one also eliminates presupposition, which is something that God would never do, since presupposition governs interpretation (Matthew 22:29, Mark 12:24). Which is why we should always expect a true scholar to state his presuppositions. I have repeatedly stated mine, but here they are again: 1) The Sovereign Creator of the universe exists; 2) He delivered a written revelation to the human race; 3) He has preserved that revelation intact to this day.

[1] B.F. Westcott and F.J.A. Hort, *The New Testament in the Original Greek* (2 Vols.; London: Macmillan and Co., 1881). The second volume explains the theory, and is generally understood to be Hort's work.

[2] For a thorough discussion of that theory, please see chapters 3 and 4 in *Identity IV*. Chapters 3 and 4 in *Identity IV* are little different from what they were in 1977. It has been over thirty-five years, and so far as I know no one has refuted my dismantling of Hort's theory. It has not been for lack of desire. Nowadays one frequently hears the argument that to criticize Hort is to flay a dead horse, since now the ruling paradigm is eclecticism (whether 'reasoned' or 'rigorous'). But eclecticism is based squarely on the same false presuppositions, and is therefore equally wrong.

however, he decided to go to Germany to study; I believe it was at Tubingen. When he returned, he was thanking God for having raised up Westcott and Hort to restore the text of the New Testament (think about the implication of 'restore'). One of his students, Archibald T. Robertson, a Baptist, followed Warfield's lead. The prestige of those two men was so great that their view swept the theological schools of the continent. I solicit the patience of the reader while I try to diagnose what happened to Warfield in Tubingen.

At Tubingen Warfield found himself among enemies of an inspired Bible. Now he was a champion of divine inspiration, but for an inspired text to have objective authority today, it must have been preserved.[1] Given the prevailing ignorance concerning the relevant evidence at that time, Warfield was simply not able to defend preservation in objective terms (and neither was anyone else—this is crucial to understanding what happened). He was faced with the fact of widespread variation between and among the extant Greek manuscripts. Even worse—far worse—was the presupposition that 'oldest equals best', because the oldest manuscripts are hopelessly at odds among themselves. For example: the two great early codices, Vaticanus and Sinaiticus, differ between themselves well over 3,000 times just in the four Gospels. Well now, they cannot both be right; one or the other **has** to be wrong, quite apart from the places where they are both wrong. So what was poor Warfield to do? Enter Westcott and Hort. Hort claimed that as a result of their work only a thousandth part of the NT text could be considered to be in doubt, and this was joyfully received by the rank and file, since it seemed to provide assurance about the reliability of that text—however, of course,

---

[1] This has always been a favorite argument with enemies of inspiration; it goes like this: "If God had inspired a text, He would have preserved it (or else why bother inspiring). He did not preserve the NT; therefore He did not inspire it." I confess that I am inclined to agree with that logical connection, except that I am prepared to turn the tables. I believe I can demonstrate that God did in fact preserve the NT Text; therefore He must have inspired it!

that claim applied only to the W-H text (probably the worst published NT in existence to this day, so the claim was false).[1] Warfield grasped at this like a drowning man grasps at a straw, thereby doing serious damage to North American Evangelicalism.[2]

Why the Defection Is Continuous

To understand the full impact of the onslaught of liberal theology, one must take account of the milieu. Reason has always been important to the historic or traditional Protestant denominations. In consequence, academic respectability has always been important to their graduate schools of theology. The difficulty resides in the following circumstance: for at least two centuries academia has been dominated by Satan, and so the terms of 'respectability' are dictated by him. Those terms include 'publish or perish', but of course he controls the technical journals. Since he is the father of lies (John 8:44), anyone who wished to tell the whole truth has always had a hard time getting an article published, no matter how good it was. To get an article published one had to toe the party line. 'Taking

---

[1] I would say that their text is mistaken with reference to 10% of the words—the Greek NT has roughly 140,000 words, so the W-H text is mistaken with reference to 14,000 of them. I would say that the so-called 'critical' (read 'eclectic') text currently in vogue is 'only' off with reference to some 12,000, an improvement (small though it be). And just by the way, how wise is it to use a NT prepared by a servant (or servants) of Satan? (On the other hand, I claim that God has preserved the original wording to such an extent that we can, and do, know what it is.)

[2] However, I should not be unduly harsh in my criticism of Warfield; no one else knew what to do either. The cruel fact was that the relevant evidence did not exist in usable form at that time. (It follows that any defense of divine preservation at that time had to be based upon faith, faith that God would produce the evidence in His time.) Part of the damage produced by Hort's theory was its disdain for the vast bulk of later manuscripts—they were not worth the bother to collate and study. Since it is precisely those disdained MSS that furnish the necessary evidence, that soporific effect of Hort's theory delayed the availability of the relevant evidence for a century. I remember one day in class (in 1957), the professor filled his lungs and proclaimed with gusto, "Gentlemen, where B and Aleph agree, you have the original." The poor man had obviously never read Herman C. Hoskier's *Codex B and its Allies: A Study and an Indictment* (published in 1914).

account of the existing literature' obliges one to waste a great deal of time reading the nonsense produced by Satan's servants, all of which was designed to keep the reader away from the truth.

The TRUTH—aye, there's the rub. Consider 2 Thessalonians 2:9-12: "The coming of the *lawless one* is according to the working of Satan, with all power, signs, and lying wonders, 10 and with all unrighteous deception among those who perish, because they did not receive the love of the truth, that they might be saved. 11 And for this reason God will send them strong delusion, that they should believe the lie, 12 that they all may be condemned who did not believe the truth, but had pleasure in unrighteousness" (NKJV). Although verse ten is in the context of the activity of the Antichrist, who will find an easy target in 'those who are wasting themselves' (my translation), it does not follow that no one will be wasting himself before that activity. Obviously, people have been wasting themselves all down through history, and the underlying cause for that 'wasting' has never changed—"they did not receive the love of the truth". (It began in the Garden.)

Please notice carefully what is said here: it is God Himself who sends the strong delusion! And upon whom does He send it? Upon those who do not receive the love of the truth.[1] And what is the purpose of the strong delusion?—the condemnation of those who do not believe the truth. Dear me, this is heavy. Notice that the truth is **central** to anyone's salvation. This raises the necessary question: just what is meant by 'the truth'? In John 14:6 Sovereign Jesus declared Himself to be 'the truth'. Praying to the Father in John 17:17 He said, "Thy Word is truth". Once each in John chapters 14, 15 and 16 He referred to the third person of the Trinity as "the Spirit of the truth". Since the Son is back in Heaven at the Father's right

---

[1] Please note that it is not enough to merely 'accept' the truth; it is required that we <u>love</u> the truth. Satan tantalizes us with fame and fortune (on his terms, of course), so to love the truth requires determination.

hand, and the Spirit is not very perceptible to most of us, most of the time, and since the Word is the Spirit's sword (Ephesians 6:17), our main access to 'the truth' is through God's Word, the Bible. The Bible offers propositional truth, but we need the Holy Spirit to illumine that truth, and to have the Holy Spirit we must be adequately related to Sovereign Jesus.

Now then, for something to be received, it must be offered; one cannot believe in something he has never heard about (Romans 10:14). The use of the verb 'receive' clearly implies an act of volition on the part of those not receiving the truth; that love was offered or made available to them but they did not want it; they wanted to be able to lie and to entertain lies told by others. But the consequences of such a choice are terrible; they turned their back on salvation. I suspect that not many Christians in the so-called 'first world' really believe what Sovereign Jesus said in Matthew 7:14: those who find the way of Life are **few**! And do not forget Revelation 22:15; "whoever loves and practices a lie" is excluded from the heavenly City [any lie, including Hort's].[1] I will here consider the implications for a student entering a graduate school of theology, because of what happens if he becomes a professor, or NT scholar, in his turn.[2]

Most such students presumably come from an evangelical environment, and were doubtless taught that the Bible is God's Word, and therefore inspired. Some may even have been taught verbal, plenary inspiration. However, in most

---

[1] Help! "A lie" is rather general, open-ended. What happens if I accepted a lie without realizing that it was one? But the text does not say 'accepts'; it says 'loves' and 'practices'. The implication is that the contrary evidence, to the lie, is available, but has been rejected, or deliberately ignored—the person sold himself to the lie.

[2] At the graduate level, a student has the responsibility to evaluate what is being taught—if it goes contrary to the Text, it should not be accepted. I remember one day in chapel, a visiting scholar was expounding Romans 10:9. He stated that the Greek Text plainly means "Jesus as Lord", but then went on to try to explain why the school didn't believe that. His effort was rather lame; so much so that I determined to delve into the question for myself.

theological schools you cannot get a job as a teacher if you do not agree to use the eclectic Greek text, with all that implies. (Just as you cannot get a teaching job in most universities unless you at least pretend to believe in evolution.) If the school is at least nominally conservative, they will still say that the Bible is inspired. But if a student brings up the question of the preservation of the text in class, there will be an uncomfortable silence. If it was preserved, no one knows what or where it is. The brainwashing has been so complete that many (most?) seminary graduates do not even know that there is any question about what they were taught. They were taught an eclecticism based on Hort's theory, and for them that is all there is.

But to go back to our student, he finds himself surrounded by professors whose job it is to destroy his faith in an inspired Bible with objective authority. Of course, presumably, very few such professors have ever thought in those terms (so they would object to my statement). They would say that they are just doing their job, doing what they are paid to do, without troubling themselves with the whys and wherefores.[1] But of course the student is not expecting that; he believes that his professors must be men of God, and so he is predisposed to believe them. Besides that predisposition (and it is powerful), what are the tools at their disposal for doing their job? Well, they have ridicule, sarcasm, brainwashing, peer pressure, the 'emperor's new clothes' gambit, and satanic assistance, for starters. (There may also be threats, failing grades, disciplinary actions, foul play, and so on—I write from experience.) Most of the terms above are self-explanatory, but some readers may not be familiar with the ancient myth about the emper-

---

[1] For older, established scholars there is also the matter of pride and vested interest; who wants to admit that he has been wrong all his professional life? Then there is the doctrine of professional ethics, one must respect his colleagues (respect for the colleague trumps respect for the truth). [One must not ask where that doctrine came from.] One other thing: where a school or institution depends on financial help from outside, it will be threatened with the loss of that help, if it does not toe the line, and its very existence may depend on that help.

or—it boils down to this: you don't want to admit that you can't 'see' it, when everyone else claims to be doing so. But by far the most serious is 'satanic assistance', and here I must needs go into detail.

Returning to 2 Thessalonians 2:10 and the 'love of the truth', as explained above, our main access to 'the truth' is through God's Word, the Bible. Our student may have gone to Sunday school, probably heard sermons with at least some biblical content, and certainly has his own copy of the Bible. In short, he has had, and continues to have, access to 'the truth'. However, the Holy Spirit does 'talk' to us, if we will listen. For example: my father was born in 1906, and in due time went to Moody Bible Institute and Wheaton College. In those days the American Standard Version (ASV) was touted as the best thing since the Garden of Eden; it was 'the rock of biblical integrity', etc. etc. Now my father had the practice of reading through the entire Bible once a year, a practice that he maintained all his life. Due to the hype surrounding the ASV, he got a copy and began to read it. It was hard going from the start, and he soon had to stop—the Holy Spirit simply would not let him go on. He returned to his trusty AV.

I imagine that at least some of my readers will have a question at this point. Am I implying that anyone who embraced the ASV was not listening to the Holy Spirit when he made that decision? The answer is, "Yes". Obviously, the same holds for the Hortian theory, etc. Unfortunately, few students of theology are in the habit of consulting the Holy Spirit, and those who do are marked for persecution. No Establishment can tolerate anyone who listens to the Holy Spirit. Surely, or have you forgotten John 3:8? "The wind blows where it wishes, and you (sg) hear its sound, but you do not know where it comes from or where it goes. So it is with everyone who has been begotten by the Spirit." Notice that the Lord is saying here that it is **we** who are to be unpredictable, like the wind, or the Spirit ("comes" and "goes" are in the present tense). If you are really under the control of the Spirit you will do unexpected things, just like He does.[1] An Establishment is defined by its 'straightjacket', and the Holy Spirit does not like straightjackets, and vice versa.

In John 8:44 Sovereign Jesus declared that "there is no truth" in Satan, and that he is the father of the lie. Since God cannot lie, Titus 1:2, it being contrary to His essence, any and all lies come from the enemy. So what happens if you embrace a lie? You invite Satan into your mind. And what does he do there? He sets up a stronghold that locks you into that lie; you become blind to the truth on that subject.[2] It is a specific application of the truth expressed in 2 Corinthians 4:4—Satan blinds minds. So what happens to our student? With very few exceptions, he succumbs to the pressure exerted by the tools already mentioned. He accepts the party line, and since it is a lie, Satan goes about blinding him to the truth. If he goes on to become an influential scholar, he will almost certainly come under demonic surveillance (since Satan is not omnipresent).

There is a common misapprehension that trips people up at this point. Since any genuinely regenerated person has the indwelling Holy Spirit, how can Satan or a demon be in that person's mind? There is a fundamental difference between presence and control. Very few Christians have consciously turned over every area of their lives to the control of the Holy Spirit. The Holy Spirit is a gentleman, he will not take over an area against your will (see John 4:23-24). Any areas not under the Spirit's control are open to the enemy's interference, and most especially if you embrace a lie. By embracing a lie you grieve the Holy Spirit; not wise (Ephesians 4:30). You also resist Him; also not wise (Acts 7:51). So why does God not protect you? Because you rejected the love of the truth, and that turned God against you! When God turns against you, what

---

[1] Since Satan is forever muddying the water with excesses and abuses, spiritual discernment is needed.

[2] On that one subject—you will not necessarily be blinded on other subjects, or at least not at first.

are your chances? Without God's protection, you become Satan's prey (1 Peter 5:8).[1]

Anyone in rebellion against the Creator is under satanic influence, direct or indirect (in most cases a demon acts as Satan's agent, when something more than the influence of the surrounding culture is required—almost all human cultures have ingredients of satanic provenance; this includes the academic culture). Anyone in rebellion against the Creator will also have strongholds of Satan in his mind. Since Satan is the 'father' of lies (John 8:44), anytime you embrace a lie you invite him into your mind—this applies to any of his sophistries (2 Corinthians 10:5) currently in vogue, such as materialism, humanism, relativism, Marxism, Freudianism, Hortianism, etc.

The selling of the lie is carried on from generation to generation, resulting in a continuous defection. Most professors are 'parrots', simply repeating what they were taught, without ever going back to check the facts. Some older scholars may have become aware of the facts, but because of vested interest they do not mention them to their students; they maintain the party line.

Is there a Way to Stop the Defection?

I believe there is, and it must begin with the TRUTH. To be more precise, it must begin with the love of the truth, which necessitates that the truth be made available. We must promote the love of the truth, and to do that we must also denounce the lie.[2] To promote something, we need vehicles for doing so. To succeed, we must be convincing. Most important,

---

[1] Please keep in mind the sequence of cause and effect—it begins with the rejection of the love of the truth. It is not enough to merely 'accept' the truth, one must love it. For those who have embraced a lie, the only 'medicine' is to return to the love of the truth, rejecting the lie. God may require a public renunciation of the lie.

[2] My own denunciation of the Hortian lie has been in print since 1977, and I continue to stand by every bit of it.

we must do something about the interference in people's minds.

Vehicles for promoting the truth:

It is modern technology that comes to our aid here. Blogs are being used to promote anything and everything. We can use them to promote the truth. I have done a fifteen-hour lecture series (in Portuguese) on the divine preservation of the NT Text. It was filmed and is available on the net via blog. Websites are being used. Most of my work is available from <u>walk-inhiscommandments.com</u>, and even more is available from my own <u>prunch.org</u>. I wish to call special attention to The Center for Study and Preservation of the Majority Text. Their site, <u>cspmt.org</u>, is receiving literally thousands of visits a day, and from dozens of countries around the world. And then there is Twitter, Facebook and so on—the fact is that the technical journals no longer have a stranglehold on any discipline; there are other ways of 'publishing' your ideas. And there has always been word-of-mouth, people telling their friends and acquaintances. I suspect that we may soon see a groundswell of this sort of thing.

The advent of self-publishing represents a real boon to those of us who reject a party line, and do not have the financial means to use an established publishing house. For various reasons it has become increasingly difficult to use a publisher. The contracts place all the onus on the author (including the cost of lawsuits). One must cover the cost of several thousand copies up front, and even so, only if the publisher decides he can make a profit on the book, not to mention an 'acceptable' content (publishers are not charitable institutions). It is the advent of 'print-on-demand' that saves those of us who have no money—copies are produced only as they are ordered. Since a machine does it all, one can order a single copy at the going price, and receive it.

Permit me to cite my own experience. My first book, *The Identity of the New Testament Text*, was published in 1977 by

Thomas Nelson Publishers. Each time they wished to do another printing, they graciously allowed me to do some revising. Their final (4th?) printing came out in 1990, so they kept the book in print for at least fifteen years, for which I give them my sincere thanks.[1] It had been out of print for some years when Wipf and Stock Publishers asked for permission to publish it as an academic reprint. So a revised edition came out in 2003, as *The Identity of the New Testament Text II*. Wipf & Stock also did *Identity III*, in 2012. It was during that interval that I tuned in to Family 35, so *Identity III* was the first edition to present and defend that family. The current *Identity IV*, with further heavy revision, I self-published with Amazon. My other books are also available there—what established publisher would have accepted *The Greek New Testament According to Family 35*?

Self-publishing also permits one to make a book available in electronic form, as I have done with mine. This allows people to download into their notebooks, or whatever, so they do not have to carry a book (or several). This is becoming increasingly important, as more and more people are joining the smartphone culture. That said, however, we should not despise the good old hard copy; for serious study many still prefer a book (you can make notes in a book). In short, we should use both, electronic and printed.

Especially in cultures where 'who you know' is more important than 'what you know', but also in others, we should promote the 'social' vehicle, the sharing with friends and acquaintances. We can invite people over for a cup of coffee (or tea), spread the word wherever we have contacts.

---

[1] By then there were well over 10,000 copies is use around the world, quietly making a difference in people's lives. Every now and again I hear from someone, thanking me for the book, including some Greek professors. Such professors are no longer destroying the faith of their students. There is a stirring at the grassroots level, that the Establishment is doing its best to ignore. When obliged to take notice, it is 'pooh-pooh'; but the time is coming, indeed now is, when that will no longer work.

A convincing presentation:

What is the best way to protect a caged lion? Just open the cage! What is the best way to promote the Truth? Just turn it loose! As Sovereign Jesus said in John 8:31-32, "If you abide in my word, you are my disciples indeed. And you shall know the truth, and the truth shall make you free" (NKJV). The truth will make us free from what? In the immediate context (verse 34), it is from sin, but with reference to the topic in hand, it is able to free us from Satan's blinding and his lies. The Word is the Holy Spirit's sword, and a sword cuts, whether someone believes it or not. That said, however, what can we do so that people will listen to us?

Bombast and ranting should be avoided. They may appeal to the emotions of those who are already on our side, but they will have a negative effect on those we are trying to reach. The truth is best served by the facts, the evidence. And the evidence should be presented in a straightforward fashion, without undue appeal to emotion. However, emotion must be distinguished from presupposition (as well as from principles of reasoned debate). It is impossible to work without presuppositions; everyone has them. It follows that if someone criticizes me for having presuppositions, while pretending that he has none, that someone is being dishonest and perverse (or perhaps just brainwashed and blinded).

Ever since Burgon, who stated his presuppositions honestly and openly (as any true scholar should), there has been a constant and insistent attack against those presuppositions, and even the stating of them. A psychosis has been created to the extent that even some modern defenders of the majority text have become paranoid on the subject; they have actually reached the point of excluding the supernatural from their model. However, in Luke 11:23 the Sovereign Creator, Jehovah the Son incarnate, declares: "He who is not with Me is against Me, and he who does not gather with Me scatters." Here is a plain statement—there are only two teams in this world; there are only two sides, two kingdoms; there is no neutral ground; there is no true agnosticism.[1] If you are not with Jesus, you are automatically against Him; if you are not gathering with Him, you are automatically scattering. If you do not receive Jesus' affirmations about Scripture, you have rejected them. Neutrality does not exist.

But how can we reach those who pretend that they have no presuppositions, who refuse, or in any case fail, to declare their presuppositions openly? If those same people criticize us for declaring ours, we may question their basic honesty; but how can we get them to listen? How can you get a blind person to see? How can you get a deaf person to hear? Something must be done about the cause of the condition. The 'cause of the condition' in the area we are discussing is the satanic interference in their thought processes that the Text, 2 Corinthians 4:4, calls 'blinding' (the brainwashing is a consequence of, and an accessory to, that blinding). Just how to address that cause will be treated in the next section. In the meantime, it is necessary to discuss the question of presupposition, but we should attempt to do so with a calm and irenic spirit.[2]

But to return to the matter of presenting the evidence in a convincing fashion, we must keep in mind that brainwashed people are generally ignorant of the evidence. Most professors are 'parrots', simply repeating what they were taught, without ever going back to check the facts. Some older scholars may have become aware of the facts, but because of vested interest they do not mention them to their students; they maintain the party line. For the truth to set people free, the truth must be presented. So I repeat: we must present the evidence in a straightforward manner.

---

[1] Agnosticism is a passive rejection; the agnostic is not accepting the claim.

[2] I am well aware that it is not easy, which is why I use 'attempt'.

The primary evidence is furnished by the continuous text manuscripts (Greek) of the NT. The evidence furnished by the lectionaries is secondary. The evidence furnished by ancient versions and patristic citations is tertiary. Genuine historical evidence (to the extent that this can be determined) is ancillary. Where the primary evidence is unequivocal, the remaining types should not come into play. For example, at any given point in the four Gospels there will be around 1,700 extant continuous text MSS, representing all lines of transmission and all locales.[1] Where they all agree, there can be no legitimate doubt as to the original wording.

It should also be evident that a variant in a single MS, of whatever age, is irrelevant—it is a false witness to its family archetype, at that point, nothing more. If a number of MSS share a variant, but do not belong to the same family, then they made the mistake independently and are false witnesses to their respective family archetypes—there is no dependency. Where a group of MSS evidently reflect correctly the archetypal form of their family, then we are dealing with a family (not the individual MSS). Families need to be evaluated just as we evaluate individual MSS. It is possible to assign a credibility quotient to a family, based on objective criteria. But of course, any and all families must first be empirically identified and defined, and such identification depends upon the full collation of MSS.

Although the discipline has (so far) neglected to do its homework (collating MSS), still a massive majority of MSS should be convincing. For example, if a variant enjoys 99% attestation from the primary witnesses, this means that it totally dominates any genealogical 'tree', because it dominated the global transmission of the text. The *INTF Text und Textwert* series, practitioners of the Claremont profile method, H.C. Hoskier, von Soden, Burgon, Scrivener—in short, anyone who has collated any number of MSS—have all demonstrated that the

---

[1] Of course we know that there are many MSS not yet 'extant', not yet identified and catalogued, so the number can only go up.

Byzantine bulk of MSS is by no means monolithic. There are any number of streams and rivulets. Frederick Wisse posited thirty-four groups within the Byzantine bulk, with seventy subgroups.[1] It is clear that there was no 'stuffing the ballot box'; there was no 'papal' decree; there was no recension imposed by ecclesiastical authority. In short, the transmission was predominantly normal.[2]

But to get back to presenting the evidence, we should call attention to the evidence that has been presented down through the years: Herman C. Hoskier's *Concerning the Text of the Apocalypse* and *Codex B and its Allies, a Study and an Indictment*; Hermann von Soden's *magnum opus*—in spite of its imperfections, it contains valuable information; S.C.E. Legg's editions of Matthew and Mark; the IGNTP's edition of Luke; Reuben J. Swanson's editions of Matthew through Galatians; Frederik Wisse on Luke; W.F. Wisselink's *Assimilation as a Criterion for the Establishment of the Text*; Tommy Wasserman on Jude; the *Text und Textwert* series from the *INTF*, and even better, their *Editio Critica Maior* series.

Last, but not least, is my own work. My Greek NT is the first to give the archetype of Family 35, and its critical apparatus is the first to offer percentages with the variants, besides including six published editions. The series on f^{35} variants, book by

---

[1] The more recent work of Frederick Wisse furnishes a strong objective demonstration of the diversity within the "Byzantine" textform. *The Profile Method for Classifying and Evaluating Manuscript Evidence* (Grand Rapids: Eerdmans, 1982), is an application of the "Claremont Profile Method" to **1,386** MSS in Luke 1, 10 and 20. He isolated 15 major groupings of MSS (which sub-divide into at least 70 subgroups), plus 22 smaller groups, plus 89 "mavericks" (MSS so mixed that they neither fit into any of the above groupings nor form groupings among themselves). One of the 15 "major" groups is the "Egyptian" ("Alexandrian")—it is made up of precisely four (04) uncials and four (04) cursives, plus two more of each that were "Egyptian" in one of the three chapters. If I understand him correctly he considers that virtually all the remaining MSS fall into the broad "Byzantine" stream. In other words, when we talk of examining the "Byzantine" text there are at least 36 strands of transmission that need to be considered!

[2] For a fuller discussion, please see my *Identity IV*, pages 367-69.

book, gives the detailed result of my collations of representative MSS, usually at least thirty per book. All of this is now freely available on the internet from my site, prunch.org (mostly in English, but also some in Portuguese). The Center for Study and Preservation of the Majority Text (CSPMT) is preparing a critical edition whose apparatus will contain new information about lines of transmission within the Byzantine bulk. We have ways of making evidence available, but how can we get people to look at it? The best, if not the only, way is to use the spiritual authority that Sovereign Jesus has given us.

Neutralizing the interference:

On what basis might we neutralize interference? The most fundamental question for human life on this planet is that of authority: who has it, to what degree, and on what terms? As the chief priests said to Jesus, "By what authority are you doing this?" (Luke 20:2). After His death and resurrection Sovereign Jesus said, "All authority in heaven and on earth has been given to me" (Matthew 28:18). So He is perfectly within His rights, clearly competent, to delegate a piece of that authority to us. Consider Luke 10:19: "Take note, I am giving you the authority to trample on snakes and scorpions,[1] and over all

---

[1] The Lord gives us the authority to "trample snakes and scorpions". Well now, to smash the literal insect, a scorpion, you don't need power from on High, just a slipper (if you are fast, you can do it barefoot). To trample a snake I prefer a boot, but we can kill literal snakes without supernatural help. It becomes obvious that Jesus was referring to something other than reptiles and insects. I understand Mark 16:18 to be referring to the same reality—Jesus declares that certain signs will accompany the believers (the turn of phrase virtually has the effect of commands): they will expel demons, they will speak strange languages, they will remove 'snakes', they will place hands on the sick. ("If they drink . . ." is not a command; it refers to an eventuality.) But what did the Lord Jesus mean by 'snakes'?

In a list of distinct activities Jesus has already referred to demons, so the 'snakes' must be something else. In Matthew 12:34 Jesus called the Pharisees a 'brood of vipers', and in 23:33, 'snakes, brood of vipers'. In John 8:44, after they claimed God as their father, Jesus said, "You are of your father the devil". And 1 John 3:10 makes clear that Satan has many other 'sons' (so also Matthew 13:38-39). In Revelation 20:2 we read: "He seized the dragon, the ancient serpent, who is a

the power of the enemy, and nothing at all may harm you." Instead of 'am giving', perhaps 2.5% of the Greek manuscripts, of objectively inferior quality, have 'have given' (as in NIV, NASB, LB, TEV, etc.)—a serious error. Jesus said this perhaps five months before His death and resurrection, addressing the seventy (not just the twelve). The Lord is talking about the future, not the past, a future that includes us!

Consider further John 20:21: Jesus said to them again: "Peace to you! Just as the Father sent me, I also send you." "Just as . . . so also"—Jesus is sending us just like the Father sent Him. So how did They do it? The Father determined and the Son obeyed: "Behold, I have come to do your will, O God" (Hebrews 10:7). And what was that will? To destroy Satan (Hebrews 2:14) and undo his works (1 John 3:8). Since Jesus did indeed defeat Satan (Colossians 2:15, Ephesians 1:20-21, etc.), but then went back to Heaven, what is left for us is the undoing of his works.[1] It seems clear to me that to undo any work we must also undo its consequences (to the extent that that may be possible).

Consider also Ephesians 2:4-6: "But God—being rich in mercy, because of His great love with which He loved us, even when we were dead in our transgressions—made us alive together with Christ (by grace you have been saved) and raised us up together and seated us together in the heavenly realms in Christ Jesus." This is tremendous! Here we have our authority. Christ is now seated at the Father's right, 'far above' the ene-

---

slanderer, even Satan, who deceives the whole inhabited earth, and bound him for a thousand years." If Satan is a snake, then his children are also snakes. So then, I take it that our 'snakes' are human beings who have chosen to serve Satan, who have sold themselves to evil. I conclude that the 'snakes' in Luke 10:19 are the same as those in Mark 16:18, but what of the 'scorpions'? Since they also are of the enemy, they may be demons, in which case the term may well include their offspring, the humanoids (for more on this see "As were the Days of Noah", below. I am still working on the question of just how the removal is done.

[1] For more on this subject see my article, "Biblical Spiritual Warfare" (available from prunch.org).

my and his hosts. This verse affirms that we who are in Christ are there too! So in Christ we also are far above the enemy and his hosts.[1] Surely, or is that not what is stated in Ephesians 1:16-21?

> I really do not stop giving thanks for you, making mention of you in my prayers: that the God of our Lord, Jesus Christ, the Father of glory, may give you the spirit of wisdom and revelation in the real knowledge[2] of Himself, the eyes of your heart having been enlightened, that you may know what is the hope of His[F] calling, and what the riches of the glory of His inheritance in the saints, and what the exceeding greatness of His power into[3] us who are believing, according to the demonstration of the extent of His might which He exercised in the Christ when He raised Him[S] from among the dead and seated Him at His[F] right, in the heavenly realms, far above every ruler and authority and power and dominion—even every name that can be named, not only in this age but also in the next.

---

[1] We should be consciously operating on that basis, but since few churches teach this, most Christians live in spiritual defeat.

[2] I finally settled on 'real knowledge' as the best way to render επιγνωσις, the heightened form of γνωσις, 'knowledge'. Real knowledge is more than mere intellectual knowledge, or even true theoretical knowledge—it involves experience. The Text goes on to say, "the eyes of your <u>heart</u> having been enlightened". Real knowledge changes your 'heart', who you are.

[3] "Into us"—that is what the Text says. Note that 'believing' is in the present tense. Consider Ephesians 3:20. "Now to Him who is able to do immeasurably more than all we ask or imagine, according to the power that is working in us." Note that "is working" is also in the present tense; having believed yesterday won't hack it, we must believe today. This tremendous power that God pours into us, as we believe, exceeds our powers of imagination. Well now, my personal horizon is limited and defined by my ability to imagine. Anything that I cannot imagine lies outside my horizon, and so obviously I won't ask for it. I sadly confess that I have not yet arrived at a spiritual level where I can unleash this power—I have yet to make the truth in this verse work for me. But I understand that the truth affirmed here is literal, and I only hope that others will get there before I do (so I can learn from them), if I keep on delaying. The whole point of the exercise (verse 21) is for God to get glory, and to the extent that we do <u>not</u> put His power in us to work we are depriving Him of glory that He could and should have.

Now then, "far above every ruler and authority and power and dominion—even every name that can be named, not only in this age but also in the next" must include Satan and his angels. If Christ, seated at the Father's right, is "**far** above" them, and we are in Him, seated at the Father's right, then we too are above all the hosts of the enemy. That is our position and authority for neutralizing interference.

Well and good, but just how are we to go about doing it? Well, at what level should we 'neutralize'? The candidates that suggest themselves are: institutions, teachers, students, church leaders, and lay people. How about working at all levels? Next, what procedures are at our disposal to do the neutralizing? I offer the following: a) forbid any further use of Satan's power, in a specific case; b) claim the undoing of the consequences of the use of that power that there has been (to the extent it may be possible); c) destroy any strongholds of Satan in their minds (including blind spots); d) bind any demons involved and send them to the Abyss, forbidding any further demonic activity; e) take their thoughts captive to the obedience of Christ. In my experience, to be efficient we need to be specific: name the institution; name the person.

But just a minute, I submit for consideration that faith is a basic prerequisite for making use of our position and authority. The theological training I myself received programmed me not to expect supernatural manifestations of power in and through my life and ministry. As a result, I personally find it to be difficult to exercise the kind of faith that the Lord Jesus demands. Consider:

In Matthew 8:5-13 the centurion understood about authority—he gave orders and they were obeyed, promptly and without question.[1] But the Lord Jesus said he had unusually

---

[1] The centurion did not say, "In the authority of Rome . . .", he just said, "Do this; do that." The Lord Jesus did not say, "In the authority of the Father . . .", He just said, "Be clean! Go!" In Luke 10:19 He said, "I give you <u>the</u> authority over all the

great faith—faith in what? Faith in the Lord's spiritual authority; He could simply give an order and it would happen. Perhaps we should understand this sort of faith as an absolute confidence, without a taint of doubt or fear. In Matthew 21:21 the Lord said, "Assuredly . . . if you have faith and do not doubt" (see Mark 11:23, "does not doubt in his heart") you can (actually "will") shrivel a tree or send a mountain into the sea. See also Hebrews 10:22, "full assurance of faith", 1 Timothy 2:8, "pray . . . without doubting", James 1:6, "ask in faith with no doubting". Mark 5:34 and Matthew 15:28 offer positive examples; while Peter blew it (Matthew 14:31, "why did you doubt?").

If someone gives a commission, they will presumably back it up to the limit of their ability. Since Christ's ability has no limit, His backing has no limit (on His end). In Matthew 28:18 He said, "All authority has been given to me in heaven and on earth." Then comes the commission: "As you go, make disciples . . . teaching them to obey all things that I have commanded you"—the pronoun refers back to the eleven apostles (verse 16). So what commands had Jesus given the Eleven? Among other things, "heal the sick, cleanse the lepers, cast out demons" (in Matthew 10:8 perhaps 94% of the Greek manuscripts do not have "raise the dead"). The Eleven also heard John 20:21. Knowing that we are being backed by the Sovereign of the universe, who has all authority and power, we can and should act with complete confidence.

A word of caution is necessary at this point. Consider James 4:7—"Therefore submit to God. Resist the devil and he will flee from you." Note the sequence: we need to verify that we are in submission to God before taking on the devil. Then we should claim our position in Christ at the Father's right hand. Since few Christians have received any remotely adequate

---

power of the enemy"—so we have the authority, so it is up to us to speak! Just like Jesus did.

level of instruction in the area of biblical spiritual warfare (most have received none), I need to explain the procedures.

a) Forbid any further use of Satan's power:

This procedure is based on Luke 10:19. Sovereign Jesus gives us 'the' authority over all the power of the enemy. Authority controls power, but since we have access to God's limitless power (Ephesians 3:20), we should not give Satan the satisfaction of our using his (and he could easily deceive us into doing things we shouldn't). We should use our authority to forbid the use of Satan's power, with reference to specific situations—in my experience, we must be specific. (I have tried binding Satan once for all until the end of the world, but it doesn't work; presumably because God's plan calls for the enemy's continued activity in this world. We can limit what the enemy does, but not put him completely out of business, or so I deem.) But just how should we go about it?

In the armor described in Ephesians 6 we find "the sword of the Spirit" (verse 17). A sword is a weapon for offense, although it is also used for defense. The Text tells us that this sword is "the ρημα of God"—ρημα, not λογος. It is God's Word <u>spoken</u>, or applied. Really, what good is a sword left in its sheath? However marvelous our Sword may be (Hebrews 4:12), to produce effect it must come out of the scabbard. The Word needs to be spoken, or written—applied in a specific way.

In the Bible we have many examples where people brought the power of God into action by speaking. Our world began with a creative word from God—spoken (Genesis, 1:3, 6, 9, 11, 14, 20, 24, 26; and see Hebrews 11:3). Moses did a lot of speaking. Elijah spoke (1 Kings 17:1, 18:36, 2 Kings 1:10). Elisha spoke (2 Kings 2:14, 21, 24; 4:16, 43; 6:19). Jesus did a great deal of speaking. Ananias spoke (Acts 9:17). Peter spoke (Acts 9:34, 40). Paul spoke (Acts 13:11; 14:3, 10; 16:18; 20:10; 28:8). In short, we need to speak!

b) Claim the undoing of the consequences of the use of that power that there has been:

This procedure is based on 1 John 3:8, allied to Luke 10:19. It should be possible for us to command Satan to use his own power to undo messes he has made, thereby obliging him to acknowledge his defeat (which will not sit well with his pride). The Son of God was manifested for the purpose of "undoing the works of the devil" (1 John 3:8), and it is incumbent upon us to continue His work here in this world (John 20:21). How can you undo a work without undoing its consequences as well? The Father sent the Son to undo Satan's works, and the Lord Jesus Christ is sending us to undo Satan's works. Again, I understand that we must be specific.

c) Destroy any strongholds of Satan in the person's mind:

This procedure is based on 2 Corinthians 10:4 and 1 John 3:8. Since strongholds, and blind spots, in the mind are a work of Satan, and we are here to undo such works, this falls within the area of our competence. It is done by claiming such destruction in so many words, being specific.

d) Bind any demons involved and send them to the Abyss:

This procedure is based on Mark 3:27 and Luke 8:31. "No one can plunder the strong man's goods, invading his house, unless he first binds the strong man—then he may plunder the house" (Mark 3:27). Since the definite article occurs with 'strong man' the first time the phrase occurs, the entity has already been introduced, so the reference is to Satan. Here is a biblical basis for binding Satan, which is now possible because of Christ's victory. If we can bind Satan, evidently we can also bind any of his subordinates. "And he[1] kept imploring Him that He would not order them to go away into the Abyss"

---

[1] The boss demon does most of the talking, representing his cohort.

(Luke 8:31).[1] I take it that Jesus did not send them to the Abyss at that time because He had not yet won the victory, and the demons were 'within their rights', under Satan, who was still the god of this world. But the demons were obviously worried! (They knew very well who Jesus was, and what He could do.) I would say that this is one of the 'greater things' (John 14:12) that we may now do—rather, that we should do. As for forbidding any further demonic activity, we have the Lord's example (Mark 9:25), and we are to do what He did (John 14:12).

e) Take their thoughts captive to the obedience of Christ:

This procedure is based on 2 Corinthians 10:5. In the context, the thoughts are of people who are serving Satan (even if unwittingly). (Of course we should always be checking to be sure that we ourselves are operating within 'the mind of Christ', 1 Corinthians 2:15-16.) Now this procedure moves away from simply neutralizing the enemy's interference, since it introduces a positive 'interference', but it is relevant to the issue being discussed here, since it is protection against falling back into the former error. Again we must be specific.

f) Some further texts that may apply: Luke 4:18-21, Psalm 149:5-9, John 14:12.

In Luke 4:18-21 Jesus includes "to set at liberty those who are oppressed" (Isaiah 58:6) as one of the things He was sent to do. Turning to Isaiah 58:6, we find Jehovah stating what kind of 'fast' He would like to see: "To loose the fetters of wickedness [a], to undo the yoke-ropes [b]; to let oppressed ones go free [a], and that you (pl.) break every yoke [b]." As is typical of Hebrew grammar, the two halves are parallel. "To loose the fetters of wickedness" and "to let oppressed ones go free" are parallel. Who placed the "fetters" and who is doing the op-

---

[1] The Text has 'the Abyss', presumably the same one mentioned in Revelation 20:3. The demons knew something that most of us do not.

pressing? Well, although people can certainly forge their own bonds through their own wicked lifestyle, I take it that the point here is that wicked beings have placed the fetters on others. "To undo yoke-ropes" and "that ye break every yoke" go together. First we should untie the ropes that bind the yoke to the neck, then we should break the yokes themselves. I gain the clear impression that this text is talking about the activity of Satan's servants, men and angels. Using culture, worldview, legal devices, threats, blackmail, lies, deception and just plain demonizing and witchcraft, they bind individuals, families, ethnic groups, etc., with a variety of fetters and instruments of oppression.

So what does this have to do with our subject? Well, fasting was an important and required component in their worship of God. So this kind of 'fasting' is something that Jehovah overtly wants to see; it is specifically His will. So when we see any work of Satan in someone's life, it is God's will that we undo it. If we know it is God's will, we can proceed with complete confidence. And it is part of our commission (John 20:21).

Notice also Psalms 149:5-9. "Let the saints exult in glory; let them sing for joy in their beds. Let the high praises of God be in their mouth, and a two-edged sword in their hand—to execute vengeance upon the nations and punishments upon the peoples; to bind their kings with chains and their nobles with fetters of iron; to execute upon them the written judgment. This honor is for all His saints." Note that the saints are in their beds, so the activity described in the subsequent verses must take place in the spiritual realm. I assume that the 'kings' and 'nobles' include both men and fallen angels. The activity described is the prerogative of "all His saints"—if you are one of those saints, it is up to you. There are a number of 'written judgments' in the Text: Zechariah 5:2-4, Proverbs 20:10, Isaiah 10:1-2, Romans 1:26-36 and 1 Corinthians 6:9-10, at least.

In John 14:12 the Lord Jesus said: "Most assuredly I say to you, the one believing into me, he too will do the works that I do; in fact he will do greater works than these, because I am going to my Father." "Most assuredly" is actually "amen, amen"—rendered "verily, verily" in the AV. Only John registers the word as repeated, in the other Gospels it is just "amen". In the contemporary literature we have no example of anyone else using the word in this way. It seems that Jesus coined His own use, and the point seems to be to call attention to an important pronouncement: "Stop and listen!" Often it precedes a formal statement of doctrine or policy, as here.

"The one believing into me, he too will do the works that I do." This is a tremendous statement, and not a little disconcerting. Notice that the Lord said, "will do"; not 'maybe', 'perhaps', 'if you feel like it'; and certainly not 'if the doctrine of your church permits it'! If you believe, you **will do!** The verb 'believe' is in the present tense; if you are believing you will do; it follows that if you are not doing, it is because you are not believing. 2 + 2 = 4. Doing what? "The works that I do." Well, Jesus preached the Gospel, He taught, He cast out demons, He healed all sorts and sizes of sickness and disease, He raised an occasional dead person, and He performed a variety of miracles (water to wine, walk on water, stop a storm instantaneously, transport a boat several miles instantaneously, multiply food, shrivel a tree—and He implied that the disciples should have stopped the storm and multiplied the food, and He stated that they could shrivel a tree [Peter actually took a few steps on water]). So how about us? The preaching and teaching we can handle, but what about the rest? I once heard the president of a certain Christian college affirm that this verse obviously could not mean what it says because it is not happening! Well, in his own experience and in that of his associates I guess it isn't. But many people today cast out demons and heal, and I personally know someone who has raised a dead person. Miracles are also happening. So how about me? And you?

"In fact he will do greater works than these." Well now, if we cast out demons, heal and perform miracles, is that not enough? Jesus wants more, He wants "greater things" than those just mentioned [do not forget what He said in Matthew 7:22-23]. Notice again that He said "will do", not maybe, perhaps, or if your church permits. But what could be 'greater' than miracles? This cannot refer to modern technology because in that event such 'greater things' would not have been available to the believers during the first 1900 years. Note that the key is in the Lord's final statement (in verse 12), "because I am going to my Father". Only if He won could He return to the Father, so He is here declaring His victory before the fact. It is on the basis of that victory that the 'greater things' can be performed. Just what are those 'greater' things? For my answer, see my outline, "Biblical Spiritual Warfare".

In verse 12 the verb 'will do' is singular, both times, so it has to do with the individual. Observe that the Lord did **not** say, "you apostles", "only during the apostolic age", "only until the canon is complete", or whatever. He said, "the one believing", present tense, so this applies to any and all subsequent moments up to our time. To deny the truth contained in this verse is to make the Lord Jesus Christ out to be a liar. Somehow I do not think that is very smart.[1]

The 'Crux' of a 'Lost' Original

Returning to the opening paragraph, is/was the original wording lost? I answer with an emphatic, **"No"**. It certainly exists

---

[1] Also, to affirm that the miraculous gifts ceased when the last shovelful of dirt fell on the Apostle John's grave is an historical falsehood. Christians who lived during the second, third and fourth centuries, whose writings have come down to us, affirm that the gifts were still in use in their day. No 20th or 21st century Christian, who was not there, is competent to contradict them. And please see the footnote at 1 Corinthians 13:12 in my translation, *The Sovereign Creator Has Spoken*. Any 'cessationist' will have a stronghold of Satan in his mind on that subject, because he has embraced a lie. Any doctrine that derives from reaction against excesses and abuses gives victory to Satan. Any argument designed to justify lack of spiritual power cannot be right.

within the Byzantine bulk. To my mind, any time at least 90% of the primary witnesses agree, there can be no reasonable question; it is <u>statistically impossible</u> that a non-original reading could score that high.[1] Any time a reading garners an attestation of at least 80% its probability is high. But for perhaps 2% of the words in the NT the attestation falls below 80% (a disproportionate number being in the Apocalypse), and at this point we need to shift our attention from MSS to families. Once all MSS have been collated and have been empirically assigned to families, then we can confine our attention to those families from the start (as I have done in the Apocalypse). I have mentioned elsewhere assigning a credibility quotient to each family, based on objective criteria, and this needs to be done. Unfortunately, there is a great deal of 'homework' waiting to be done in this area. So far as I know, only Family 35 has an empirically defined profile (defined by a complete collation of a representative number of the MSS that make up the family), at least to this date.[2]

About the 2% with attestation below 80%, in a heavy majority of the cases the difference can hardly be reflected in a translation. A reader will understand the intended meaning with either variant. But within Family 35 there is very little significant variation, and the archetypal form is demonstrable. For example, of the forty-three family members I have collated for the

---

[1] See Appendix C in my *Identity IV*.

[2] So far as I know, neither f^1 nor f^{13} exists outside of the Gospels, but even there, has anyone ever produced an empirically defined profile for either one? Consider the following statement by Metzger:

> It should be observed that, in accord with the theory that members of f^1 and f^{13} were subject to progressive accommodation to the later Byzantine text, scholars have established the text of these families by adopting readings of family witnesses that differ from the Textus Receptus. Therefore the citation of the *siglum* f^1 and f^{13} may, in any given instance, signify a minority of manuscripts (or even only one) that belong to the family. (*A Textual Commentary on the Greek New Testament* [companion to UBS³], p. xii.)

Would it be unreasonable to say that such a proceeding is unfair to the reader? Does it not mislead the user of the apparatus? At least as used by the UBS editions, those *sigla* do not represent empirically defined profiles.

General Epistles, twenty-eight are identical (perfect) for 2 & 3 John (but not always the same MSS), twenty-two are identical for Jude, five for 2 Peter, four each for James and 1 John, and three for 1 Peter.

For my article, "Copyist Care Quotient" (see prunch.org), I collated fifty-one (now 53) representatives of Family 35 for Mark. I analyzed the variants contained in MS 1384 (eapr, XI, Andros)—of the fifty-three MSS I collated, at least forty-four are better than 1384, so it is only a mediocre representative. However, with four exceptions, only a single letter or syllable is involved, and nowhere is the meaning seriously affected. **Someone reading MS 1384 would not be misled as to the intended meaning at any point in the book.** I say this is noteworthy, and it is typical of almost all f^{35} MSS. Down through the centuries of transmission, anyone with access to an f^{35} representative could know the intended meaning of the Autograph.[1] Not only that, most lines of transmission within the Byzantine bulk would be reasonably close, good enough for most practical purposes. This is also true of the much maligned *Textus Receptus*; it is certainly good enough for most practical purposes. Down through the centuries of Church history, most people could have had reasonable access to God's written revelation.

Some years ago now, Maurice Robinson did a complete collation of 1,389 MSS that contain the P.A. (John 7:53-8:11),[2] and I had William Pierpont's photocopy of those collations in my

---

[1] Since f^{35} MSS are scattered all over, or all around, the Mediterranean world, such access would have been feasible for most people.

[2] 240 MSS omit the P.A., 64 of which are based on Theophylact's commentary. Fourteen others have lacunae, but are not witnesses for total omission. A few others certainly contain the passage but the microfilm is illegible. So, 1389 + 240 + 14 + 7(?) = about 1650 MSS checked by Robinson. That does not include Lectionaries, of which he also checked a fair number. (These are microfilms held by the *INTF* in Münster. We now know that there are many more extant MSS, and probably even more that are not yet 'extant'.) Unfortunately, so far as I know, Robinson has yet to publish his collations, thus making them available to the public at large.

possession for two months, spending most of that time studying those collations. As I did so, it became obvious to me that von Soden 'regularized' his data, arbitrarily 'creating' the alleged archetypal form for his first four families, $M^{1,2,3,4}$ —if they exist at all, they are rather fluid. His $M^{5\&6}$ do exist, having distinct profiles for the purpose of showing that they are different, but they are a bit 'squishy', with enough internal confusion to make the choice of the archetypal form to be arbitrary. In fact, I suspect that they will have to be subdivided. In contrast to the above, his M^7 (that I call Family 35) has a solid, unambiguous profile—the archetypal form is demonstrable, empirically determined.

As for the Apocalypse, of the nine groups that Hoskier identified, only his Complutensian (that I call Family 35) is homogenous. Of the others, the main ones all have subdivisions, which will require their own profile.

Given my presuppositions, I consider that I have good reason for declaring the divine preservation of the precise original wording of the complete New Testament Text to this day. That wording is reproduced in my edition of the Greek NT. My presuppositions include: the Sovereign Creator exists; He inspired the biblical Text; He promised to preserve it for a thousand generations (1 Chronicles 16:15); so He must have an active, ongoing interest in that preservation [there have been fewer than 300 generations since Adam, so He has a ways to go!]. If He was preserving the original wording in some line of transmission other than f^{35}, would that transmission be any less careful than what I have demonstrated for f^{35}? I think not. So any line of transmission characterized by internal confusion is disqualified—this includes **all** the other lines of transmission that I have seen so far![1]

On the basis of the evidence so far available I affirm the following:

---

[1] Things like M^6 and M^5 in John 7:53-8:11 come to mind.

1. The original wording was never 'lost', and its transmission down through the years was basically normal, being recognized as inspired material from the beginning.

2. That normal process resulted in lines of transmission.

3. To delineate such lines, MSS must be grouped empirically on the basis of a shared mosaic of readings.

4. Such groups or families must be evaluated for independence and credibility.

5. The largest clearly defined group is Family 35.

6. Family 35 is demonstrably independent of all other lines of transmission throughout the NT.

7. Family 35 is demonstrably ancient, dating to the 3rd century, at least.[1]

8. Family 35 representatives come from all over the Mediterranean area; the geographical distribution is all but total.[2]

9. Family 35 is not a recension, was not created at some point subsequent to the Autographs.

10. Family 35 is an objectively/empirically defined entity throughout the NT; it has a demonstrable, diagnostic profile from Matthew 1:1 to Revelation 22:21.

11. The archetypal form of Family 35 is demonstrable—it has been demonstrated (see Appendix B in my *Identity IV*).

12. The Original Text is the ultimate archetype; any candidate must also be an archetype—a real, honest to goodness, ob-

---

[1] Family 35 readings are attested by early witnesses, but without pattern, and therefore without dependency. But there are many hundreds of such readings. So how did the f^{35} archetype come by all those early readings? Did its creator travel around and collect a few readings from Aleph, a few from B, a few from p^{45,66,75}, a few from W and D, etc.? Is not such a suggestion patently ridiculous? The only reasonable conclusion is that the f^{35} text is ancient (also independent).

[2] And for some places in Greece, based on their surviving copies, it was all they used.

jectively verifiable archetype—there is only one (so far), Family 35.[1]

13. God's concern for the preservation of the biblical Text is evident: I take it that passages such as 1 Chronicles 16:15, Psalm 119:89, Isaiah 40:8, Matthew 5:18, Luke 16:17 and 21:33, John 10:35, 1 Peter 1:23-25 and Luke 4:4 may reasonably be taken to imply a promise that the Scriptures (to the tittle) will be preserved for man's use (we are to live "by *every* word of God"), and to the end of the world ("for a thousand generations"), but no intimation is given as to just how God proposed to do it. We must deduce the answer from what He has indeed done—we discover that He **did**!

14. This concern is reflected in Family 35; it is characterized by incredibly careful transmission (in contrast to other lines). [I have a perfect copy of the Family 35 archetypal text for most NT books (22); I have copies made from a perfect exemplar (presumed) for another four (4); as I continue to collate MSS I hope to add the last one (Acts), but even for it the archetypal form is demonstrable.]

15. If God was preserving the original wording in some line of transmission other than Family 35, would that line be any less careful? I think not. So any line of transmission characterized by internal confusion is disqualified—this includes **all** the other lines of transmission that I have seen so far.

16. I affirm that God used Family 35 to preserve the precise original wording of the New Testament Text; it is reproduced in my edition of the Greek Text. (And God used mainly the Eastern Orthodox Churches to preserve the NT Text down through the centuries—they have always used a

---

[1] If you want to be a candidate for the best lawyer in your city, you must be a lawyer, or the best carpenter, or oncologist, or whatever. If there is only one candidate for mayor in your town, who gets elected?

Text that was an adequate representation of the Original, for all practical purposes.)

I claim to have demonstrated the superiority of Family 35 based on <u>size</u> (number of representatives), <u>independence</u>, <u>age</u>, <u>geographical</u> <u>distribution</u>, <u>profile</u> (empirically determined), <u>care</u> (see my "Copyist Care Quotient") and <u>range</u> (all 27 books). I challenge any and all to do the same for any other line of transmission!

"As were the days of Noah"

Mathew 24:37—"Just as were the days of Noah, so also will be the coming of the Son of the Man"[1]—spoken by the Lord Jesus Christ.

According to Ezekiel 33:6-7, a watchman who sees danger approaching has the obligation to warn the populace. I believe that God has designated me as a watchman with reference to the matter in hand—most unpleasant but terribly serious—so I consider that I am obligated to sound the alarm. Unfortunately, I myself have taught error on this subject in the past (in Portuguese, if not in English).

The Fact

1. Sovereign Jesus declares that at the time of His second coming the situation in the world will be similar to what it was in Noah's day (Matthew 24:37-44, Luke 17:26-35). Many of us believe that the Second Coming is upon us, so let us consider the reality of our day.

---

[1] That is what the Text says, "the Son of the Man", which appears to be a phrase coined by the Lord Jesus to refer to Himself; the phrase does not make very good sense in English, at first glance, but if "<u>the</u> man" refers to pristine Adam and "<u>the</u> son" to an only pristine descendent, it makes great sense. It seems to indicate a perfect human prototype, like Adam was before the fall—the human side of the God-man.

2. The people were completely evil and perverse: "Jehovah saw that the wickedness of man was great in the earth, and that every intent of the thoughts of his heart was only evil continually" (Genesis 6:5). If a person is as he thinks in his heart (Proverbs 23:7), then in Noah's time a majority (evidently) of the people practiced only evil, were incapable of doing good. And what about our day? 2 Timothy 3:1-5—"Now understand this: In the last days there will be grievous times; because people will be self-lovers, money lovers, boasters, arrogant, blasphemers, disobedient to parents, ungrateful, unholy, without family affection, unforgiving, slanderers [or, 'devils'], without self-control, brutal, despisers of good, betrayers, reckless, conceited, lovers of pleasure rather than lovers of God; wearing a form of godliness while having denied its power! You must avoid such people."[1] Now is that not a faithful picture of our present day society at large? (See also Romans 1:28-32.)

3. Sovereign Jesus affirmed that marriage would be similar. So how was that marriage? "The sons of God saw the daughters of men, that they were beautiful; and they took wives for themselves of all whom they chose" (Genesis 6:2). The phrase, 'the sons of God', is a translation of the Hebrew phrase, *bene-haelohim*, that in the other places where it occurs—Job 1:6, 2:1 and 38:7—clearly refers to angelic beings, apparently of

---

[1] Note that the order is to avoid such people. But, wait a minute—how can we evangelize them if we are ordered to avoid contact with them? Could it be that they have passed a point of no return, or might they be a type of being that is not an object of salvation? Matthew 7:6 comes to mind; this verse may be a chiasmus, ab,ba. But just who are 'the dogs' and 'the pigs'? A pig will sniff the pearl and perhaps think it a stone—it not being edible the pig will ignore it and it will get trampled into the mud. So a 'pig' is someone who is incapable of recognizing or appreciating the 'pearl' (perhaps a materialist with a completely closed mind) —the reaction will be one of total indifference. So do not waste your time. In contrast a 'dog' reacts in an aggressively hostile manner against what is 'holy'. So a 'dog' is presumably someone who is committed to evil and will therefore attack what is holy. So do not innocently offer what is holy to a 'dog'—you will get chewed up! Anyone who has sold out to Satan will almost certainly have a resident demon, and we have the authority to bind such.

high rank. The inspired commentary in the New Testament, Jude 6-7 and 2 Peter 2:4-7, makes clear that they were in fact angelic beings, albeit in rebellion against the Creator.[1] (In Luke 20:36 the Lord Jesus said, with reference to the resurrected, that "they are equal to angels and are sons of God".) Note that the fallen angels acted on their own initiative, taking 'whom they chose'. And what was the result of those 'marriages'? "There were giants [Hebrew *Nephilim*] on the earth in

---

[1] Jude makes clear that the phrase in Genesis 6:2 is not an exception. "And the angels who did not keep their proper domain but deserted their own dwelling He has kept bound in everlasting chains under darkness for the judgment of the great day. So also Sodom and Gomorrah and the surrounding towns—who gave themselves up to fornication and went after a different kind of flesh [Greek ετερος] in a manner similar to those angels—stand as an example, undergoing a punishment of eternal fire" (Jude 6-7). The author, inspired by God, affirms that the people of Sodom did what certain angelic beings had done; they wanted sex with a different kind of flesh. Recall that the men of Sodom, old and young, from every quarter, wanted to rape the angels that were with Lot (Genesis 19:4-5). Whatever kind of flesh an angel has (when he materializes), it is not human flesh; it is precisely "a different kind of flesh". The parallel text in 2 Peter 2:4-6 links the crime of those angels to the Flood. (In Matthew 22:30 [Mark 12:25, Luke 20:35-36] the Lord does not say that angels do not have a sex/gender. Evidently no baby angels are born [whether good or bad], but if angels are of only one gender then they cannot reproduce in kind. In the Bible, whenever an angel materializes it is in the form of a man, not a woman.)

The argument that 'the sons of God' would be a reference to the male descendants of Seth, while 'the daughters of men' would be a reference to the female descendants of Cain, is totally unfounded. Genesis 6:1 says that the men (Hebrew *haadam*, 'the man' or 'Adam', but in 5:1 we find *adam* twice without the article, referring to 'Adam' and 'the man' respectively) began to multiply, which included daughters. It should be obvious that the reference is to the human race as a whole, not just to the descendants of Cain—surely, otherwise there would be no male descendants of Seth to take the female descendants of Cain (on that hypothesis). Verse 2 goes on to say that 'the sons of God' saw those daughters of men (Hebrew *haadam*, just as in verse 1)—if *haadam* in verse 1 refers to the human race as a whole, then the identical vocabulary item in verse 2 ought to have the same meaning. Further, in verse 3 Jehovah declares that He is not going to strive with man (*adam*) forever and in verse 7 further declares that He will destroy man (*haadam*) from the face of the earth. It is clear that the Flood destroyed the descendants of Seth just as much as those of Cain. So then, the Hebrew word *haadam* refers to the human race as a whole. (Will anyone argue that the female descendants of Seth were not also 'daughters of men'?)

those days, <u>and also afterward</u>,[1] when the sons of God came in to the daughters of men and they bore children to them" (Genesis 6:4). A race of 'humanoids' was born, half-breeds of demon and woman, beings that were totally perverse, malignant, and of impressive size. And what about our day? Is our society at large not replete with beings that are totally perverse and malignant? The impressive size is lacking, but I think I can explain why.

4. An objection will probably be raised: "But, but, but, didn't Jesus say that angels don't marry?" Let us check it out; the text is: "When they rise from the dead, they neither marry nor are given in marriage, but are like angels in heaven" (Mark 12:25; see also Matthew 22:30 and Luke 20:35-36). Jesus was answering the captious question posed by the Sadducees, who denied the existence of resurrection; He affirms that in Heaven marriage, as we know it, does not exist; once there we will no longer procreate (since no one will die, there will be no need to produce new people to replace the old). In Heaven the angels do not procreate either, but that could be the consequence of there being only one sex (Jesus did not say that angels do not have gender, or a sex). Whenever an angel materializes in the appearance of a human being in the Bible, it is always as a male or man, never as a woman.[2] The lack of females among them could explain why angelic beings are fasci-

---

[1] Unfortunately, I once taught all over Brazil that apparently God had changed the rules after the Flood, with the result that we no longer see that happening; at least we no longer have giants, and although demons are certainly having sexual relations with women, we do not hear of anything being born as a result. But, just a minute, how would I know that no offspring of demons were being born? In Brazil we have a great many single mothers (and presumably that is not just here), and are they going to trumpet to the world that their baby's father is a demon? How can we know? [And what about the babies found in the trash or in the brush; might they be demonic offspring that the mother did not want?] But the Text is clear, "and also afterward", and I am to blame for having ignored this plain statement.

[2] The women in Zechariah 5 are part of a vision, not materializations; what Zechariah saw was women, not angels. In contrast, the Text says plainly that it was an angel who was talking with him.

nated by the female of our species (see 1 Corinthians 11:10, that I will discuss below).

5. Before proceeding, let us go back to the "and also afterward" to check out what happened after the Flood. Based on Deuteronomy 2:10-12 and 20-21 we may understand that already in Abraham's day, and even before, other mongrel races had appeared, and of impressive size. Deuteronomy 3:11 states overtly that Og, king of Bashan, was the last of his race, the *Rephaim*, that were similar to the *Anakim*; it states further that his bed was some 4½ meters in length, which allows us to deduce that Og himself was around four meters tall. Thirty-eight years before, the spies, wishing to badmouth the land, spoke of a number of giants, sons of Anak, that are overtly called *Nephilim* (Numbers 13:33). Four hundred years later David still had to face Goliath, and others of his race (1 Chronicles 20:4-8), but his height was 'only' three meters, no longer four (1 Samuel 17:4). As soon as God promised the land of Canaan to Abraham, it was entirely predictable that Satan would attempt to louse things up.[1] So much so, in fact, that although all the fallen angels who married women before the Flood had been confined in Tartarus (2 Peter 2:4), which would have been a rather severe warning to the rest, Satan obliged (so I imagine) a number of others to repeat the stunt. The severity used by God in the case of Sodom and Gomorrah indicates that the level of perversity there had reached uncommon proportions—Genesis 13:13 affirms that "the men of Sodom were exceedingly wicked". Although the Text does not make direct mention of giants in Sodom, we may deduce that yes there were, because Deuteronomy 2:10-12 says that Moab, that occupied what was left of the area controlled by Sodom and Gomorrah (that was not under the Dead Sea), took the area away from the *Emim* (who were the same size as the *Anakim*—it becomes evident that there were several mongrel

---

[1] And with the reappearing of Israel as a nation in that land, will anyone suppose that Satan is doing nothing?

races). God's severity with reference to the Amalekites, commanding Saul to annihilate them, including babies and even animals (1 Samuel 15:3), is probably to be explained by a massive demonic infestation of some sort. Just as we destroy animals and poultry to keep an epidemic from spreading, perhaps the contamination of the Amalekites was such that the only solution was destruction. (Cancerous cells cannot be recovered, returned to normal; they need to be destroyed in order to save the organism as a whole.)

6. And now about the size: why do we not have giants in our day? To begin, the phrase 'sons of God' evidently referred to angelic beings of high rank. Next, in Noah's day the women would have numbered in the thousands, or tens of thousands, certainly not more than hundreds of thousands; but there are over 50 million fallen angels (Revelation 12:4 and 5:11).[1] There simply were not enough women to go around! So then, it seems to me to be perfectly logical that it would be the biggest/strongest demons that got the women. However, all that gang was imprisoned in Tartarus as punishment for their incredible crime; so all of a sudden thousands of high-ranking demons are removed from the scene, which would open up the opportunity for the lesser ones. I cannot prove it, but it seems to me logical that the size of the offspring would reflect the size of the 'father', just as with us. (However, everything was bigger before the Flood than after—people, animals,

---

[1] We understand that 'the dragon' (12:3-4) refers to Satan. The term 'star' frequently refers to an angel, and in the context it should be obvious that the reference cannot be to literal luminaries—since the stars are many times larger than our planet, just one would have blown it to smithereens, and the Text refers to a third of them. Therefore we understand that Lucifer managed to recruit a third of the original angels to join him in his rebellion against the Creator. In 5:11 the Greek Text says that the angels around the throne of God numbered ten thousand times ten thousand and thousands of thousands. Well, 10,000 X 10,000 = 100,000,000 (one hundred million), but there were more than that. It follows that if the two thirds that remained true to the Creator number a hundred million, then the one third that went with Satan must number over 50 million. What a calamity!

plants—so the pre-Flood women were much larger than women today.) In any case, Goliath was certainly smaller than Og, who was probably smaller than the *Nephilim* destroyed by the Flood. Although the Text is silent, it would not be strange for God to keep on sending to Tartarus any other high-ranking demons that perpetrated the same crime. Since Satan needs his high-ranking subordinates for other purposes, he himself would tell them to stop.[1] It could be that lesser demons are allowed to escape, and their offspring would not be of abnormal size. Further, with the return of Christ bearing down upon us, God may be permitting a renewing of that activity. In any case, based on the declaration of the Lord Jesus, something similar to what precipitated the Flood must exist in our world today. He who hath an ear, let him hear!

Implications

1. Consider Jude 18-19: "<u>In the end time</u> there will be scoffers who live according to their own godless desires; these are the division-causers;[2] they are soulish [characterized by soul], not having a spirit." That is what the Text says. Our Bibles generally read, "not having the Spirit", but there is no article with 'spirit' in the Greek text; translators have supposed that the reference is to the Holy Spirit, and in that event the 'soulish' people would be the unconverted. But the description of such persons that occupies verses 8-16 is almost violent—they are totally perverse. One is reminded of Genesis 6:5 and 2 Timothy 3:1-5. The crucial question is precisely this: would the offspring of a demon have a human spirit? The Sacred Text informs us that the human spirit is transmitted by the sperm of

---

[1] There is another possibility. Jude 6 affirms that the *bene-haelohim* of Genesis 6 "deserted their own dwelling". The idea of deserting or abandoning implies that there is no return. It may be that those fallen angels, in order to be able to procreate with women, had to make an irreversible choice. Upon taking on human form they could never return to their former condition. Following this hypothesis, again Satan would command them to stop, since he needs his high-ranking subordinates for other purposes.

[2] The 'divisions' they cause would be in the society at large, not in the church.

the father, in which event that hybrid race would have lost the human spirit, and presumably the 'image of God' as well. Let us check it out.

In Genesis 5:3 the Text affirms that Adam "begot a son in his own likeness, after his image", that reminds us of Genesis 1:26. "Then God said: Let us make man in our image, according to our likeness." In all the genealogies it is always the man who begets; women conceive and gestate. I take it that Hebrews 7:9-10 is clear enough. "Even Levi, who receives tithes, paid tithes through Abraham, so to speak, for he was still in the loins of his father when Melkizedek met him." When Abraham paid the tithe to Melkizedek, not even Isaac had been begotten, much less Jacob and Levi. Still, the inspired author affirms that the person of Levi was in Abraham's reproductive system. It follows that it is the sperm of the man that transmits the human spirit and the image of the Creator. That is why Romans 5:12-21 teaches that Adam's sin was transmitted to all his descendants, and death as well.[1] As David explains, "Behold, I was brought forth in iniquity, and in sin my mother conceived me" (Psalm 51:5). (It should be obvious that the reference is not to the reproductive process itself, since the Creator Himself commanded them to "be fruitful and multiply"—Genesis 9:1.)

Consider also Genesis 38:8-10. The Text affirms that God killed Onan. Why? It was not because he did not want to perpetuate his brother's name—even under the more stringent demands of the Law of Moses the penalty for that was 'only' public humiliation, not death (Deuteronomy 25:5-10). In Onan's day there was no Law of Moses. Up to that point only one crime carried the death penalty, precisely murder (Genesis 9:6). Since the life is in the seed, when Onan spilled the seed on the ground, before having intercourse with the widow, he was deliberately killing the human life in the seed—it was murder.

---

[1] When Eve sinned, she sinned alone. When Adam sinned, we did too, because we were in his reproductive system. It was Adam who degraded the race.

And God exacted the penalty![1] We may add Exodus 21:22-23 here as well. A human fetus is a person, and whoever caused the death of a fetus was liable to the death penalty.[2] It is the seed of the man that transmits the human spirit; so the off-spring of a demon will not have one. The essence of a woman being her soul, the offspring has the mother's soul. Not having spirit, it most probably will not have any conscience either.[3] Here in Brazil, where I live and work, the papers and news-casts are full of cases where the criminals appear to have no

---

[1] To be sure, the life latent in the sperm is only set in motion when a spermatozoon joins an ovum. Since a man produces many billions, if not trillions, of spermato-zoa during his life, almost all of them are wasted, one way or another. It is mainly a perverse intention that the Creator punishes. However, if I am not badly mis-taken, He is not pleased when people go after pleasure without assuming the accompanying responsibility.

Leviticus 18:6-30 prohibits certain practices because they contaminate the earth, and the situation can reach a point where the earth 'vomits' the people. Now there is a dramatic picture for you: the very ground gets nauseated at the people that walk it! And what are those practices? Every kind of incest (verses 6-17), sex with a woman in menstruation (verse 19), adultery (verse 20), human sacrifice (verse 21), homosexualism (verse 22) and sex with an animal (verse 23). Verse 29 decrees the death penalty for all those practices. Leviticus 20:1-22 is a parallel passage. The Text states plainly that innocent blood shed without punishment contaminates the ground, and God demands the death penalty for murderers. But why does the Creator react the same way to the practices listed above? I suppose for the following reason: sex with an animal, anal sex and sex with a menstruating woman destroys the man's seed, and it is the seed that transmits 'the image of God', human life. So they are kinds of homicide—remember the case of Onan. Human sacrifice is obvious murder. Incest and adultery degrade the seed. In short, the Creator attaches considerable importance to His 'image'!

[2] In verse 22 the correct rendering is a premature birth, not a miscarriage. The baby lives. In verse 23 the baby dies.

[3] Down through the years many Christian writers have affirmed that every human being has a 'space' in the soul that only the Creator can fill. Analogously, human-oids probably have a demon-specific 'socket', being open to demonic influence at any moment.

Modern medicine informs us that each person has the father's blood, not the mother's; so the mixed race mentioned in Genesis 6:4 had demonic blood in their veins, not human. Had Satan succeeded in contaminating everyone, the Messiah, the second Adam, could not have been born, and Genesis 3:15 could not have been fulfilled. The maneuver that Satan devised against God's plan was so incredible, and came so close to succeeding, that the response was to destroy everything and start over, using eight human beings not yet contaminated.

conscience at all—they say they would do it again, and with pleasure![1]

2. 1 Corinthians 11:9-10—"Nor was man created for the woman, but woman for the man. For this reason the woman ought to have authority upon her head, because of the angels." Our Bibles generally add 'a symbol of' before 'authority'—there being nothing of the sort in the Text, it is an unwarranted addition. The woman needs the protection of male authority, precisely because of the angels. In Numbers 30:3-15 Jehovah makes clear that the man exercises spiritual authority over the woman. Recall that in Genesis 6:2 the angelic beings simply took the women that they wanted, at their own initiative. A woman without male protection is an easy target. In our day, the feminist women who peremptorily reject any semblance of male authority are asking for a demon (and what little demon is going to object?). [It would not surprise me in the least if 100% of such feminists have a demon.] And what about the lesbians that want sex, but without a man—are they not an open invitation? Well, and so what? Well, our society ought to be full of single mothers, and many of the children would be humanoids.[2] I understand that the return of Christ is upon us, and He Himself declared that things would be like they were in Noah's day. In that event, a significant percentage of the population today is probably made up of humanoids, that mongrel race of demon with woman. All of a sudden we are faced with an urgent necessity—we need to be able to distinguish the

---

[1] Please note, I am not suggesting that every perverse and violent individual is a humanoid. Persons who turn themselves over to Satan grow progressively worse. And then, there are the 'robots', people who voluntarily and deliberately turn themselves over to the complete control of a demon; they become under 'remote control'. Over fifteen years ago I was informed that at that time there was a network of thousands of 'robots' distributed around the United States (we also have them in Brazil). I must confess that I never troubled myself to study the problem and find a way to neutralize such 'persons'—it would be a welcome asset toward the subject in hand.

[2] Of course married women can also produce humanoids.

imitation. We need the gift of discerning spirits! On the way, let us think about the probable characteristics of such beings.

The females, not having a spirit, will be very sensual, and will be used by Satan to ruin men. A human male who has sex with one of them will certainly be demonized, and if he marries her he will be tormented; he can never be happy, and any children will be perverse. As for the males, without a spirit, they will also be sensual, as well as given to violence, to lying and to corruption. The Lord Jesus affirmed that Satan is a murderer and a liar (John 8:44), as well as a thief and a vandal (John 10:10).[1] The description of Lucifer in Ezekiel 28:13 includes musical instruments, and I think it is obvious that Satan uses music as a favorite tool to destroy young people. Some time ago there was a rock group called KISS (Knights in Satan's Service) whose 'music' was openly satanic, and so on. The description given in 2 Timothy 3:1-5 is precisely to the point. They will be beings without conscience, without remorse. They will kill their parents without any emotion, etc. etc.

3. "As it was in the days of Noah"—never before had I paused and tried to imagine the emotions of Noah and the other 'decent' people of his time as they saw their world being taken over by those *Nephilim*, as they watched their culture being destroyed, apparently without being able to do anything to stop, much less reverse, the trend. There would be frustration, anger, perplexity, melancholy and at last despair and panic. So how about us in today's world—are we not beginning to have the same emotions as we observe a world without the political will to confront the organized Islamic terror, organized crime running loose, violence rampant in the streets, corruption at home in all levels and all areas of society, the growing lack of shame and modesty in customs and culture, in short, a 'church' that is absent and unable to promote biblical values in the public sector and society at large?

---

[1] "Brood of vipers", "your father is the devil"—like father, like son; if the father is a 'snake', the children are too.

For some time now Canada has had a law whereby if you voice a criticism of the homosexual life style you go to prison. I believe similar laws are in place in several European countries. The militant 'gay' lobby is hard at work to get similar laws in the US and here in Brazil—a similar law has been passed by the House of Representatives here and is presently being debated in the Senate. According to the proposed law, moral or religious objections to homosexualism will not be tolerated; a church would not be able to fire a pastor for being 'gay', and so on. The 'gay' lobby is openly working for an inversion of cultural values, the destruction of any moral principles left over from our former civilization. Those who study the militant 'gay' agenda are telling us that the movement is no longer concerned for the person, but rather with the pleasure derived from their destructive program itself—the pleasure of perverting what is natural, of transforming the right into wrong and the wrong into right (see Isaiah 5:20), of destroying the human being as a whole.[1] It is simply satanic.

Our turn to live Hebrews 13:12-13 is coming, something that Christians in China, North Korea, Islamic countries and those persecuted elsewhere have known for some time. "Jesus also, so that He might sanctify the people by His own blood, suffered outside the city gate. So then, let us go out to Him, outside the camp, bearing His disgrace." I doubt that even 5% of the so-called evangelicals here in Brazil are prepared to actually suffer physical persecution for Jesus Christ. Do you suppose that the percentage in North America will be any higher? Martin Luther wrote the following:

> If I profess with loudest voice and clearest exposition every portion of the truth of God except precisely that little point which the world and the devil are at the moment attacking, I am not confessing Christ, however boldly I may be professing Christ. Where the battle rages, there the

---

[1] I have used material from an e-mail written by Rozangela Justino.

loyalty of the soldier is proved, and to be steady on all the battlefield besides, is merely flight and disgrace if he flinches at THAT point.

Well then, I would say that the "little point" that the world and the devil are presently attacking in Brazil, and elsewhere, is the position on anal sex.

The position of the Bible is clear enough. God created two sexes, male and female, and He expects that they be respected. Homosexualism is not a work of the Creator—so much so that He decrees the death penalty for the practice (Leviticus 18:22 & 29, and to this day, Romans 1:32). Whose work is it then? Romans 1:18-32 is to the point; homosexualism is a result of denying the existence of the Creator (Romans 1:26). Since God wants adoration that is in spirit and truth (John 4:24), He will not force us to adore; when people reach the point of actually denying His existence (the ultimate stupidity), He removes His hand, abandoning them to their disgraceful passions, that Satan knows how to manipulate very well.

I believe that Hebrews 2:7 is relevant here: "You made him [man, verse 6] lower than the angels, for a little while" (quoting Psalm 8:5). The human being is superior to the angelic being in essence; we bear the Creator's image and they do not, and once glorified that superiority will be obvious, but only for the redeemed. Those who serve Satan subordinate themselves to him, and thus can never rise above him. If Lucifer's rebellion was provoked, as I suppose, by the creation of a being superior to himself, he is doing very well at getting his 're-venge', by depriving the vast majority of humanity of that superiority [and so verse 8 would not apply to them]. Now Satan is controlled by spite; he was demoted. Since he is unable to create, he gets his satisfaction by degrading and destroying. His greatest 'pleasure' must be to drag the image of the Creator through the mire, and for that purpose anal sex is just the ticket. Since it is a man's seed that transmits the 'image', anal sex mixes the image of God with feces—a monstrous insult!

The practice of anal sex is the equivalent of spitting in the face of the Creator; it is an extremely serious offense (worse than a buck private spitting in the face of a four star general). So then, as soon as God removes His hand, Satan pushes men toward anal sex.[1]

Several years ago Dr. James Dobson, founder and president of Focus on the Family, on the television program Larry King Live, said that he never taught that the homosexual tendency was a choice of the person. That made me stop and think. If the tendency is not a choice (just supposing), where would it come from? I see two possibilities: either someone is born with it, or he gets it from a demon. Going on from there, in a society dominated by a relativistic humanism, starting from pluralistic presuppositions, there will be no perceived basis for combating homosexualism.

But, can it be that someone is actually born with the tendency? By an act of the Creator, no. Well, how about by an act of evolution? I owe to Dr. Ney Augusto de Oliveira (a surgeon) the following observation: Even for someone who believes in evolution as an explanation of origins [even though it is scientifically impossible], it would be a contradiction for the organism to evolve a homosexual gene, because that gene would condemn the organism to extinction. It should be obvious to all that anal sex will never produce life—if during 50-60 years not a single woman gave birth, our race would disappear from this planet. Bye, bye. So then, if neither God nor evolution has produced, or would produce, a homosexual gene, how can someone be born with the tendency? Only as a work of Satan, that I understand to be entirely possible.[2] Actually, the am-

---

[1] Here in Brazil, people who come out of the various forms of spiritism affirm that most of the men in those groups are homosexual; Satan pushes them in that direction—they teach that anal sex gives power, and it becomes necessary for those who wish to climb the hierarchical ladder.

[2] See my essay, "Concerning Pathogens—Origin and Solution".

bush that the enemy has prepared for us is a whole lot worse than we have gotten around to imagining. Consider.

The inspired commentary links Sodom to the Flood. The Sodomites were known for their appetite for anal sex. If there was a mixture of humanoids in Sodom, as I understand (Deuteronomy 2:10), they were probably born with the tendency. It seems to me obvious that many (if not all) of the humanoids in our day will have been born with the tendency, precisely in order to create a social climate where approval for the practice becomes irresistible. Which, of course, will cause the Creator to abandon that society more and more, which will turn that society over to Satan more and more. It is a vicious cycle of evil, a downward spiral. Since we do not know how to distinguish between human beings and humanoids, the sexual acrobatics of the humanoids become part of the culture at large and influence the behavior of the real humans. Such perversity![1]

I was recently informed that soybeans (if not fermented) contain a good deal of female hormone, so that too much soy represses the masculine libido, reducing the virility. During centuries, if not millennia, Buddhist monks have taken soy precisely to smother their sexual desire. There are no end of articles available on the internet telling about the bad effects of soy, that go beyond sex. (The Japanese make their soy sauce and tofu out of soy that has been properly fermented, that removes the harm.) In North America and Europe soy is sold to the public as 'health food', and the negative effects are beginning to appear.[2] Here in Brazil the vast majority of the population cooks with soybean oil, including the bars and res-

---

[1] Freud's theory that sex is the mainspring of human life has been, and continues to be, a most useful fool for Satan.

[2] Women who do not wish to be bothered with breastfeeding their babies and fill the poor things with soy milk do special harm to the boys. And it might be that the girls reach puberty sooner—the number of eleven-year-olds that get pregnant seems to be growing.

taurants.[1] So then, the negative effects of soy will not result in sodomites, those who take the male role in anal sex. Since soy inhibits precisely that capacity, it will be the number of catamites that increases, those who take the female role in anal sex. A catamite tendency could come from soy, rather than a demon. Obviously such a person can refuse to participate in anal sex, but it becomes difficult to blame him for the tendency (he could be the victim of an irresponsible mother).

4. Jude 22-23: "Now be merciful to some, making a distinction; but others save with fear, snatching them out of the fire."[2] The implication is clear: there is a third category, the without-mercy ('some' plus 'others' does not equal 100%; in fact, one gains the impression that the third category could be sizeable). 1 John 5:16-17 speaks of fatal sin, such that there is no point in praying for the culprit. Such culprits would presumably be among the 'without-mercy'. (See Solution, point 5, with special attention to the discussion of Deuteronomy 7:10, Psalm 34:16 and 2 Peter 2:17.)[3] We need discernment in order

---

[1] Every so often the local press comments on a growing level of impotence among the men, now approaching 40% (which would help to explain the increase in lesbianism among the women).

[2] I confess that I do not understand how it could be possible to rescue someone who is already in the fire, but that is what the Text says.

[3] It may be that the 'without-mercy' category includes two types: the mortal sin in 1 John 5:16-17 is presumably committed by a human being; but the third class in Jude 22-23 may be made up of humanoids, since a major share of the letter is describing them (as I see it).

A theological question presents itself: can a humanoid without a human spirit be saved? The demons cannot be recovered; their final destiny is sealed (Matthew 25:41). So, will the son of a demon fare any better? A type of being with soul, but without spirit, would be very similar to an animal (mammal), that also has soul but not spirit. As far as I can understand the Sacred Text, when an animal dies it simply stops existing. Since a humanoid did not choose to be so born, and is not a candidate for salvation (as best I can see), would it not be unjust to condemn it to spend eternity in the Lake? The angels who fell chose to rebel against the Creator, and so have guilt. A human being has the option of submitting to the Creator and receiving salvation. But a humanoid, ... A rabid animal needs to be destroyed, for the benefit of the rest. Just as we have the option of sending a demon to the Abyss, so I understand the Text, stopping it from continuing with its evil around here, perhaps we can find a way to get rid of a humanoid as well,

to do the triage. Yes, but, what can or should we do after that. According to the Sacred Text, Jehovah the Son took on flesh and blood in order to abolish Satan (Hebrews 2:14) and to undo his works (1 John 3:8). To undo a work one needs to also undo its consequences—is that not so? If someone crumples a fender of my car, how can we undo that 'work'? Someone has to take out the wrinkles, re-paint, restore the fender to its former condition. If someone kills my son, how can we undo that 'work'? Only by bringing him back from the dead, restoring his life. If someone rapes my daughter, making her pregnant, how can we undo that 'work'? I doubt that even God could restore her virginity, but the fetus could be aborted.[1] A son of a demon is an obvious work of Satan; so, how can we undo that 'work'?

A more or less literal translation of the Hebrew Text of Psalm 92:7 would be: "When the wicked flourish like grass, and all the workers of iniquity blossom, it is for them to be destroyed forever." The preceding verse speaks of persons who ignore and despise the Creator—for such there is no cure, only destruction. Since a humanoid is not a candidate for salvation, and is in this world for the sole purpose of doing evil, it is like a gangrene in the body—if the gangrene is not excised, it will kill the body. But, what if we get to the place where we can identify a humanoid with certainty? So far as I know, there is no country in the world whose civil law distinguishes between human beings and humanoids. And many countries no longer

---

with the same objective, precisely. The question of discernment becomes crucial. Why waste time 'evangelizing' a humanoid? It would be like offering something holy to a dog, that will respond by attacking you (Matthew 7:6). (Actually, I believe the Holy Spirit has confirmed to me that the 'dogs' in Matthew 7:6, and possibly in Philippians 3:2 and Revelation 22:15, can include humanoids.) If there have always been humanoids, throughout human history, there must have been some in Jesus' day. In that event, it would be strange if He never touched on the subject, and dangerous for His followers. See Asides, item1.

[1] If the rape was perpetrated by a demon or humanoid, might aborting the result not be an obligation to society? Why give birth to a being that will only do evil in this world, and only be extinguished in the end anyway?

have capital punishment. So then, we must find a solution in the spiritual realm. (If God removes someone, there is nothing the law of the land can do.)

Consider also Matthew 6:22-23—"The lamp of the body is the eye. So if your eye is sound your whole body will be full of light. But if your eye is evil your whole body will be full of darkness. So if the light that is in you is darkness, how great is that darkness!" Of course we have two eyes, but the Text has "eye" in the singular. I take it that the Lord Jesus is referring to the way we interpret what we see, which is our real 'eye'—two people, one pure and one vile, observing the same scene will give different interpretations to it. Someone with a malignant mind will give an evil interpretation to everything he sees, and in consequence his being will be filled with unrelenting darkness. (Cf. Titus 1:15.) Such persons reach a point where they are beyond help, beyond recovery, and should be removed, for the good of society.[1]

Solution

1. First, let us consider our incumbency, what Sovereign Jesus intends for us to do: "Just as the Father sent me, I also send you" (John 20:21)—just as. It is the Lord Jesus Christ, our Commander-in-chief, who is speaking. He is expecting, rather requiring, that we do as He did. So, **what** did He do? The Father ordered and the Son obeyed: "I have come to do Your will, O God" (Hebrews 10:7). (John 4:34—"My food is to do the will of Him who sent me and to complete His work.") Brothers, we too must experience Hebrews 10:7. An effective participation in the spiritual war begins with a total commitment to the Lord Jesus, and that needs to be renewed daily. Just like the Lord Jesus, our life must revolve around the Father's will. And what was that will, in specific terms? It is stat-

---

[1] Perhaps we should distinguish between two types of bad people: those who deliberately devise evil and those who gradually lost the ability to distinguish between good and bad; perhaps these might still have a chance.

ed in Hebrews 2:14—the Son took on flesh and blood in order to abolish the devil; also to undo his works (1 John 3:8).

So then, why are we here? To give continuity to the work of Christ. He came to abolish Satan, and He succeeded, Hallelujah! (Colossians 2:15, John 16:11, Ephesians 1:20-21, John 12:31, 1 Peter 3:22, 1 John 4:4). Yes indeed, Satan has been defeated, his final destination has been decreed (Matthew 25:41), but for His own sovereign reasons the Creator still allows the enemy to operate in this world. It is up to us to 'pay to see'—we must impose the defeat on the devil, in practice (Matthew 18:18). Christ came to undo Satan's works, and since he continues to produce evil in this world, it is up to <u>us</u> to undo it. As soon as Jesus won the victory He returned to Heaven, leaving the undoing on our plate. Since the Church has been calamitously absent in this area, we are all obliged to live with the negative consequences of that neglect. **We are here to undo the works of the devil!**

"Just as He is, so are we in this world" (1 John 4:17)—in <u>this</u> world, not the next. The Church is the body of Christ, and so it is mainly through her that He deals with this world. (When you look at someone what you see is the person's body.) We are the Creator's spokesmen in this world. (That could include the Trinity!—1 John 4:13-14, Genesis 1:26.) <u>Attention please</u>: it is time to wake up. It is time to really understand that we represent the Creator down here, and He expects us to conduct ourselves in a manner worthy of our office.

2. Second, let us consider our competence, as stated in Psalm 149:5-9. "Let the saints exult in glory; let them sing for joy on their beds. Let the high praises of God be in their mouth, and a two edged sword in their hand, to execute vengeance upon the nations, and punishments upon the peoples; to bind their kings with chains, and their nobles with fetters of iron; to execute upon them the written judgment—this honor is for all His saints."[1]

Here are some observations based on the Text:

a) we are looking at commands (not optional points);

b) the commands are to be obeyed in bed—the point being, presumably, that we operate in the spiritual realm;

c) the battle is allied with praise, and the praise comes first (see 2 Chronicles 20:21-22);

d) the 'honor', a consequence of the positive results of obedience to the commands, is for "all His saints". It follows that if you are one of those saints, to obey those orders is on your plate, within your competence (so they will be required);

e) since our activity takes place in the spiritual realm, the 'kings' and 'nobles' presumably refer not only to the men who occupy positions of authority but also to the fallen angels (demons) who are behind them. In fact, a thorough job must get rid of the demons, as well as the men;

f) the scope includes entire nations, whole peoples; in short, any geographic or political entity that has a ruler;

g) since the battle is part of worshipping God, the 'vengeance' and 'punishment' need to be in accord with His character. It is where norms established by the Creator are being blatantly rejected that we should concentrate our action. NB: the point is to impose the Creator's norms, not our pet peeves;

h) since we operate in the spiritual realm, the authorities we bind may not literally wind up in the penitentiary, but they will be removed from power; being bound hand and foot they cannot function;

---

[1] The type of warfare ordered in Psalm 149 is at the highest level, including against fallen angels of high rank, 'world rulers'. A woman should not attempt it unless she is under the spiritual protection of a competent man (an unbelieving or backslidden husband will not hack it; nor a pastor who does not understand the subject [and does not want to learn]). (See 1 Corinthians 11:9-10 and Numbers 30:3-15.)

i) there is no lack of 'written judgment'—Zechariah 5:2-4, against thieves and perjurers; Proverbs 20:10 against diverse weights and measures; Isaiah 10:1-2, against whoever makes unjust laws; Romans 1:26-32, against homosexualism and a sad list of other perversities (note that verse 32 says that they **are** deserving of death, by the righteous judgment of God; 'are', not 'were'—and this within the age of Grace, since Romans was written decades after Pentecost). (See also 1 Corinthians 6:9-10, Revelation 21:8 and 22:15.) Since humanoids are here to do evil, they come within our jurisdiction, without doubt.

Further, 1 Corinthians 6:2-4 affirms that saints judge the world; the verb 'judge' is in the present tense (the first occurrence is ambiguous with the future, but not the second one). Verse 3 adds that our jurisdiction includes angels. Well now, if we can judge an angel, then we can judge the son of an angel. Conclusion: judging humanoids is within our jurisdiction, our competence.

3. Third, let us consider our authority and power. In Luke 10:19 the Lord Jesus said: "Behold, I <u>give</u> [so 98% of the Greek manuscripts] you **the** authority to trample on snakes and scorpions, and over all the power of <u>the</u> enemy, and nothing shall by any means hurt you." The Lord is addressing the Seventy, not the Twelve, and others were doubtless present; further, this was said perhaps four months before His death and resurrection. It follows that this authority is not limited to the apostles, and there is no indication of a time limit. The Lord Jesus affirms that He gives us **the** authority over all the power of the enemy. In Matthew 28:18 He declares that He holds "all authority . . . in heaven and earth", and so He has the right and the competence to delegate a portion of that authority to us. We may have any number of enemies, but <u>the</u> enemy is Satan. The phrase, "all the power", presumably includes his works, followed by their consequences. Someone with authority can forbid an action, and therefore we can stop Satan from acting in a specific case.[1]

I link Ephesians 3:20 to Luke 10:19. "Now to Him who is able to do immeasurably more than all we ask or imagine, according to the power that is working in us, . . ." "Is working" is in the present tense; so it is valid for us today. There exists a power in us (the redeemed) that even surpasses our ability to imagine. It follows that to bring about something written should be easy.

Returning to Luke 10:19, the Lord gives us the authority to "trample snakes and scorpions". Well now, to smash the literal insect, a scorpion, you do not need power from on High, just a slipper. To trample a snake I prefer a boot, but we can kill literal snakes without supernatural help. It becomes obvious that Jesus was referring to something other than reptiles and insects. I understand Mark 16:18 to be referring to the same reality—Jesus declares that certain signs will accompany the believers (the turn of phrase virtually has the effect of commands): they will expel demons, they will speak strange languages, they will remove 'snakes', they will place hands on

---

[1] Can we command Satan to undo his own works (including those of his servants)? I know a pastor here in Brazil whose car was stolen, so he ordered Satan, by name, to return it within 24 hours, and within the stipulated time it was parked in front of his house. But what about disease, would it not be better to use God's power (Ephesians 3:20)? I gather that the Lord Jesus always used God's power (not the enemy's), and we should follow His example. Since we have access to Christ's limitless power, we do not need Satan's, and should not give him the satisfaction of seeing us use it. And, recalling how subtle he is, there is the distinct possibility that he could deceive us and have us doing what we shouldn't.

(There are those who argue that Satan was stripped of his power, based on texts like Hebrews 2:14, Revelation 1:18, Colossians 2:15 and Matthew 28:18. The cruel facts of life that surround us and fill the world would seem to weigh inconveniently against that thesis, but the Text itself goes against it—what Satan will yet do through the Antichrist and the false prophet reflects considerable power. I understand the texts above to refer to the fact of Satan's having been demoted and deposed from his position as god/prince of this world, along with the privileges and perks that go with the office. Now he is obliged to act as a usurper, bluffing his 'rights'.)

the sick.[1] ("If they drink . . ." is not a command; it refers to an eventuality.) Your Bible probably reads "they will take up serpents", or something similar. It happens that the Greek verb 'take up' covers a fairly wide semantic area, and one of the main meanings is 'to remove'—a garbage collector picks up a bag in order to remove it, get rid of it, not to keep it (he holds on to it only long enough to throw it into the truck). I believe that is the intended meaning here in Mark 16:18, but what did the Lord Jesus mean by 'snakes'?

In a list of distinct activities Jesus has already referred to demons, so the 'snakes' must be something else. In Matthew 12:34 Jesus called the Pharisees a 'brood of vipers', and in Matthew 23:33, 'snakes, brood of vipers'. In John 8:44, after they claimed God as their father, Jesus said, "You are of your father the devil". And 1 John 3:10 makes clear that Satan has many other 'sons'. In Revelation 20:2 we read: "He seized the dragon, the ancient serpent, who is a slanderer, even Satan, who deceives the whole inhabited earth, and bound him for a thousand years." If Satan is a snake, then his children are also snakes. So then, I take it that our 'snakes' are human beings who chose to serve Satan, who sold themselves to evil—the term could also include 'humanoids', who are literally devils' children. I conclude that the 'snakes' in Luke 10:19 are the same as those in Mark 16:18, but what of the 'scorpions'? Since they also are of the enemy, they may be demons, in which case the term may well include their offspring, the humanoids.[2] So then, whether as snakes or as scorpions, hu-

---

[1] 1 Corinthians 12:29-30 leaves clear that no gift is given to everybody; we need the community, where all the gifts should be present.

[2] Since a snake is more dangerous than a scorpion (usually), and since a human being is superior to an angelic one in essence, and a human being in Satan's service can produce more damage in the world than a demon can, to associate scorpion with demon in this context is not unreasonable. I understand the Text to affirm that we have the authority to free ourselves from demons, humanoids, 'robots' and 'snakes' (human beings given over to evil).

manoids will be included, and therefore Luke 10:19 grants us the authority over them, explicitly so.[1]

In Matthew 8:5-13 the centurion understood about authority—he gave orders and they were obeyed, without question or delay (but only within the sphere of his competence). But the Lord Jesus said that he had great faith, to an unusually high degree—but faith in what? Faith in Jesus' spiritual authority; all He had to do was give an order and it would happen. Perhaps we should understand this type of faith as being an absolute confidence, beyond a shadow of a doubt or a fear. In Matthew 21:21 the Lord said, "Assuredly I say to you, if you have faith and do not doubt" (see Mark 11:23, "and does not doubt in his heart") you also can dry up a tree, and even transport a mountain into the sea. See also Hebrews 10:22, "full assurance of faith" and James 1:6, "ask in faith, with no doubting". Mark 5:34 and Matthew 15:28 offer positive examples, and Matthew 14:30-31 the opposite.

If an authority gives a commission to someone, he will presumably back that commission up to the limit of his capacity. Since Christ's capacity is without limit, His backing should be so as well (as far as He is concerned). In Matthew 28:18 He said: "All authority in heaven and on earth has been given to me." Then comes the commission: "As you go make disciples . . . teaching them to obey everything that I commanded **you**"—the pronoun refers to the eleven apostles (verse 16). Very well, so what commands had Jesus given to the Eleven? Among others, "heal the sick, cleanse the lepers, cast out demons" (in Matthew 10:8—perhaps 94% of the Greek MSS do not have "raise the dead"). The Eleven also heard John 20:21. Knowing that we have the backing of the Sovereign of the universe, who has all authority and all power, we can and should do our duty with tranquil confidence.

---

[1] Yes, but the authority is to trample them; the intent is to kill or destroy. Evidently the Lord Jesus is talking about eliminating those things.

4. Very well, we have the incumbency, the competence and the authority to face and solve the problem posed by humanoids in our world. It remains to know how to proceed, in terms both specific and concrete. I really cannot imagine that it could be God's will for His Church to be defeated or humiliated in this matter. So there must be a solution, and we need to keep calling out to God until He gives us a clear answer on this. Still, I believe that a few observations may already be made.

In the armor described in Ephesians 6 we find "the sword of the Spirit" (verse 17). A sword is a weapon for offense, although it is also used for defense. The Text tells us that this sword is "the ρημα of God"—ρημα, not λογος. It is God's Word <u>spoken</u>, or applied. Really, what good is a sword left in its sheath? However marvelous our Sword may be (Hebrews 4:12), to produce effect it must come out of the scabbard. The Word needs to be spoken, or written—applied in a specific way.

In the Bible we have many examples where people brought the power of God into action by speaking. Our world began with a creative word from God—spoken (Genesis, 1:3, 6, 9, 11, 14, 20, 24, 26; and see Hebrews 11:3). Moses did a lot of speaking. Elijah spoke (1 Kings 17:1, 18:36, 2 Kings 1:10). Elisha spoke (2 Kings 2:14, 21, 24; 4:16, 43; 6:19). Jesus did a great deal of speaking. Ananias spoke (Acts 9:17). Peter spoke (Acts 9:34, 40). Paul spoke (Acts 13:11; 14:3, 10; 16:18; 20:10; 28:8). In short, we need to speak!

The centurion did not say, "In the authority of Rome . . ."; he just said, "Do this; do that". The Lord Jesus did not say, "In the authority of the Father . . ."; He just said, "Be clean! Go!" In Luke 10:19 He said, "I give you **the** authority over all the power of the enemy"—so we have the authority; so let us speak!! Just like Jesus!

In Luke 17:6 we have a 'contrary to fact' condition, that in a literal translation would be: So the Lord said, "If you had faith [but you don't] like a mustard seed *has*,[1] you would say [but you don't] to this mulberry tree, 'Be pulled up by the roots and be planted in the sea,' and it would have obeyed you." The second apodosis is in a past tense, whereas the protasis and the first apodosis are in the present tense.[2] It is a curious grammatical construction, but I suppose that the Lord is emphasizing the certainty of the response—if they would only speak!!

I would translate Hebrews 11:1 like this: "Now faith is a realization of things being hoped for, an evidence of things not (being) seen." The concept of 'hope' in the New Testament includes an element of certainty (it is not mere wishful thinking). To declare as fact something we do not see is difficult for many (including myself), but I believe that to be the meaning of the Text. True faith is able to declare the existence of something before seeing it. When the centurion gave an order he was declaring what was going to happen, before the fact. He spoke, and it happened.[3] Of course the Lord Jesus did precisely the same thing; He would speak and it happened. I cannot help but wonder if some day people will say about me, "Of

---

[1] I rather doubt that the Lord is commenting on the size of the faith; rather it is a quality of faith. But, what type of 'faith' might a mustard seed have? Although so small, it responds to the climatic circumstances without hesitation, and grows to a remarkable size. If we would respond without questioning to the nudges of the Holy Spirit, our 'climatic circumstances', we could literally transport a tree, just with our word. In Matthew 17:20 the Lord Jesus said, "If you have faith as a mustard seed *has*, you <u>will</u> say to this mountain, 'Move from here to there,' and it <u>will</u> move; and nothing will be impossible for you." That is what He said, but we just don't believe it.

(But why then did Jesus emphasize the size of the seed? However small a seed may be, it can germinate and produce. However small a person may be [or appear to be] in the Kingdom of God, if he has the faith of a seed he will produce marvelously.)

[2] Well, actually some 30% of the Greek manuscripts, including the best line of transmission, have the protasis in the imperfect tense.

[3] We do well to remember, however, that it only worked, or would work, within the reach of his authority. That is why he appealed to Jesus—he himself could not heal the servant.

course he did the same thing; he would speak and it happened."

5. Perhaps someone will say: "Sure, sure, we have to speak; but exactly what are we going to say, and how and when and where?" Good questions. On the way to an answer we need to consider the following. Among all the sacrifices and burnt offerings in the Old Testament there is nothing for premeditated sin—something done with the intention of challenging or disdaining the Creator ('with a raised fist' in Hebrew), in short, rebellion. Thus, Deuteronomy 17:12 imposes the death penalty for rebellion; there was no sacrifice for that. According to Numbers 15:27-28, there was indeed sacrifice for unintentional sin, but now notice verse 30: "But anyone who sins defiantly, whether native-born or alien, blasphemes Jehovah, and that person must be cut off from his people." To insult Jehovah carried the death penalty, there being no sacrifice for that. Exodus 21:12-17 determines that those guilty of certain crimes must be executed. Notice especially verse 14: "But if a man schemes and kills another deliberately, you must take him away from my altar and execute him." Imagine that! At that time the altar represented precisely the means for expiating sins. To run to the altar was a way to plead for God's mercy and protection, but the Creator does not allow this recourse to a murderer—a murderer must be executed. People can object all they like, but the Creator is resolute—whoever deliberately kills the image of God (without due cause) must be killed in his turn; there is no indemnity. I have already commented on Leviticus 18:6-30 and 20:1-22, where incest, adultery, human sacrifice, homosexualism and sex with an animal received the death penalty. To be sure, since it was the society that applied, or was to apply, the penalty, it would only happen in the community of God's people. Pagan peoples were ignorant of God's laws. But none of that alters the fact that there was no sacrifice for such practices.

But how about the New Testament, does not the age of Grace change the picture? To try to argue that God's grace annuls

His moral law will not work. Note Romans 1:18-32, where it is clear that the application is current. In verse 32 'the righteous judgment of God' is that those who practice the things mentioned (including the list in Leviticus 18) "**are** deserving of death". "**Are**", not "were"—the verb is in the present tense, as in the original Text. In other words, Paul affirms that the penalty has not changed; even in the Church age, the age of grace, certain persons continue to be subject to death—by divine sentence. 1 Corinthians 10:6-12 declares that the experiences of Israel in the desert are "examples for us" and "were written for our admonition" (verse 11), and concludes with: "Therefore let him who thinks he stands take heed lest he fall." All the examples given resulted in physical death, and if they were recorded for our admonition, it is because we may face something similar. We cannot be too careful! 1 Corinthians 6:9, Revelation 21:8 and 22:14-15 were also written after the day of Pentecost. And notice Hebrews 10:26, "For if we sin willfully after we have received the knowledge of the truth, there no longer remains a sacrifice for sins" (see verses 26-31). We cannot be too careful!

As for blood guiltiness (see Deuteronomy 21:1-9, 19:13 and Numbers 35:33), 1 Corinthians 11:27-30 makes clear that the New Testament does not change the Creator's position regarding it. According to verse 27, whoever drinks the cup of the Lord in an unworthy manner will be <u>guilty of the blood</u> of the Lord. And what is the consequence? The answer is in verse 30: "For this reason . . . many sleep." 'Sleep' means they are dead; in other words, God executed them. The apostle Paul, inspired by the Holy Spirit, declares that with reference to "many" the Creator had exacted the penalty of blood guiltiness, literally—the culprit died. I confess that God's severity in this case surprises me, but there it is. Let no one kid himself; the Creator is still punishing blood guiltiness!

The Bible declares that God created man in His own image, and from then till now men have tried to return the favor, creating their own 'god' in their minds (of course any god you create will be smaller than you are, inescapably—totally worthless). Something similar happens to God's love, concerning which the vast majority of people, including believers, have a mistaken view. "Whom the Lord loves He chastens, and **scourges** every son whom he receives" (Hebrews 12:6; see also Revelation 3:19). [I myself have been on the business end of a horsewhip, and can assure the reader that it isn't pleasant.] In Deuteronomy 33:2-3 the "fiery law" is an expression of God's love for the people. Precisely because He is concerned for our true wellbeing, the Creator imposes the earthly consequences of our sins. The love of God **necessarily** includes hating evil, because of the consequences of the evil that will harm His 'image'.

Hebrews 1:8-9 cites Psalm 45:6-7, declaring that it refers to the Son: among other things it is affirmed that He hates iniquity. The glorified Christ Himself declares that He hates the works of the Nicolaitans (Revelation 2:6). Jehovah hates stealing (Isaiah 61:8), divorce (Malachi 2:16) and seven other transgressions (Proverbs 6:16-19). "The fear of Jehovah is to hate evil" (Proverbs 8:13; and see 9:10). In Psalm 97:10 we have a command: "You who love Jehovah, hate evil!" Are we going to obey?

Psalm 5:5 informs us that Jehovah hates all workers of iniquity. We are in the habit of teaching that God hates sin but loves the sinner. It seems so, up to a point. But when someone decides to join Satan, and makes a point of practicing evil, he attracts God's wrath—Deuteronomy 7:10. (See Psalm 26:5; 31:6; 101:3; 119:104, 113, 128, 163—these help us to understand David's attitude in Psalm 139:21-22; it is because they act with wicked intent [verse 20] that he hates them.) We must learn to hate sin, evil in any and all forms, Satan and his angels—since they are beyond recovery (Matthew 25:41, 2 Peter 2:4, Revelation 20:10), we are in a war without pity, without quarter, to the death.

The Sacred Text is clear: the character of God does not change, cannot be altered. In Malachi 3:6 Jehovah Himself declares that He does not change. James 1:17 affirms the same thing in other words. Hebrews 13:8 affirms something similar about Jesus Christ. Let us give special attention to 2 Timothy 2:13. "If we are faithless, He remains faithful; He cannot deny Himself." He cannot deny Himself—is it not obvious? He cannot go against His very nature, His own essence; it is one thing that God cannot do. He is Truth, and so cannot be unfaithful. It is precisely for that reason that He is incapable of lying (Titus 1:2).

Now let us consider Deuteronomy 7:9-10: "Therefore know that Jehovah your God is **God**; He is the faithful God who keeps covenant and mercy for a thousand generations with those who love Him and keep His commandments; and He repays those who hate Him to their face, to destroy them. He will not be slow to repay to his face the one who hates Him." If God repays hate with destruction, and without delay, then He does not offer salvation to that hater.[1] Obvious. Palm 34:16 reads like this: "The face of Jehovah is against those who do evil, to cut off the remembrance of them from the earth" (quoted in 1 Peter 3:12). Well now, to erase the memory of someone you must begin by erasing that someone himself. Any question? When a person chooses to become an ally of evil, he is challenging the Creator to kill him, literally. 2 Peter 2:17 affirms this about the allies of evil described in verses 9-17: "for whom the blackest of the darkness has been reserved forever".[2] We find the same expression in Jude 13.

---

[1] In Joel 3:4 Jehovah expresses Himself like this: "Indeed, what have you to do with me, O Tyre and Sidon and all the coasts of Philistia? Will you retaliate against me? But if you retaliate against me, swiftly and speedily I will return your retaliation upon your own head." God demonstrates the same attitude as in Deuteronomy 7:10—He does not tolerate perversity.

[2] This darkness is associated with Satan's kingdom, because "God is light and in Him is no darkness at all" (1 John 1:5). Peter is affirming that they will share the same destiny as their boss.

With an eternal reservation like that, what are their chances? John 3:16 declares that giving His Son was an expression of God's love for the world. So He offers salvation to those He loves, not those He hates. Whoever decides to hate God receives the hate back, and remains without salvation. In John 6:44 (and verse 65) the Lord Jesus declares, "No one can come to me unless the Father who sent me draws him", and it should be obvious that the Father is not going to draw someone whom He hates.[1] Actually, when you stop and think about it, for someone who hates God, being in Heaven would really be a sort of 'hell'.

In Matthew 10:25 the Lord Jesus affirms: "It is enough for a disciple that he be like his teacher, and a slave like his owner." 1 John 4:17 says that "just as He is, so are we in this world". So then, if He hates those who work iniquity, Psalm 5:5, we have the obligation to do the same thing. To permit a malevolent person to continue doing damage in this world, when it is incumbent upon us to remove him, turns us into his accomplices. An accomplice to a crime is a criminal. In Luke 10:19, when the Lord Jesus gives us the authority to trample snakes and scorpions, it follows that He is also giving us the incumbency— otherwise, why give the authority? To 'trample' involves hostile intent. Just to step on a scorpion, even without wanting to, will crush the insect, will kill it. How much more if you do it with hostile intent! The purpose of trampling a snake is also to kill it. Conclusion: it is up to us to rid the world of 'snakes' and 'scorpions'; it is our responsibility; it is our incumbency! So, God is waiting on us—we are the ones who have to do it! And we will do it by speaking.

6. Conclusion: Humanoids are not candidates for salvation, do only evil, and therefore need to be eliminated, for the public

---

[1] John 3:36 is also to the point: "The one believing into the Son has eternal life, but the one disobeying the Son will not see life, but the wrath of God remains upon him." Will the Father 'draw' someone who remains under His wrath? How? The Text declares that the person **will not see life**—not ever.

good. Human beings who have chosen Satan, who have sold themselves to him to devise and do evil, are haters of God and therefore cannot be saved—they need to be eliminated for the public good. The partisans of the militant 'gay' agenda are a case in point; they are in open rebellion against the Creator and His values. Since it is their declared intention to destroy our culture, making it impossible for decent people to live in peace, we are facing a question of life or death. If we do not react adequately, we will lose the game.

At least three times the Lord Jesus referred to the Holy Spirit as being "the Spirit of the Truth" (John 14:17, 15:26, 16:13). It follows that to deliberately reject the Truth is to blaspheme the Holy Spirit, the unpardonable sin (Mark 3:29). It adds to our case. The enemies of God are without pardon, without salvation, do only evil, and are therefore a type of cancer or gangrene in society—if the society does not get rid of it, the society will be killed. Since the society at large does not have the slightest idea of the danger it faces, and even less of the solution, it is up to us to save the day, we who know and can. Recalling the exposition of Psalm 149 (Solution, 2.), I understand that all the texts that speak of the divine intention to eliminate partisans of evil enter the list of texts that state a 'written judgment'. And it is up to us to impose written judgment.

I invite attention to Psalm 91. The context is one of war. Since God offers protection to those who take refuge in Him, the terror, the arrow, the pestilence, the destruction come from the enemy. Verse 13 says: "You shall tread upon the lion and the cobra, the young lion and the serpent you shall trample underfoot", which reminds us of Luke 10:19. Verse 7 speaks of a thousand falling on our left and ten thousand on our right. Why the difference? Most people being right handed, a sword is normally held in the right hand. So a soldier would normally kill more to the right than to the left.

Asides

2 Corinthians 10:4 teaches us that "the weapons of our warfare are not carnal". So we must do our duty in the spiritual realm, using God's power. I understand that this is done verbally in the presence of the Righteous Judge of the whole earth (2 Timothy 4:8, Genesis 18:25, Hebrews 12:23), citing the written judgments specifically and applying them by name to those who deserve them. I myself am claiming before God the removal of eleven thousand of Satan's servants, and I am not alone in this.

1. More than one person has asked: "If humanoids were a reality that the Christians would have to face, why did not the Lord Jesus teach about them, why did Paul not write about them, nor any of the other authors of the New Testament?" The question is based on a false premise, that the New Testament is silent on the subject, but I will argue that it is not. Let us see.

It is a simple fact that the Bible frequently uses the term 'man' to refer to a materialized angel. In Genesis 18:2 Abraham saw three 'men', two being angels and the third Jehovah Himself (and the three ate the meal he prepared). As the story goes on, 19:1 says plainly that they were angels, but in verses 5, 10, 12 and 16 they are called 'men'. Once more in Genesis 32:24 the term 'man' refers to Jehovah Himself (see also Joshua 5:13). In Judges 13:6 Samson's mother refers to the Angel of Jehovah, who had appeared to her, as a 'man' (also in verses 8, 10 and 11). See also Daniel 3:25 and 28, 8:15-16, 9:21, 10:5 and 16, 12:5-7; Ezekiel 2:26; Zechariah 1:8-11, 2:1-3. In the New Testament angels had an important role at Jesus' empty tomb, sometimes appearing as angels, sometimes as men (Matthew 28:2-7, Mark 16:5-8, Luke 24:4-7, John 20:12-13). See also at the ascension of Jesus, Acts 1:10-11. Well now, if an angel can be called a 'man', why not, and all the more, the offspring of an angel? Quite so.

In Genesis 6:4 the hybrid race, the half-breeds, are called 'men', as also in the description that follows. Since the description in 2 Timothy 3:1-5 parallels the description in Genesis 6, the 'men' here presumably includes humanoids. The same holds for the description in Jude 10-19 and in Romans 1:28-32. Consider also 1 John 2:18—"Children, it is the last hour, and just as you have heard that the Antichrist is coming, even now many antichrists have appeared, by which we know that it is the last hour." Well, the Lord Jesus was a hybrid being, Holy Spirit with woman. I do not doubt that the actual Antichrist will also be a hybrid, Satan with woman (his 'thing' is to be like God). So what about the 'many antichrists' to which John refers, what might they be? It seems to me to be perfectly possible that they also were hybrids, precisely our 'humanoids'.

Once we start 'chewing' on this subject, I think we are obliged to conclude that humanoids themselves will marry and procreate—perhaps with another humanoid, but I imagine that the preference would be with a human. In that way the miscegenation would become increasingly diluted, and such subsequent generations would certainly be called 'men'. If we stop and think, the cultures where the parents choose a mate for their children may not be so 'stupid' as some might like to imagine. Really, to check out the lineage of a prospective mate is an important proceeding, in fact necessary (an impulsive marriage with a humanoid equals disaster).

Further, as I have already maintained, the 'snakes' in Mark 16:18 and Luke 10:19 and the 'scorpions' in Luke, presumably include humanoids. Also, I understand that the Holy Spirit has confirmed to me that the 'dogs' in Matthew 7:6 (and probably in Philippians 3:2 and Revelation 22:15) include humanoids.[1]

---

[1] Although the Jews were in the habit of referring to Gentiles as 'dogs', the context here calls for a different meaning.

Over twenty-five years ago, when I started ministering on the subject of biblical spiritual warfare, I soon realized that not a single text that treats of our 'weapons' or procedures explains how to do it. For example: Mark 3:27 teaches that we must bind Satan; but does not say how! In James 4:7 we have the <u>command</u> to resist the devil; but it does not say how. 2 Corinthians 10:4 says we have some great weapons; but does not identify them—if they are the gerundive clauses in verses 5 and 6, again we are not told how to do it!! I take it that God uses Satan and his angels (the demons) to test and train the successive generations of people, and if all the procedures were clearly laid out, God's people would have wiped out the enemy long since. So, it is cheerfully foreseeable that the references to humanoids in the New Testament will be veiled, none of which justifies the claim that the New Testament does not mention the subject.

2. In John 14:12 the Lord Jesus said: "Most assuredly I say to you, the one believing into me, he too will do the works that I do; in fact he will do greater works than these, because I am going to my Father. "Most assuredly" is actually "amen, amen"—rendered "verily, verily" in the AV. Only John registers the word as repeated, in the other Gospels it is just "amen". In the contemporary literature we have no example of anyone else using the word in this way. It seems that Jesus coined His own use, and the point seems to be to call attention to an important pronouncement: "Stop and listen!" Often it precedes a formal statement of doctrine or policy, as here.

"The one believing into me, he too will do the works that I do." This is a tremendous statement, and not a little disconcerting. Notice that the Lord said, "will do"; not 'maybe', 'perhaps', 'if you feel like it'; and certainly not 'if the doctrine of your church permits it'! If you believe you **will do!** The verb 'believe' is in the present tense, 2nd person singular; if you (sg.) are believing you will do; it follows that if you are not doing, it is because you are not believing. 2 + 2 = 4. Doing what? "The works that I do." Well, Jesus preached the Gospel,

He taught, He cast out demons, He healed all sorts and sizes of sickness and disease, He raised an occasional dead person, and He performed a variety of miracles (water to wine, walk on water, stop a storm instantaneously, transport a boat several miles instantaneously, multiply food, shrivel a tree—and He implied that the disciples should have stopped the storm and multiplied the food, and He stated that they could shrivel a tree [Peter actually took a few steps on water]). So how about us? The preaching and teaching we can handle, but what about the rest? I once heard the president of a certain Christian college affirm that this verse obviously could not mean what it says because it is not happening! Well, in his own experience and in that of his associates I guess it isn't. But many people today cast out demons and heal, and I personally know someone who has raised a dead person. Miracles are also happening. So how about me? And you?

"In fact he will do greater works than these." Well now, if we cast out demons, heal and perform miracles, is that not enough? Jesus wants more, He wants "greater things" than those just mentioned [do not forget what He said in Matthew 7:22-23]. Notice again that He said "will do", not maybe, perhaps, or if your church permits. But what could be 'greater' than miracles? This cannot refer to modern technology because in that event such 'greater things' would not have been available to the believers during the first 1900 years. Note that the key is in the Lord's final statement (in verse 12), "because I am going to my Father". Only if He won could He return to the Father, so He is here declaring His victory before the fact. It is on the basis of that victory that the 'greater things' can be performed. Just what are those 'greater' things? For my answer, see my outline (essay), "Biblical Spiritual Warfare". Now I would add to the list 'get rid of humanoids' ('robots' and 'snakes' should also receive appropriate attention).

In verse 12 the verb 'will do' is singular, both times, so it has to do with the individual. Please note that the Lord did **not** say, 'you apostles', 'just during the apostolic era', 'only until the Canon is completed', or whatever. What He did say is, "the one believing", present tense, and so it applies to any subsequent time including the present day. To deny the truth contained in this verse is to call the Lord Jesus a liar. Not a good idea![1]

3. In Luke 4:18-21 Jesus includes "to set at liberty those who are oppressed" (Isaiah 8:6) among the things He was sent to do. Turning to Isaiah we find that Jehovah is declaring what type of 'fast' He wants to see: "To loose the fetters of wickedness [a], to untie the yoke thongs [b]; to set the oppressed free [a], and that you break every yoke [b]." As is typical of Hebrew grammar, the two halves are parallel. "To loose the fetters of wickedness" and "to set the oppressed free" are parallel. Who placed the fetters and who is doing the oppressing? Well, although people can certainly forge their own chains through a sinful lifestyle, it seems to me that in this context it is evil beings putting the fetters on others. "To untie the yoke thongs" and "that you break every yoke" go together. First we should untie the thongs/cords that bind the yoke to the neck, and then we should break the very yokes. It seems clear to me that this text treats of the activity of Satan's servants: men, demons, humanoids. Using culture, worldview, legal maneuvers, threats, blackmail, lies, deceit and plain demonization and witchcraft, they bind individuals, families, ethnic groups, etc. with a variety of fetters and instruments of oppression.

Well, but so what? What does that have to do with our subject? Well, fasting was an important/obligatory component of their worship of God. It follows that this kind of 'fasting' is something that Jehovah overtly wants; it is His declared will.

---

[1] One other point: to affirm that the miraculous gifts ceased when the last clod of dirt fell on the Apostle John's grave is an historical falsehood. Christians who lived during the 2nd, 3rd and 4th centuries, whose writings have come down to us, affirm that these gifts still existed in their time. No Christian of the 20th or 21st century, who was not there, is competent to contradict them.

And so, whenever we see the work of Satan in someone's life, it is God's will that we undo it. If we know that it is God's will, we can proceed with complete confidence. It is also included in our commission (John 20:21).

Well, and what if we do nothing?

James 4:17—"Therefore, to the one knowing to do good and not doing it, to him it is sin." So, if I do not undo Satan's works, it shows up on my bill as sin, and I will have to answer for it. Ezekiel 22:30-31—"I sought for a man among them who would make a wall, and stand in the gap before me on behalf of the land, that I should not destroy it; but I found no one. Therefore I have poured out my indignation on them; . . ." The Text is clear: just one person could have made the difference, and averted the destruction. See also Malachi 1:10, that asks for just one person to act. So then, if I do not undo Satan's works, people will continue to suffer, without need. If I reject the plain meaning of the Text, I am closing my mind against the Truth, and thereby condemning myself to continue living with error and its consequences. Condemning myself and any others who depend on me or follow me. Help!

We need the gift of discerning spirits! [Note that 'spirits' is plural.][1]

---

[1] I regret that I must confess that during 20 years of ministering on Biblical spiritual warfare around Brazil I never taught this gift, and I never heard anyone else explain it. We must try to diminish the damage. To deny the existence of cancer, AIDS, aviary flu, etc., would be to guarantee that a solution would never be found. Analogously, to deny the existence of humanoids will carry the same guarantee. Not a valid option! To ignore the word of Sovereign Jesus can only bring negative consequences—it was He who said, "As were the days of Noah"!!

www.ingramcontent.com/pod-product-compliance
Lightning Source LLC
Chambersburg PA
CBHW051816090426
42736CB00011B/1508